CAMBRIDGE LIBRARY COLLECTION

Books of enduring scholarly value

Religion

For centuries, scripture and theology were the focus of prodigious amounts
of scholarship and publishing, dominated in the English-speaking world by
the work of Protestant Christians. Enlightenment philosophy and science,
anthropology, ethnology and the colonial experience all brought new
perspectives, lively debates and heated controversies to the study of religion and
its role in the world, many of which continue to this day. This series explores
the editing and interpretation of religious texts, the history of religious ideas
and institutions, and not least the encounter between religion and science.

Hermas in Arcadia and the Rest of the Words of Baruch

Much of the work of James Rendel Harris (1852–1941), palaeographer and
biblical scholar, focused on the translation and understanding of early Christian
writing, and this collection of two volumes of essays examines two key texts.
The first work in this reissue, published in 1896, discusses the book known
as 'The Shepherd of Hermas'. This early work, thought to be written in Rome
around the first or second century CE, is composed of three parts: visions,
commandments and similitudes. Harris examines aspects of the work, such as
how to interpret the ninth similitude – as allegory or literally – and discusses in
detail questions about translation. Themes of other essays include the legendary
library of Prester John in Abyssinia, the third-century writer Gaius the
Presbyter and problems surrounding the fourth-century Codex Euthalianus.
The second work, published in 1889, is concerned with the apocalyptic
language in the book of Baruch.

T0345398

Cambridge University Press has long been a pioneer in the reissuing of out-of-print titles from its own backlist, producing digital reprints of books that are still sought after by scholars and students but could not be reprinted economically using traditional technology. The Cambridge Library Collection extends this activity to a wider range of books which are still of importance to researchers and professionals, either for the source material they contain, or as landmarks in the history of their academic discipline.

Drawing from the world-renowned collections in the Cambridge University Library, and guided by the advice of experts in each subject area, Cambridge University Press is using state-of-the-art scanning machines in its own Printing House to capture the content of each book selected for inclusion. The files are processed to give a consistently clear, crisp image, and the books finished to the high quality standard for which the Press is recognised around the world. The latest print-on-demand technology ensures that the books will remain available indefinitely, and that orders for single or multiple copies can quickly be supplied.

The Cambridge Library Collection brings back to life books of enduring scholarly value (including out-of-copyright works originally issued by other publishers) across a wide range of disciplines in the humanities and social sciences and in science and technology.

Hermas in Arcadia
and
The Rest of the
Words of Baruch

J. RENDEL HARRIS

CAMBRIDGE
UNIVERSITY PRESS

CAMBRIDGE UNIVERSITY PRESS

Cambridge, New York, Melbourne, Madrid, Cape Town,
Singapore, São Paolo, Delhi, Tokyo, Mexico City

Published in the United States of America by Cambridge University Press, New York

www.cambridge.org
Information on this title: www.cambridge.org/9781108039734

© in this compilation Cambridge University Press 2012

This edition first published 1896
This digitally printed version 2012

ISBN 978-1-108-03973-4 Paperback

This book reproduces the text of the original edition. The content and language reflect
the beliefs, practices and terminology of their time, and have not been updated.

Cambridge University Press wishes to make clear that the book, unless originally published
by Cambridge, is not being republished by, in association or collaboration with, or
with the endorsement or approval of, the original publisher or its successors in title.

HERMAS IN ARCADIA

AND OTHER ESSAYS.

London: C. J. CLAY AND SONS,
CAMBRIDGE UNIVERSITY PRESS WAREHOUSE,
AVE MARIA LANE,
Glasgow: 263, ARGYLE STREET

Leipzig: F. A. BROCKHAUS.
New York: MACMILLAN AND CO.

HERMAS IN ARCADIA

AND OTHER ESSAYS

BY

J. RENDEL HARRIS, M.A., D.Litt. (Dubl.),

FELLOW OF CLARE COLLEGE, CAMBRIDGE.

CAMBRIDGE:
AT THE UNIVERSITY PRESS.

1896

[*All Rights reserved.*]

𝔊𝔞𝔪𝔟𝔯𝔦𝔡𝔤𝔢:

PRINTED BY J. AND C. F. CLAY,

AT THE UNIVERSITY PRESS.

PREFACE.

IN the following pages I have reprinted two essays which throw some light on critical problems connected with the text and interpretation of that famous early Christian book, known as the Shepherd of Hermas. Each of them has been the starting point for important investigations by the leading scholars of our time; and I have endeavoured to indicate the accretions or corrections which they have made to my first statements, so that the student may not only have before him the texts of my researches, which are extant, sometimes in very brief form, in journals not very easy of access, but may also be able to bring the investigations up to their latest point of development.

Of these two essays the first appeared in June 1887 in the *Journal of the Society for Biblical Literature and Exegesis* (Boston, U.S.A.); the second is three years earlier in date; it was first printed in the *Circulars of the Johns Hopkins University* for April 1884, a publication containing many valuable notes on all branches of science, but not generally accessible, nor easy to handle. If the brief paper in question were estimated by the combat of giants which it provoked, I think it would be admitted that it was worth reprinting.

To these I have added a number of other pieces which may, perhaps, be found useful by the critics. Where they do not permanently instruct, they may transitorily please; and where the matter of them may seem to be unimportant, the method will sometimes be found deserving of consideration.

CONTENTS.

HERMAS IN ARCADIA.

THE object of the present paper is to set at rest a critical difficulty which has been raised concerning the interpretation of the tract of Hermas which goes under the heading of the Ninth Similitude; and to indicate a direction in which further light may be obtained on the vexed question of the date of this remarkable writer. The difficulty is in the first instance one of interpretation: we find in the writings of Hermas a blending of the real experiences of life with imaginary importations from current mythologies which render it hard to decide whether the writer wishes us to take him seriously, or to apply to his works an allegorical interpretation such as was common enough in early times, both in pagan and Jewish and Christian circles. And it is probably this perplexity rather than a mere personal fondness for such interpretations which led Origen to explain even the most strongly defined personal allusions in Hermas, the names of Clement and Grapte, in a spiritual manner. We may at least conclude that the subject invited such treatment. We may easily agree that the allusions to his life in Rome in the first Vision are genuine history, from which the step to the second Vision, which contains a visit to Cumæ, seems natural, as does also the account of the walk on the Via Campana in the third Vision. But if we admit these passages to be meant for a literal acceptation, we certainly cannot admit the interview with the Church-Sibyl to be anything but a work of imagination based on popular religious mythology. And we should not find it easy to determine where the literal ends and the allegorical begins. We are thus in much the same case as an interpreter of the Pilgrim's Progress would be who had sufficient knowledge of Bunyan's history to see that the "certain den" with which the book opens is the Bedford prison, and who had sufficient insight to determine that the rest of the book was allegorical, but who was wanting both in the historical information and in the intuitive perception by which to detect the traces of Bunyan's personal history which lurk behind the folds of the Allegory. It is however generally held that the mention of places not very remote from Rome ought to be accepted as sufficient evidence that the writer is giving us history rather than romance. The Via Campana, at least, scarcely admits of being allegorized, nor the mile-stones which Hermas passes on the road: with Cumæ the question is a little more involved, but even here the general opinion has been, and probably will remain in favour of the positive geographical acceptation of Hermas' words.

Such being the case, it is not a little surprising that, when we have so many Italian allusions in the book of Visions, we should find ourselves transported in the Ninth Similitude into Arcadia, and there regaled with an allegorical account of the building of the Church, which outdoes in fantastic detail the whole of the previous accounts. Are we to assume that, as in the case quoted from the Pilgrim's Progress, the initial note of place is to be accepted literally, and that from that point we plunge into allegory; or is the whole a work of imagination from the start? In the latter case, how can we explain the change of literary method involved in the comparison between a real Rome, Cumæ, Via Campana, and a poetic Arcadia? In the former case, how did the Roman Hermas find his way into the most inaccessible part of Greece? It was no doubt through some such questioning that Zahn was led to propose an emendation in the text of Hermas so that instead of reading

$$\kappa a\grave{\iota} \ \mathring{a}\pi\acute{\eta}\gamma a\gamma\acute{\epsilon}\nu \ \mu\epsilon \ \epsilon\mathring{\iota}\varsigma \ \mathrm{'A}\rho\kappa a\delta\acute{\iota}a\nu$$

we should put 'Αρικίαν for 'Αρκαδίαν. The advantage of this correction was that it transferred the scene again to the neighbour-hood of Rome, and restored the literary parallelism between the Ninth Similitude and the book of Visions. To support this conjecture, Zahn first brought forward a case where the word 'Αρικίαν had been corrupted in transcription, viz.: a passage in the Acts of Peter and Paul, c. 20, where the scribe has in error given 'Αραβίαν. If Arabia, why not Arcadia?

Then he proceeds to shew that the country around Aricia corresponds to the description given by Hermas of Arcadian scenery, and, in particular, he identifies the "rounded hill" (ὄρος μαστῶδες) to which Hermas was transported, with the Italian *Monte Gentile.* I do not know whether this suggestion of Zahn has met with any great favour, although it is ingenious, and not outside the bounds of possibility. The objection to it is chiefly that which falls to the lot of the majority of conjectural emendations, viz.: that it is not necessary; for, as I shall shew presently, the whole description of the country visited by Hermas, corresponds closely with the current accounts of Arcadian scenery, and is probably based upon them. So that if I do not discuss Zahn's hypothesis directly, it is because it is a last resort of criticism to which one must not look until the normal methods of interpretation have broken down. Let us then examine the scene into which Hermas introduces us; and the interpretation which he puts upon what he sees. We are told in the first place that his guide led him away into Arcadia and there seated him upon the top of a rounded hill from whence he had a view of a wide plain surrounded by mountains of diverse character and appearance. We will indicate the description of these mountains by the following diagram, in which the successive eminences are ranged in a circular form, and attached to each is the leading characteristic which is noted by Hermas:—

$$\zeta'$$
$$\times$$

| πηγῶν πλῆρες | ή× | εἶχε βοτάνας ἱλαρὰς καὶ πᾶν γένος κτηνῶν καὶ ὀρνέων | ×ϛ' | σχισμῶν ὅλον ἔγεμεν .. εἶχον δὲ βοτάνας αἱ σχισμαί |

θ′×
ὅλον ἐρημῶδες
.. ἕρπετα θανατώδη

×ε'
ἔχον βοτάνας
χλωρὰς καὶ
τραχὺ ὄν

εἶχε δένδρα μέγιστα ί×
... καὶ πρόβατα

×
ὄρος μαστῶδες

×δ'
βοτάνας ἔχον
ἡμιξήρους

δένδρα κατάκαρπα ια′×

×γ'
ἀκανθῶν καὶ
τριβόλων πλῆρες

ὅλον λευκόν ιβ′×

×β' ψιλόν, βοτάνας μὴ ἔχον

×
α'
μέλαν ὡς ἀσβόλη

Now before we begin to look for identifications with the scenery of any particular country or neighbourhood, we should try to subtract from the description those details which are artistically inserted by Hermas in order to bring certain views of his own before the minds of his reader under the cover of his allegory. The matter of the Ninth Similitude so far as it concerns the building of the tower and the shaping of the various stones is already present in the third Vision; and there is much in the description that is parallel to the account given of the various stones which are brought from the twelve mountains. For example, just as in the third Vision we find stones brought for building that are white, and some that are speckled (ἐψωριακότες); some that are squared, and some that are round; some that are sound, and some that have cracks in them. When we find, therefore, that in his Ninth Similitude Hermas makes his first mountain black as soot and his twelfth perfectly white, we know that it is more likely to be an expansion of the previous allegory than a natural feature; and when we find him saying that some of the mountains had chasms (σχισμαί) in them, we must rather refer to the stones that have cracks in them (σχισμὰς ἔχοντες) than to any peculiarity of the mountain region, however the description may seem to invite the identification with the peculiar characteristic of Arcadia, the κατάβαθρα or underground passages and hollows of the mountains into which the rivers of that country so commonly precipitate themselves.

A similar process of subtraction must be made on account of the similarity between this Ninth Similitude and the one that precedes it. In this case the allegory turns upon the distribution by the angel of the Lord of a number of branches which he had cut from a great willow-tree. After a while the angel summons the people to whom he had given them and scrutinizes them carefully. Some brought back their branches withered, others half-withered and with cracks on their surface, (ἡμιξήρους καὶ σχισμὰς ἐχούσας,) others again were green, (χλωράς,) others had fruit, and so on. A comparison of these terms with those used by Hermas of his mountains will shew that there has been a use made of the Eighth Similitude in the Ninth.

Nor must we suppose that there is any special identification with the particular number twelve. The number is introduced artificially and for the following reason: the mountains out of which the stones are taken are declared to represent the peoples of the earth out of whom the church is builded; now the idea prevailed at an early period that since the Jewish Ecclesia was composed of twelve tribes, something of a similar nature was to be predicated concerning the Christian world which had replaced and comprehended the Jewish world. Otherwise how was an explanation possible of the sealing of the 144,000 in the Apocalypse? But then these twelve tribes could not be identified with nationalities and must therefore represent so many different types of character.

This is undoubtedly Hermas' idea, and it shews us that we must not suppose any geographical enumeration to be involved in the number twelve. The author of the *Opus Imperfectum in Matthaeum* amongst his many traces of antiquity gives us the following on Matt. xix. 28: "Adhuc autem audeo, et subtiliorem introducere sensum, et sententiam alterius cuiusdam viri referre. Exponit autem sic: Quoniam sicut Judaeorum populus in duodecim tribus fuit divisus, sic et universus populus Christianus divisus est in duodecim tribus secundum quasdam proprietates animorum et diversitates cordium, quas solus deus discernere et cognoscere potest, ut quaedam animae sunt de tribu Reuben, quaedam de tribu Simeon vel Levi vel Juda."

These twelve classes according to Hermas are

α. Blasphemers and traitors.

β. Hypocrites and wicked teachers.

γ. Rich men and those who are involved in the business of life[1].

δ. The double-minded.

ε. Badly-trained, self-willed people.

ς. Slanderers and keepers of grudges.

ζ. Simple, guileless, happy souls who give of their toils without hesitating and without reproach. (Cf. Teaching of Apostles.)

η. Apostles and teachers.

θ. Bad deacons who have plundered the widow and orphan. Lapsi who do not repent and return to the saints.

---

[1] Note that these are said to be πνιγόμενοι ὑπὸ τῶν πράξεων αὐτῶν, and correspond to the mountain covered with thorns and briars; the reference to the Gospel (the thorns sprang up and choked them) seems indisputable.

ι. Hospitable bishops who entertain the servants of God.

ια. Martyrs for the Name, including those who thereby obtain a remission that was otherwise inaccessible to them.

ιβ. Babes of the Kingdom who keep all the commands of God.

These, then, are the twelve tribes of the new Israel; and, as I have said, we do need to identify twelve mountains.

When we have made the deductions intimated from the imagery, we are left to identify the locality from the remaining data; and this we shall proceed to do. And to begin with, let us observe that the idea of Arcadia presented itself early in connection with Christianity. For example, that beautiful composition which passes under the name of the second epistle of Clement, but which seems rather to be an early Christian homily, declares (c. xiv) the pre-existence of the Church in the following terms: "Wherefore, my brethren, if we do the will of God our Father we shall be of the first Church, viz.: the spiritual one, which *was created before the sun and moon*... For the Church was spiritual as was also our Jesus[1], and was manifested in the last times." No doubt this language is in part to be explained like the Valentinian Syzygy of Man and the Church by reference to a gnosis on Genesis i. 27. The writer of the homily says as much; the first Adam having been created male with female, so was the second; but what should be noticed is that the terms used to describe the pre-existence are not borrowed from Genesis, but from the Arcadian tradition that they existed in their mountain fastnesses before the moon, and it was thus that they explained their name of Προσέληνοι. What the writer of the homily means is that the Christian Church is the true Arcadia. And thus we have at once the explanation of the ideal journey which Hermas makes into Arcadia. For we find the same view held in the second Vision of Hermas (Vis. ii. 4. 1), where we are told even more decidedly that the Church was created first of all things. Similar ideas must have been common enough in the earlier centuries. So much being premised, let us put ourselves into the position of Hermas on the supposition that he has no more than the ordinary notions concerning Arcadia. We should simply be

---

[1] That Christ was before "the Sun and Moon" is proved by Justin, *Dial.* 76, apparently from Ps. 72. 17, 110. 3.

able to say that Arcadia was the innermost part of the Peloponnesus, and that it was shut in on every side by a ring of mountains. The rudest idea that could be formed would therefore be that of a plain within a circular mountain-wall; precisely the kind of view with which the Ninth Similitude opens. Here dwell the remnants of the primitive and virtuous race of men whom the gods loved to visit, whose chief virtues were, according to Polybius, $\phi\iota\lambda o\xi\epsilon\nu\acute{\iota}a$ and $\phi\iota\lambda a\nu\theta\rho\omega\pi\acute{\iota}a$. It may be noticed in passing, though I do not attach any importance to it, that Hermas makes one of his spiritual tribes, the good bishops, representative of the virtue of hospitality.

But it is plain that Hermas' knowledge goes beyond the elementary notion sketched above. This can be seen best by noticing the points which occur in the description of the mountains which have no special parallel in the allegorical explanation of the characters whom the mountains represent. For example, he adds to his description of his seventh mountain the fact that there were found on it all manner of beasts and birds; the eighth mountain is full of springs; the tenth mountain has sheep resting under the shade of its timber; the ninth is full of snakes and evil beasts; the eleventh shews fruit trees, and so on. But especially one should draw attention to the sixth mountain, whose description is $\emph{\"{\epsilon}\chi ov}$ $\beta o\tau\acute{a}\nu a\varsigma$ $\chi\lambda\omega\rho\grave{a}\varsigma$ $\kappa a\grave{\iota}$ $\tau\rho a\chi\grave{v}$ $\emph{ov}$. The same language is used again in c. 22 $\tau o\hat{v}$ $\emph{\"{\epsilon}\chi ov\tau o\varsigma}$ $\beta o\tau\acute{a}\nu a\varsigma$ $\chi\lambda\omega\rho\grave{a}\varsigma$ $\kappa a\grave{\iota}$ $\tau\rho a\chi\acute{\epsilon}o\varsigma$ $\emph{ov\tau o\varsigma}$. Here all the editors print the word $\tau\rho a\chi\acute{v}$ as an adjective, and it may be so; but if an adjective it is suggested by the name of one of the mountains of Arcadia. A reference to a map of Arcadia will shew this mountain on the eastern side of the plain of Orchomenos: E. Curtius in his Peloponnesos (i. 219) describes it as follows: "Den östlichen Berg nannten die Alten seiner rauhen und schroffen Form wegen Trachy."

I suppose it will hardly be maintained to be an accidental coincidence that Hermas, writing of Arcadia, or professing to do so, should twice describe a particular mountain by the name which the ancients used to designate one of the mountains of Arcadia. So far from any such assumption being likely, the mere mention of the name Trachy would be sufficient to intimate that we were in Arcadia.

This identification being then made, we are able to take the next step, and to determine the plain in which the scene is laid and the rounded hill from which the scenery is viewed. This seems at first sight to be difficult, because, although to an outsider Arcadia might be pictured as a happy valley within mountains, in reality, like Switzerland, with which it has often been compared, it does not furnish any one central plain, but innumerable valleys and small plains; and although there are one or two larger and more spacious than others, none seems to correspond to the rounded form which Hermas' language would at first lead us to expect.

But the mention of Mount Trachy shews that the plain must be the plain of Orchomenos, in the midst of which stands, dividing it into upper and lower respectively, the hill of Orchomenos, the strongest natural fortress of Arcadia and perhaps of ancient Greece. This then must be the ὄρος μαστῶδες of Hermas; it rises to a height of nearly 3000 feet immediately from the plain, and was famous even in Homeric times as one of the early Greek strongholds and cities[1].

Thus far we might have arrived from a study of the itinerary of Pausanias, from whose description of Arcadia we must make not a few references. Thus in xiii. § 2 we have the following notes: Ὀρχομενίοις δὲ ἡ προτέρα πόλις ἐπὶ ὄρους ἦν ἄκρᾳ τῇ κορυφῇ καὶ ἀγορᾶς τε καὶ τειχῶν ἐρείπια λείπεται: and in § 3. ἔστι δὲ ἀπαντικρὺ τῆς πόλεως ὄρος Τραχύ. τὸ δὲ ὕδωρ τὸ ἐκ τοῦ θεοῦ διὰ χαράδρας ῥέον κοίλης μεταξὺ τῆς τε πόλεως καὶ τοῦ Τραχέος ὄρους κάτεισιν ἐς ἄλλο Ὀρχομένιον πεδίον· τὸ δὲ πεδίον τοῦτο μεγέθει μὲν μέγα, τὰ πλείω δέ ἐστιν αὐτοῦ λίμνη. It appears, therefore, that the name Trachy was current for the mountain on the east of Orchomenos in the second century: Pausanias seems to have given us here a careful and correct description of the country.

Some of the other mountains to which Hermas makes reference may now be identified by the aid of Pausanias. For example, the ninth mountain is said to be full of serpents and noxious beasts. The mountain referred to is Mt. Sepia. The name is supposed to be derived from the venomous viper that was found there; and there were legends enough about the neighbourhood, even in Pausanias' time, to make it appear a country which was formerly something like Ireland before the arrival of St. Patrick.

---

[1] Curtius, *Peloponnesos*, i. 220. "Die orchomenische Berg, eine Kuppe von 2912 F. Höhe, welche Ithome ähnlich ist, und wie diese zwei Ebenen beherrscht, steigt unmittelbar aus dem Nachlande empor."

MAP ILLUSTRATING HERMAS' VISIT TO ARCADIA

Here they said that Æpytus, the son of Elatos, met his death from the bite of a serpent. Cf. Pausan. *Arcad.* iv. 4, Κλείτορι δὲ τῷ ᾿Αζᾶνος οὐ γενομένων παίδων ἐς Αἴπυτον ᾿Ελάτου περιεχώρησεν ἡ ᾿Αρκάδων βασιλεία. τὸν δὲ Αἴπυτον ἐξελθόντα ἐς ἄγραν θηρίων μὲν τῶν ἀλκιμωτέρων οὐδὲν, σὴψ δὲ οὐ προϊδόμενον ἀποκτίννυσι. τὸν δὲ ὄφιν τοῦτον καὶ αὐτός ποτε εἶδον· κατὰ ἔχιν ἐστὶ τὸν μικρότατον, τέφρᾳ ἐμφερής, στίγμασιν οὐ συνέχεσι πεποικιλμένος κτέ. xvi. 1, Τρικρήνων δὲ οὐ πόρρω ἄλλο ἐστὶν ὄρος Σηπία καὶ Αἰπύτῳ τῷ ᾿Ελάτου λέγουσιν ἐνταῦθα γενέσθαι τὴν τελευτὴν ἐκ τοῦ ὄφεως κτέ.

Now, I think, if we compare Pausanias' account of Æpytus' death while hunting, through no great beast, but by the bite of a viper, with Hermas' statement that in the ninth mountain there were ἕρπετα θανατώδη, διαφθείροντα τοὺς ἀνθρώπους, he will have little doubt that the mountain meant is Mt. Sepia.

The identification of these two mountains, Trachy and Sepia, I regard as established. They are respectively the fifth and ninth of Hermas' series, and whatever further progress in identification is possible, the results must harmonize with these so that the other mountains enclose a plain with them, and from an examination of the situation of these two on a map of Arcadia it is not difficult to infer that the order in which Hermas reckons his mountains is East—North—West—South. I am not, however, very sanguine of making any further identifications that would be equally convincing. It would be, however, possible to detect the origin of Hermas' many-fountained mountain. For we are informed by Pausanias that the emperor Adrian brought water for the city of Corinth all the way from Stymphalus: Paus. ii. iii. 5, Κρῆναι δὲ πολλαὶ μὲν ἀνὰ τὴν πόλιν πεποίηνται πᾶσαι, ἅτε ἀφθόνου ῥέοντός σφισιν ὕδατος, καὶ ὃ δὴ βασιλεὺς ᾿Αδριανὸς ἐσήγαγεν ἐκ Στυμφήλου. The language of Pausanias is in close correspondence with Hermas, and the mountain is located in the eighth place in the field of view. The umbrageous mountain under the shade of which flocks of sheep were gathered might find its identification in the Mt. Skiathis, described by Pausanias as follows, xiv. 1, Καρυῶν δὲ στάδια πέντε ἀφέστηκεν ἥ τε ᾿Όρυξις καλουμένη καὶ ἕτερον Σκίαθις. ὑφ᾿ ἑκατέρῳ δὲ ἔστι τῷ ὄρει βάραθρον τὸ ὕδωρ καταδεχόμενον τὸ ἐκ τοῦ πεδίου.

According to this identification Mt. Skiathis should be the next in order to Mt. Sepia, since it is the tenth on Hermas' circle; and a reference to the map will shew that this conclusion is not contradicted by the geography of the region, except that I think Skiathis would appear a little to the right of Mt. Sepia to an observer on the hill of Orchomenos[1]. As to the other characteristics, it is not worth while to discuss the animal and vegetable products of Arcadia more at length: it is sufficient to say that Hermas' description shews a very fair acquaintance with ancient Greek geography: and we may naturally go on to enquire what were the sources of his knowledge.

I think that it will be sufficiently evident from what has gone before that there is at least a suspicion that the description is taken from Pausanias. When we remove from our minds those details which I have shewn to be artificial creations of Hermas, and such generalities as attach themselves naturally to the idea of Arcadia as seen from the outside, we are left with peculiarities that at once fall in with the notes in the Itinerary of Pausanias. And these peculiarities are not the striking features of the Arcadian scenery, such as the lofty Mt. Cyllene[2] and the like, but somewhat insignificant details which would hardly have been noted except by a close observer who was making his own notes carefully as he went along, nor would they have been repeated except by some one who had carefully perused such an itinerary[3].

Now here a difficulty presents itself. No doubt we may admit a certain amount of agreement between Pausanias and Hermas, and it would be strange if two second-century writers, both dealing with the subject of Arcadia, had not expressed themselves in a

---

[1] Note that Curtius says (i. 210), "Σκίαθις ist der schattige Waldberg, gleich σύσκιον ὄρος bei Dikaearch. 75. Diesem Bergnamen entspricht der Name des Dorfes Skotini das am Abhange unseres Skiathis liegt."

[2] We cannot even be sure whether Hermas alludes to Mt. Cyllene at all; yet it must have been the most conspicuous feature of the landscape. The fact that it is not actually on the borders of the plain of Orchomenos, proves nothing; Mt. Sepia overlooks the valley of Stymphalus rather than the plain of Orchomenos, yet it is clearly alluded to by Hermas. Is Mt. Cyllene intended by the seventh mountain upon whose slopes are found all kinds of cattle and of birds?

[3] For example, in addition to what has been said, notice that the leading feature in the southwest of the landscape is Mt. Ostrakina, and compare the description in Hermas where the pastor bids those who build the tower to bring ὄστρακον and ἄσβεστος in order that they may make the neighbourhood of the tower clean against the day of its inspection: ὕπαγε καὶ φέρε ἄσβεστον καὶ ὄστρακον λεπτόν. Is this Ostrakina the twelfth mountain of Hermas?

manner which suggested peculiar coincidences in minor points, but in that case how could it be possible that Hermas could have utilized Pausanias, when that writer had not completed his Arcadia before the year 167 (as we shall shew)?

For determining the date of Pausanias' Itinerary we have, I believe, no facts besides those which are contained in the work itself. The chronological landmarks are as follows : In the seventh book of the Itinerary (Achaia 20, § 6) Pausanias explains that the Odeion at Athens was not described in his first book on Attica because Herodes Atticus had not built it at the time when the first book was written. Now Atticus is one of the leading figures of the second century, sufficiently known by his reputation as a rhetorician, an executor of magnificent public works all over Greece, and as a teacher and friend of Marcus Aurelius. The period of his life is supposed to be A.D. 104–180. Since the close of his life was embittered by the plots and complaints of an opposing faction at Athens, we may suspect that his liberality in public building at Athens does not belong to the last years of his life. And, whatever date we may assign to the structure, we have the following sequence :—

> Pausanias writes his Attica.
> Herodes builds the Odeion.
> Pausanias writes his Arcadia.

The other landmark is as follows: Pausanias alludes in his Itinerary of Arcadia to Marcus Aurelius and, perhaps, to his victory over the Quadi which took place in A.D. 174. The passage is as follows :

Τοῦτον Εὐσεβῆ τὸν βασιλέα ἐκάλεσαν οἱ Ῥωμαῖοι, διότι τῇ ἐς τὸ δεῖον τιμῇ μάλιστα ἐφαίνετο χρώμενος· δόξῃ δὲ ἐμῇ καὶ τὸ ὄνομα τὸ Κύρου φέροιτο ἂν τοῦ πρεσβυτέρου, πατὴρ ἀνθρώπων καλούμενος. Ἀπέλιπε δὲ καὶ ἐπὶ τῇ βασιλείᾳ παῖδα ὁμώνυμον· ὁ δὲ Ἀντωνῖνος οὗτος ὁ δεύτερος καὶ τούς τε Γερμάνους, μαχιμωτάτους καὶ πλείστους τῶν ἐν τῇ Εὐρώπῃ βαρβάρων καὶ ἔθνος τὸ Σαυρομάτων πολέμου καὶ ἀδικίας ἄρξαντας τιμωρούμενος ἐπεξῆλθε.

The language here used has generally been taken to mean that Pausanias was writing his eighth book subsequently to the defeat of the Quadi in 174. But it seems to me that while the passage has an air of having brought recent history down to date, that date is the date of the departure of the expedition against the Germans and not of its return. It becomes therefore possible to push back the date of the Arcadia nearly seven years earlier. We proceed on the supposition that Pausanias wrote his history and published it as he went along; this appears from the fact that the eighth book was written at a time when the first book was out of reach of correction. But even, on the earliest hypothesis, does it seem likely that Hermas could have written so late in the second century as to copy Pausanias? And if this seem too difficult an assumption, especially in view of the Muratorian canon, is there any other hypothesis that will explain the apparent coincidence? The alternative that first offers itself is the depression of the date of this portion of Hermas.

It has been noticed by Hilgenfeld that the writings attributed to Hermas fall, upon critical examination, into three groups: the first of these which Hilgenfeld calls *Hermas apocalypticus*, comprises the first four Visions; the second part, which comprises Vis. v to Sim. vii, having Vis. iii for its prologue, and Similitude vii for its epilogue, is the true *Hermas pastoralis* or book of the Shepherd. The third division comprises Similitudes viii and ix with the tenth for an epilogue. This part of the book Hilgenfeld calls *Hermas secundarius*, and attributes to his editorial care (whoever he may be) the massing together of the whole series of writings. Now there is something to be said for this division, even if we may not feel like abandoning altogether the theory of the single authorship. May it not be that the last division is the later workmanship of the same hand as wrote the two former groups? In that case we are able still to hold to the Muratorian statement with the single restriction that it applies only to the earlier parts of the book. This would require us to assume that Hermas outlived his brother Pius by a number of years, depending, in part, upon the (doubtful) date of the death of Pius, or at least of the close of his episcopate. And even if this explanation be considered insufficient, it is still possible to adopt Hilgenfeld's theory of a later writer who re-edits and makes an appendix to the earlier Hermas (I do not of course mean to imply that Hilgenfeld makes Hermas fall so late as my theory would imply). And even if Pausanias should turn out not to be the true authority, the identification of the water sources of Corinth brought by Hadrian remains and lowers the date of Hermas accordingly.

It becomes proper now to return to the Arcadian allegory and see whether there is any other point where the comparison can be made geographically correct. And I should like, though in a somewhat tentative manner, to suggest that in the details of the building of the tower, Hermas has had some reference to the early Cyclopean buildings of which the ruins were still to be seen in Greece and especially in the Peloponnesus. Perhaps the best way to make my meaning clear will be to compare a passage in Hermas with descriptions taken from Pausanias and modern writers. In Sim. ix. vii. 4, we find Hermas speaking as follows: "I said to the Shepherd, How can these stones which have been condemned enter into the building of the tower? He answered and said unto me, Dost thou see these stones? I see them, sir, said I. Said he, I will cut away the greater part of these stones and put them into the building, and they shall fit in with the rest of the stones. How, sir, said I, can these stones when cut occupy the same room? He answered and said unto me, Those which are found to be small for their place shall be put into the middle of the building, while the larger ones shall be put outside, and so they will hold one another together."

Now let us compare with this the description which Pausanias gives of the wonderful Cyclopean walls of Tiryns. He tells us that these walls are made of unwrought stones of such size that a team of mules would not be able to shake even the smallest ones; and that smaller stones to these are fitted into the interstices of the larger ones, so as to produce the closest union between them[1].

I understand Hermas to mean to describe in his builded tower a work of Cyclopean character (which, by the way, appears also from the fact that there are only ten stones in the first course of the building), and the small stones which result from the process of cutting, to correspond to those which Pausanias describes as producing a union between the larger blocks. And it is clear from the description in Hermas that the larger blocks are unwrought stones (ἀργά). Those who wish to see the appearance of such a wall depicted will find it in Schliemann, *Mycenæ and Tiryns*, p. 29, where it is called a "wall of the first period."

Similar Cyclopean remains may be found at other points in

---

[1] τὸ δὴ τεῖχος, ὃ δὴ μόνον τῶν ἐρειπίων λείπεται, κυκλώπων μέν ἐστιν ἔργον, πεποίηται δὲ ἀργῶν λίθων, μέγεθος ἔχων ἕκαστος λίθος ὡς ἀπ' αὐτῶν μηδ' ἂν ἀρχὴν κινηθῆναι τὸν μικρότατον ὑπὸ ζεύγους ἡμιόνων· λίθια δὲ ἐνήρμοσται πάλαι ὡς αὐτῶν ἕκαστον ἁρμονίαν τοῖς μεγάλοις λίθοις εἶναι. Paus. ii. 25, 8.

the Peloponnesus, such as the top of the mountain of Orchomenos, and the ruins of the ancient city of Lycosura in Southwest Arcadia.

And this identification helps us to explain a detail in Hermas' account; viz.: the way in which his tower is said to be built over the rock and *over the gate* (ἐπάνω τῆς πέτρας καὶ ἐπάνω τῆς πύλης). Special attention is given in these early buildings, such as the acropolis of Mycenæ and the like, to the defences of the entrance. The entrance to the gate of the Lions at Mycenæ is an illustration of this, the gate being placed at right angles to the wall of the citadel and approached through a passage formed by the citadel wall and a nearly parallel outer wall which formed part of the masonry of a tower by which the entrance was guarded. Schliemann adds to his description of this gateway an approving reference to Leake for pointing out that "the early citadel builders bestowed greater labour than their successors on the approaches to the gates." Another instance of a gate defended by a tower which projects over it is given by Curtius from the ruins of Lycosura: "On the east side of the city there is preserved a gate with a projecting tower (ein Thor mit einem Thurmvorsprunge)."

I venture the suggestion, then, that Hermas in the Ninth Similitude, when working up again the subject of the Church-Tower, has been influenced by accounts of the Cyclopean buildings of the Peloponnesus. If his authority was a written one, it may have been Pausanias, as in the previous cases; unless some point can be brought forward to show that Pausanias was unacquainted with what Hermas describes elsewhere, and that Hermas must have had written authority for the same.

To sum up the whole course of the preceding arguments: the scene of the Ninth Similitude of Hermas is really laid in Arcadia, probably in the plain of Orchomenos. Some of the mountain scenery which he describes is capable of exact identification by means of the Itinerary of Pausanias; and he has been influenced in his architecture by the Cyclopean remains of the Peloponnesus. Either the whole or at all events the latter part of the writings of Hermas should therefore be held of later date than the Arcadia of Pausanias. But the objection will be made that recent researches of German investigators and archæologists have shown reason for believing Pausanias himself to be a wholesale thief and plunderer of previous guide-books to Greece. So that our investigation may lead rather to the reopening of the Pausanias question than to the solution of the Hermas chronology and geography.

The attack upon Pausanias was commenced by Wilamowitz-Möllendorf (*Hermes* xii. 72) and sharply reinforced by Hirschfeld in an article in the *Archäologische Zeitung* (XL = 1882, f. 97). Hirschfeld brings a good deal of evidence to shew that the list of statues of Olympian victors does not reach later than the second century B.C.; and that the series stops here, not because there were no more Olympian victories commemorated, but because Pausanias is copying an earlier writer (probably Polemo), who does not pass this point of time in his descriptions: so that we may almost say that there is no evidence that Pausanias ever visited Olympia at all; but that both he and Pliny drew upon earlier writers.

Now this problem is a very many-sided one, and the archæological world is still divided over it, and, until the discussion subsides somewhat, it is not easy to determine whether the defenders of Pausanias or his severe critics have won the day. My own judgment is still reserved upon the point. Hence we must also be careful in reference to Hermas. We may be reasonably sure that if Pausanias was never at Olympia, he was never in Arcadia; but the preliminary hypothesis is not yet settled. Hence we content ourselves in the Hermas problem with affirming that Hermas really describes Arcadian scenery, but whether he takes his description from Pausanias or from some earlier Baedeker's Guide to Arcadia is as yet uncertain.

After the appearance of the foregoing paper, I received the following remarks upon it from Dr Hort, the characteristic caution of which will be evident to the reader, as I hope it will also be evident presently that the caution was undue and unnecessary.

CAMBRIDGE,
23 Dec. 1887.

. . . . . The first reading interested me much, but not with conviction; for the time, at least, the coincidences seemed too slight. The passage from *Op. Imperf.* at p. 73, a book which has much from Origen, is probably founded on some lost passage of him. There is a reference, though in somewhat ambiguous terms in the *Comm. in Matt.* p. 688 Ru. (1325 A, Migne); cf. 480 (912 A) . . . . .

Dr Lightfoot was more favourable in his view of the argument, but he demurred (as we shall see, rightly) to the assumption that Hermas was indebted to Pausanias.

He wrote as follows:

AUCKLAND CASTLE, BISHOP AUCKLAND,
Nov. 14, 1887.

MY DEAR SIR,

I am much obliged to you for your very interesting paper on *Hermas in Arcadia.*

You seem to me to make out a very strong case for Arcadia. As for Pausanias, I am less able to follow you. But you do not insist on this, nor does it affect your main point. If his information had been derived from Pausanias, I should have expected to find the resemblances go much further.

Yours very sincerely,

J. B. DUNELM.

At this point the argument was taken up by Mr (now Prof.) Armitage Robinson, who published, in an Appendix to his edition of Lambros' collation of the Athos Codex of the Shepherd of

Hermas, some further considerations, which will be found sufficient to dissipate the suspicions aroused by Dr Hort, and to confirm those expressed by Dr Lightfoot.

Over and above the identifications which I had suggested between the Arcadian mountains and the scenery described by Hermas, Mr Robinson suggested four further positive identifications as well as some of a more shadowy character. These are as follows:

(i) Mt Knakalus described by Pausanias (viii. 23. 3, 4); κνᾶκος is the Doric form of κνῆκος a kind of thistle, and consequently this mountain is to be equated with the mountain which Hermas describes as ἀκανθῶδες καὶ τριβόλων πλῆρες (Sim. ix. 1. 5).

(ii) A ridge close to Mt Sepia, called Τρίκρηνα.

'This no doubt was an abbreviation of Τρικάρηνα, the three-peaked ridge; but its popular explanation is all that we have to do with, and that is shewn by the legend that is attached to it: ὄρη Φενεατῶν ἐστὶ Τρίκρηνα καλούμενα· καὶ εἰσὶν αὐτόθι κρῆναι τρεῖς· ἐν ταύταις λοῦσαι τεχθέντα Ἑρμῆν αἱ περὶ τὸ ὄρος λέγονται νύμφαι, καὶ ἐπὶ τούτῳ τὰς πηγὰς ἱερὰς Ἑρμοῦ νομίζουσιν' (Paus. viii. 16. 1).

Accordingly Mr Robinson identified this with the mountain which Hermas describes as πηγῶν πλῆρες...καὶ πᾶν γένος τῆς κτίσεως τοῦ κυρίου ἐποτίζοντο ἐκ τῶν πηγῶν τοῦ ὄρους ἐκείνου.

The next two identifications are less satisfactory:

(iii) A mountain is mentioned by Pausanias, called Phalanthus, and since φάλανθος is synonymous with φαλακρὸς which, like ψιλός, means 'bald,' Mr Robinson proposed to identify this with a mountain which Hermas describes as ψιλὸν, βοτάνας μὴ ἔχον. This seems to me too artificial; if Hermas had been describing this mountain, it is much more likely that he would have preserved its Greek name, in the same way as he preserved the name of Τραχύ.

(iv) The next identification I am almost ashamed to cast a suspicion upon. Mr Robinson replied to my question as to the omission of Mt Kyllene from the panorama of Hermas, when it must have been the most conspicuous feature in the landscape, by suggesting that Mt Kyllene is the twelfth mountain of Hermas, the great white, glad-faced mountain, 'unreached by either cloud or wind, so that the very ashes on the altar of Hermes were found undisturbed whenever the worshippers returned for the annual sacrifice.'

There is no doubt that this profound calm of the mountain of Hermes was a favourite thought with the ancients; it has survived for us in modern poetry in the beautiful lines of Wordsworth, where he praises

> . . . . the perpetual warbling that prevails
> In Arcady, beneath unaltered skies,
> Through the long year in constant quiet bound,
> Night hushed as night, and day serene as day.
>
> *Excursion*, Bk. iii.

Unfortunately, however, and this is the only serious objection to the identification, the mountain Kyllene is, as Mr Robinson knows from an actual visit to the spot, invisible from the hill of Orchomenos; and it seems unlikely that Hermas would have thrust into his panorama a mountain which did not properly form a part of it. He might, perhaps, have done so, if he had been simply working from a geography or a guide-book; but the result of Mr Robinson's additions to my identifications is such as to make it impossible for me to hold any longer the theory of borrowing from Pausanias. Hermas must have been in Arcadia, and in that case, it is very unlikely that he would have given us an incorrect landscape. I will not say it is impossible, and I should be glad if further consideration should make it appear more probable.

But enough has been said to dissipate the suspicions which Dr Hort had expressed to me in private. We take it as proved that the scenery of Hermas' vision is actually laid in Arcadia, and we have not the slightest right to substitute Aricia, or to try to Italianize the vision.

Not only so, but as Mr Robinson has shewn by a number of considerations, the net result of the investigation is to shew that Hermas must have come from Arcadia; his geography is a part of himself and not a loan from Pausanias or some other guide-book. 'May he not,' asks Mr Robinson, 'have been a Greek slave of Arcadian origin? In this case his name, a common one for Greek slaves, would seem specially fitting for a native of this particular district, when we remember that Pausanias tells us of the worship of Hermas at Pheneos, twelve miles distant from Orchomenus..., when we remember also the story of the Nymphs who bathed him at his birth in the sacred fountains of Trikrena, one of the spurs of Mount Kyllene; and above all when we recall the epithet 'Cyllenius' derived from the worship of Hermas on the windless summit of the great mountain-king of Arcadia, who reared his head, as it was firmly believed, right up into the eternal calm above the clouds and above the storms which darkened and distressed the world at his feet.'

The conclusion seems to me to be correct as well as highly eloquent; and I am quite prepared to admit that we have in Hermas a Greek slave from Arcadia. And in this connexion, it is worthy of note that it explains certain features in Hermas' personal history. Arcadian slaves were commonly sold in pairs, and we may get some light on the situation by recalling an instance from the century before Hermas, where two brothers, Arcadian slaves, rose to great eminence in the Roman Empire. The case to which I allude is that of Pallas and Felix, who were sold to Antonia, the mother of the emperor Claudius; both of them attained their freedom; Pallas became a leading figure in the life of imperial Rome, and Felix is known to us as the procurator of Judaea who trembled before the preaching of Paul. Now Tacitus tells us (*Ann.* xii. 53) that Pallas was 'regibus Arcadiae ortus,' no doubt because he was named after one of the Arcadian kings, Pallas the son of Lycaon; and if this be so, we have an exact parallel to the naming of Hermas after the great deity of Arcadia. But it may be asked, where is the brother of Hermas to complete the parallel? The answer is in the Muratorian Canon which tells us that Hermas is the brother of Pius, who occupied the episcopal chair of the Roman Church.

We thus arrive at a picturesque series of parallels between the two pairs of Arcadian brothers, who, in two successive centuries, attained eminence in Roman life; and while we do not wish to press coincidences which may be accidental, such as the sale of slaves to Roman ladies (cf. Herm. Vis. i. 1 ὁ θρέψας με πέπρακέν με Ῥόδῃ) and the like, we may at least illustrate by the successful rise from slavery into political eminence of the two freedmen of Claudius, the similar liberation which took place in the case of Hermas and Pius, and which set one of them on the chair of St Peter, and gave the other an even greater place than the chair of Peter, as representative in the Church's literature of one of the most interesting periods in her history.

ON THE ANGELOLOGY OF HERMAS.

(*Johns Hopkins University Circulars, April* 1884.)

THERE is a passage in the Shepherd of Hermas, Vis. iv. 2, 4, which has occasioned a great deal of perplexity to the commentators. Hermas is met by a fierce beast with a parti-coloured head, which beast symbolizes an impending persecution or tribulation, and makes as though it would devour him. But the Lord sends his angel who is over the wild beasts, whose name is Thegri, and shuts the mouth of the creature, that it may not hurt him.

Θεγρὶ according to Gebhardt and Harnack is 'nomen inauditum'; it appears in the Vulgate Latin as *Hegrin* and in the Palatine version as *Tegri*. The Ethiopic translation has *Tégêri*. Jerome seems to have read *Tyri*, since in his comments on Habac. i. 4 we have 'ex quo liber ille apocryphus stultitiae condemnandus est, in quo scriptum est quemdam angelum nomine Tyri praeesse reptilibus.' Much ingenuity has been expended over the origin of the word and in particular the following is the solution of Franciscus Delitzsch as given in Gebhardt and Harnack's edition : 'Si sumi possit, Hermam nomen angeli illius ex angelologia Judaica hausisse, quae angelos maris, pluviae, grandinis etc. finxit iisque nomina commentitia indidit, θεγρί idem est quod תִּגְרִי, *instimulator* h. e. angelus, qui bestias (contra homines) instimulat atque, si velit, etiam domat (Taggar = dissidium, discordia ; cum î = Tigrî, quod bene descripsit H. : θεγρί etc.).'

I assent to the Hebrew origin of the name, but am unwilling to explain a *nomen inauditum* by a *nomen vix auditum*. A more simple solution presents itself; if for θ we write σ, according to the confusion common in uncial script, we have Σεγρὶ for the

name of the angel: which immediately suggests the root סָגַר,
to close. The angel is the one that *closes* or *shuts*. This is
immediately confirmed by the language of Hermas, ὁ κύριος
ἀπέστειλεν τὸν ἄγγελον αὐτοῦ τὸν ἐπὶ τῶν θηρίων ὄντα, οὗ τὸ
ὄνομά ἐστιν θεγρί, καὶ ἐνέφραξεν τὸ στόμα αὐτοῦ ἵνα μή σε
λυμάνῃ.

If any doubt remained as to the correctness of this solution it
would be swept away by reading the passage in Hermas side by
side with the LXX of Daniel vi. 23; ὁ θεός μου ἀπέστειλεν τὸν
ἄγγελον αὐτοῦ καὶ ἐνέφραξεν (וּסֲגַר) τὰ στόματα τῶν λεόντων
καὶ οὐκ ἐλυμήναντό με.

The curious parallelism of the language employed in the two
passages is decisive as to the etymology, and further we may be
sure that the language of Hermas is an indirect quotation from
the book of Daniel.

The result arrived at is an important one in many respects,
and has a possible bearing upon the genealogy of the MSS. and
versions of Hermas: so far as we are concerned we may simply
say that those copies and versions which read θεγρὶ or any
variation of the same bear conclusive marks of a Greek original.
It might seem unnecessary to make such a remark, but the fact is
that grave suspicions have been thrown out in some quarters as
to the character of the original text of Hermas. Upon further
consideration I am inclined indeed to conclude that all the versions
came from an original which read θεγρί, for even the Vulgate
Latin which has *Hegrin* seems to have arrived at it by dropping
the reduplicated T in the words

NOMEN EST THEGRI.

There is, however, another way in which the Latin variant
might be explained: for, as Dr Haupt points out to me, we have
a similar transformation in the Hebrew סַפַרְוַיִם (2 Kings xviii. 34)
which appears in Berosus as Σίσπαρα, in Ptolemy v. 18 Σίπφαρα,
but in Pliny vi. 123 as Hipparenum.

At this point the argument was taken up by Dr Hort, in a communication which appeared in the *Johns Hopkins University Circulars* for Dec. 1884, as follows :

Hermas and Theodotion ;

a communication from Professor Hort with regard to an emendation of the text of Hermas.

The note on the Angelology of Hermas printed by Professor Rendel Harris in the *Johns Hopkins University Circular* for April contains a discovery of considerable interest in itself, and further noteworthy as having at once enabled the discoverer to find a satisfactory answer to an old riddle. There cannot be a doubt that he is right in tracing back the language of Hermas in Vis. iv. 2—4 to Daniel 6₂₂; and it is hardly less certain, I think, that he has given the true explanation of Θεγρί, the mysterious name of the angel who is sent to protect Hermas, by reading it as Σεγρί taken as a derivative from *sagar*, the verb employed in that verse for the shutting of the lions' mouths.

The best known repositories of Jewish angelology do not appear to contain the name of *Segri* : but Sigron (סגרון) is recorded by Lévy-Fleischer (p. 478) from the Talmudic Tract Sanhedrin as an accessory name of Gabriel, given him 'because, if he shuts the doors of heaven, no one can open them.' The designation would seem to belong more naturally in the first instance to some such high function as this than to the shutting of lions' mouths—an office not to be confounded with the general charge of lions or other beasts, said to have been appropriated to different angels ; and the occurrence of Gabriel's name in Dan. 8₁₆; 9₂₁ may easily have been taken as determining the identity of the angel of 6₂₂. By what channel the Hebrew application of an obscure name belonging to Jewish tradition came to be accepted, though apparently misunderstood, by the Roman Hermas, is a question easier to ask than to answer.

My chief purpose, however, in writing this supplementary note, which is sent by Prof. Rendel Harris' request, is to point out that his discovery may have an important bearing on the disputed question of the Shepherd's date. The language of Hermas follows not the true Septuagint version of Daniel, but that of Theodotion, which superseded it in the course of the second century. The Septuagint drops the angel altogether: and in v. 22 has merely

σέσωκέν με ὁ θεὸς ἀπὸ τῶν λεόντων,

while it transfers the shutting of the lions' mouths to v. 18 by the insertion of an interpolated clause ending

ἀπέκλεισεν τὰ στόματα τῶν λεόντων καὶ οὐ παρηνόχλησαν τῷ Δανιήλ.

This clause, shortened in the opening words, was retained by Theodotion, with ἔκλεισεν (according to the best MSS.) substituted for ἀπέκλεισεν; but he corrected v. 22 by the Aramaic text reading ὁ θεός μου ἀπέστειλεν τὸν ἄγγελον αὐτοῦ καὶ ἐνέφραξεν τὰ στόματα τῶν λεόντων καὶ οὐκ ἐλυμήναντό με. Now Hermas has retained not only the angel, but the two characteristic Greek verbs, for he writes ὁ κύριος ἀπέστειλεν τὸν ἄγγελον αὐτοῦ...καὶ ἐνέφραξεν τὸ στόμα αὐτοῦ ἵνα μή σε λυμάνῃ.

It follows that Hermas cannot be older than Theodotion. To discuss the other evidence for the date of either Hermas or Theodotion would be beyond my present purpose.

F. J. A. HORT.

CAMBRIDGE, ENGLAND.
July 8, 1884.

This attempt to place the date of Hermas lower than that of Theodotion provoked the opposition of Dr Salmon who, in the following year in a note on Hermas and Theodotion which will be found appended to his Introduction to the New Testament, defended the antiquity of Hermas relatively to Theodotion. Dr Salmon had already in an article on Hermas in Smith's *Dictionary of Christian Biography* rejected the evidence of the Muratorian Canon which places the time of the composition of the Shepherd in the episcopate of Pius, i.e. c. A.D. 140—155. (The Canon itself must be later than this by some years, and we shall perhaps not be far wrong if we date it approximately in A.D. 180.) Salmon was now obliged to face new and, at first sight, conclusive evidence for the lateness of Hermas. True, the date of Theodotion is not a fixed point, being almost as much in dispute as the date of Hermas. But the evidence of the Patristic literature goes to shew that the Church abandoned the use of the Septuagint Daniel somewhere between the time of Justin and the time of Irenaeus, substituting for it the more exact version of Theodotion. And certainly the translation made by Theodotion is earlier than Irenaeus, for it is alluded to by the latter writer in his work against Heresies (iii. 21), and there are traces of the use of the Theodotion Daniel in the quotations of Irenaeus from the book itself. It follows, therefore, that Theodotion's text was known in the West as early as 180 A.D. And if we grant the use of Theodotion by Irenaeus why should we deny it in the case of Hermas?

The answer to this, from Dr Salmon's point of view, is that we have no right to assume that the only translations of Daniel current in the early Church were those of the LXX and of Theodotion. An examination of the quotations made from Daniel in the Apocalypse shews some singular agreements with the text of Theodotion as against the LXX, from which it is a natural inference that Theodotion remodelled an earlier version of Daniel. But in that case we have no right to say positively that Hermas has quoted from the text of Theodotion. Even in the very verse which is supposed to furnish the test case, we find a curious agreement with Daniel as quoted in the Epistle to the Hebrews, which suggests the use of a version like the Theodotion version by a writer a century earlier than Theodotion (cf. Heb. xi$_{33}$ ἔφραξαν στόματα λεόντων).

The argument must be traced at length in Dr Salmon's own pages, and it will, I think, leave the impression upon the mind of the student that a fair case has been made out for a suspense of judgment in regard to inferences drawn from the Segri passage. Probably it will also be felt that Dr Salmon went too far when he suggested that even the quotations in Irenaeus, which were supposed to come from Theodotion, might be from some lost early version to which that of Theodotion was closely related. If these quotations are to be disputed, in the light of the known fact of Irenaeus' acquaintance with the version of Theodotion, we should almost be obliged to go further, and deny the use of Theodotion by Irenaeus' pupil Hippolytus. But this step is too extreme for any one who was not prepared to abolish Theodotion altogether. But without denying the use of Theodotion by Irenaeus we might hold the posteriority of Hermas to be *non-proven,* and the question then arises as to whether there is any further light to be obtained upon the disputed points from fresh points of view.

PRESTER JOHN'S LIBRARY.

A Lecture delivered in the Divinity School, Cambridge, in October 1892.

THE newspapers have from time to time during the last two years informed us that the King of Abyssinia has begun to collect books for a Royal Library, and that he has made requisition from the monks of the various monasteries in his kingdom for the leading works which are extant among them, or for copies of the same. One suspects that some traveller is there who has been urging the King to make collections with the view of rendering the recovery of lost Ethiopic books more easy. If that be so, he is a wise traveller and deserves our best thanks.

The suggestion, however, of a royal library for Abyssinia takes us back as well as invites us forward; for one of the features of the great kingdom of Prester John, the Christian King of Ethiopia, whom the Portuguese discovered holding the faith in the mountains that border on the southern end of the Red Sea, was a magnificent library. Abyssinia was reported to be a paradise of books, as well as a Christian country with a Happy Valley in it[1]. And the description which the English writer Purchas gives of this collection of rare books is enough to make the mouth of every scholar and bibliophile to water. Let me draw your attention, as mine has been drawn by a friend, to the following extract from *Purchas his Pilgrimage or Relations of the*

---

[1] Rasselas is no mere imagination of Johnson; he wrote the novel shortly after he had been doing the hack-work of translating Lobo's *Voyage to Abyssinia* for Bettesworth and Hicks of Paternoster Row, who published it in 1735. Johnson received five guineas for this piece of work and devoted his first earnings to the funeral expenses of his mother. The translation was made from the French edition.

World and the Religions observed in all Ages, London, 1613; pp. 565 ff., Of the Hill Amara: and the rarities therein. After describing the natural features of the hill, the stately buildings of the two churches with their monasteries, he goes on to speak of the library thus (p. 567):

"In the monastery of the Holy Crosse are two rare peeces, whereon Wonder may justly fasten both her eies; the Treasury and Library[1] of the Emperour, neither of which is thought to be matchable in the world. That Librarie of Constantinople[2] wherein were 120000 bookes, nor the Alexandrian Library, wherein Gellius[3] numbereth 700000, had the fire not been admitted (too hastie a student) to consume them, yet had they come short, if report over-reach not, this whereof we speake, their number is in a maner innumerable, their price inestimable. The Queene of Saba (they say) procured Bookes hither from all parts, besides many which Solomon gave her, and from that time to this, their Emperors have succeeded in like care and diligence. There are three great Halls, each above two hundred paces large, with Bookes of all Sciences, written in fine parchment, with much curiosity of golden letters, and other workes, and cost in the writing, binding, and covers: some on the floore, some on shelves about the sides; there are few of paper: which is but a new thing in Ethiopia[4]. There are the writings of Enoch copied out of the stones wherein they were engraven, which intreate of Philosophie, of the Heavens and Elements. Others goe under the name of Noe, the subject whereof is Cosmographie, Mathematickes, ceremonies and prayers; some of Abraham which he composed when he dwelt in the valley of Mamre, and there read publikely Philosophie and the Mathematikes. There is very much of Salomon, a great number passing under his name; many ascribed to Job, which he writ after the recovery of his property[5]; many of Esdras, the Prophets and high Priests. And besides the four canonicall Gospels, many others ascribed to Bartholomew, Thomas, Andrew, and many others; much of the Sibylles, in verse and prose; the

---

[1] "The library of the Prete." [Margin.] [2] "Zonar. Ann. to. 3." [Margin.]
[3] "Gell. li. 6 c. 17." [Margin.]
[4] "Fr. Luys hath a very large catalogue of them l. 1, c. 9 taken out (as he saith) of an Index, wh. Anthony Gricus and L. Cremones made of them, being sent hither by the Pope Gregory 13 at the instance of Cardinall Zarlet, which sawe and admired the varietie of them, as did many others then in their company." [Margin.]
[5] Qu. prosperity.

workes of the Queen of Saba; the Greek Fathers all that have
written, of which many are not extant with us; the writers of
Syria, Egypt, Africa, and the Latine Fathers translated, with
others innumerable in the Greeke, Hebrew, Arabike, Abissine,
Egyptian, Syrian, Chaldee, far more authors, and more of them
than we have; few in Latin; yet T. Livius is there whole, which
with us is imperfect, and some of the works of Thomas Aquinas;
Saint Augustines workes are in Arabike: Poets, Philosophers, Physicians, Rabbines, Talmudists, Cabalistes, Hierogliphikes, and others
would be too tedious to relate.   When Jerusalem was destroyed
by Titus; when the Saracens over-ranne the Christian world;
many books were conveyed out of the Eastern partes into Ethiopia;
when Ferdinand and Isabella expelled the Jewes out of Spaine,
many of them entered Ethiopia and for doing this without licence,
enriched the Pretes library with their Bookes; when Charles V
restored Muleasses to his kingdom, the Prete hearing that there
was at Tunis a great Library sent and bought more than 3000
books of divers arts.   There are about 200 monks whose office
it is to looke to the Librarie, to keep them cleane and sound; each
appointed to the Books of that language which he understandeth;
the Abbot hath streight charge from the Emperor, to have care
thereof, he esteeming this Library more than his treasure."

The foregoing statements of Purchas are astonishing enough,
and it may well be supposed that the range of the literature
declared to be extant in the library of Prester John would be
sufficient, of itself, to destroy all faith in the authority of the
narrator: and indeed this seems to have been the impression
produced upon the minds of many scholars of the day, who, while
they were not unwilling to believe that lost books might be
recovered from Abyssinian libraries, not unnaturally shrank from
the belief that all the lost works of ancient Christian literature,
to say nothing of pagan letters, were to be found under a single
roof in the library of Rasselas.

But we must admit that the statements made by Purchas
have an air of verisimilitude to a modern scholar.   Take the
very first statement made by the Elizabethan writer, that the
books are all on vellum, and that paper is a new thing in Ethiopia.
Does that look like an invention?   Take Wright's Catalogue of
the Ethiopic MSS. in the British Museum: and examine whether
there are any paper MSS.   You will find that they are sur-

prisingly few, and of those which exist almost all are of a
more recent date than Purchas' Pilgrims: e.g. No. 127 is written
in the xviiith century; No. 151 is dated 1630; No. 318 was
written in the xixth century; No. 357 was written about the
beginning of the xixth century; No. 392 was written in A.D. 1861;
No. 395 was written in 1810 (and the paper is dated 1807), and
so on. In fact I have not noted any copy in the British Museum
on paper which was not written later than Purchas' day. Is not
this remarkable? How did Purchas' informant know that things
were so different in Abyssinia to what they were in Syria, for
example?

In the next place notice that the first of the books referred to
by Purchas as extant in the Abyssinian Library is "the writings
of Enoch, copied out of the stones on which they were engraven,
which intreate of Philosophie, of the Heavens and Elements." Is
it not strange that the front rank should have been assigned to
the very book which was actually brought back a century and
a half later from Abyssinia by the traveller Bruce? Further
the reference to the heavenly tablets is in agreement with the
language of the book of Enoch; for example, compare c. 81 "and
he said unto me, O Enoch, observe the writing of the heavenly
tablets, and read what is written thereon and mark every indi-
vidual fact. And I observed everything on the heavenly tablets,
and read everything which was written thereon and understood
everything." Compare with it the manner in which the book of
Enoch is cited in the Testament of the Twelve Patriarchs: "and
now, O my sons, I have read in the tablets of heaven."

Last of all the description which Purchas gives is not a bad
summary of the contents of the lost book. The most recent
editor of Enoch (Mr Charles) describes a certain section of the
book as a Book of Celestial Physics, which is not unlike Purchas'
language concerning the Heavens and the Elements. For example,
the 62nd chapter entitles itself "The Book of the courses of the
luminaries of the heaven and the relations of each, according to
their classes &c."

It must, I think, be admitted that Purchas' account of the
book of Enoch is not inconsistent with the belief that he derived
his knowledge from some one who had seen the book.

A little lower down in the list we are told that the library
contained the works of the Queen of Saba. Now this, at all

events, could hardly have been derived from notices of the earlier
Greek and Latin literature. The Queen of Sheba, however, is one
of the stock figures in Abyssinian History; for instance in the
book called Kebra Nagast (the Glory of Kings) fourteen chapters
are devoted to the legends concerning the Queen of Sheba[1].
Further the Abyssinian literature contains amongst the laws and
statutes of the kingdom, a collection brought from Jerusalem
by Menelek the son of Solomon. Menelek's mother is the Queen
of Sheba.

Now we can hardly regard it as a pure accident that Purchas
has thrust the Queen of Sheba in amongst the ecclesiastical
authors known in Abyssinia; he must have had some knowledge
or tradition at the very least with regard to the historical and
literary position assigned to the elect lady in question by the
Abyssinians.

It becomes proper for us, therefore, to investigate as far as
possible the sources from which Purchas drew his wonderful
account of the Ethiopian literature.

Now, as will be seen from our quotation, Purchas gives a
marginal reference which betrays his authority: he tells us that
" Fr. Luys hath a very large catalogue of them (the Abyssinian
treasures) taken out, as he saith, of an Index, which Anthony
Gricus and L. Cremones made of them, being sent hither by the
Pope Gregory 13 at the instance of Cardinall Zarlet, which sawe
and admired the varietie of them, as did many others then in
their company."

Cardinal Zarlet is, of course, the famous Sirletus, Librarian of
the Vatican, and just the very man to have instituted a literary
hunt in connexion with the Apostolic missions to the Ethiopes.
But who is Fr. Luys, that tells the tale?

Amongst the historians who have written of Ethiopia in
modern times, we find the name of Luys de Urreta. His work
' Historia de la Etiopia ' was published at Valencia in the year
1610, just three years before the first edition of Purchas. In
those days Englishmen travelled in Spain and talked Spanish
and read Spanish. One has only to recall the allusions in
Shakespeare to Spanish customs and the borrowing of Spanish
words in a manner which would be unintelligible now-a-days

[1] These chapters were edited by Pretorius in 1870 under the title ' Fabula de
Regina Sabaea apud Æthiopes.'

and to compare similar phenomena in Ben Jonson and other Elizabethan writers, in order to assure oneself that in the golden age of English literature learned men were familiar with Spanish[1]. There is then no difficulty *a priori* in the use of a Spanish author by Purchas, two or three years after the date of production of his work. But we need not speculate, for we have only to read Purchas side by side with Fr. Luys de Urreta in order to see that practically everything in the one is translated from the other. The very description of the Monasteries, and their location on the sacred mountain of Amara, comes out of Urreta, and so does the whole account of the library and its contents.

In proof of these statements we transcribe some sentences of Urreta, and reproduce his account of the Library, from which it will be seen that it is indeed, as Purchas described it, a *very large catalogue*, too large apparently for the faith˙ of Purchas, and his was no slight faith, to judge from the number of lost books which he advertised out of Urreta.

In lib. i. c. 9 Urreta tells us all about Prester John's library under the heading De los dos Monasterios que ay nel Monte Amarà, y la famosa libreria que tiene en uno de ellos el Preste Juan....Estas dos Iglesias que la una se intitula del Espiritu Santo, y la otra de Santa Cruz, son las mas sumptuosas y magnificas q̄ ay en toda la Etiopia.

He then gives a sketch of the most famous libraries in the world, from Aulus Gellius, Epiphanius, Plutarch, Galen, Nicephorus and Zonaras. Two of his references, viz. to Zonaras and Gellius will be found on the margin of Purchas. He goes on to describe the buildings: *Son tres salas grandissimas, cada una de mas de dozientos passos de largo*, donde ay libros de todas scientias, *todos en pergamino* muy sutiles, delgados y bruñidos, con mucha curiosidad de lettras doradas y otras labores y lindezas; unos enquadernados ricamente, con sus tablas; otros estan sueltos, como processos, rollados y metidos dentro de unas bolsas y talegas de tafetan: *de papel ay muy pocos, y es cosa moderna y muy nueva entra los de Etiopia.*

The passages which I have printed in italics shew the source from which Purchas derived his information about the size of the

---

[1] Cf. George Herbert's playful allusion :

    "It cannot sing or play the lute,
    It never was in France *or Spain*."

three separate halls, and the predominance of vellum books over paper, and the whole of his statements may be further compared with Urreta.

Next comes the Catalogue made for Gregory XIII.

El aranzel que se traxo al Sumo Pontifice Gregorio decimotercio, es el siguiente. Hay escrituras de *Enoch*, q̄ fue el septimo nieto de Adam, las quales está en pergaminos, façadas de piedras y ladrillos donde se escriuieron primeramente, que tratan de cosas de Philosophia, de cielos y elementos. Hay otros libros q̄ van cō nombre de *Noe*, que trata de Cosmographia, y Matematicas d̄ cosas naturales y de algunas oraciones y ceremonias. Hay libros de *Abraham*, los que el compuso quando estuuo en el valle de Mambre, donde tenia discipulos y leya publicamente Philosophia y las Mathematicas; estos discipulos fueron con cuya ayuda vencio a los quatro Reyes que lleuauan preso a su sobrino Loth. De *Salomon* muchissimos, unos traydos por la Reyna Saba, otros por Melilec hijo de Salomon, y otros q̄ el mismo Rey Salomon embiaua, y assi son en grande numero los que van con titulo de Salomon. Hay muchos libros con titulo de *Job*, y dizen que el los compuso despues que boluio en su antigua prosperidad.

So far we can see that Purchas has taken practically everything in Urreta. But it will be noticed that Urreta is not destitute of information which could not have been obtained except from people conversant with Ethiopian life. The allusion to Melilec the son of Solomon agrees closely with what we have noted above from the Kebra Nagast or book of the Glory of Kings.

Urreta continues as follows; and we shall see that Purchas is with him for a part of the account:

Hay muchos libros de *Esdras*, y de muchos *Prophetas y Sumos Sacerdotes*. Muchas epistolas extraordinarias de *San Pablo*[1], de las quales no se tiene en la Europa noticia. Muchos Evangelios fuera de los quatro Canonicos y Sagrados, que son san Matheo, san Lucas, san Marcos, y san Juan, como *el Evangelio secundum Hebraeos, secundum Nazaraeos, Encratitas, Ebionitas, y Egipcios;* y Evangelio *secundum Bartholomaeum, Andream, S. Thomam,* y otros.

Compare this with Purchas' account, and you will see that the English transcriber has begun to abbreviate. Urreta's account grows more and more wonderful.

[1] The italicized authors are either those mentioned above by Purchas, or they are names to which we shall refer a little later on. See note on p. 40.

Aunque es verdad que todos estos Evangelios y libros nombra-
dos sean apocriphos, de muy poca, o ninguna autoridad, con todo
los pongo aqui por curiosidad que por tal los guardan en esta
libreria, que tambien los tienen por apocriphos en toda la Etiopia;
solo los guardan por grandeza, y lo es sin duda para una libreria.
Hay muchos libros de *las Sybillas* en verso y en prosa, y otros
compuestos por *la reyna Saba y Melilec.*

By this time Purchas had got as much as he could carry, and
he summarizes what remains in Urreta, by telling us that all the
Greek and Latin fathers, and all the Philosophers, Physicians and
Rabbis are there. Urreta's account proceeds as follows:

Historias de la vida y muerte de Jesu Christo, y otras cosas
que sucedieron despues de su muerte, compuestas por algunos
Judios de aquellos tiempos. Hay tambien muchos libros de
Abdias[1], San Dionysio, fuera de los que por Europa tienen de
Origines, y de su maestro Clemente Alexandrino, y el maestro de
este Panteno, de todos estos ay muchas obras; de solo Origines ay
mas de dozientos libros. Tertulliano, san Basilio, san Cypriano,
san Cyrillo, san Hilario, san Hilarion, san Anastasio, san Gregorio
Niceno, y Nazianzeno, Epiphanio Damaceno, y todos los Dotores
Griegos, sin que aya ninguno de los que han escrito que no este
en esta libreria: no solo los que comunmente andan entra las
manos, pero otros muy esquisitos que no se tiene de ellos noticia,
cōpuestos per los mismos Dotores. De San Ephrem Siro, Moyses
Bar cepha, y de otros de la Iglesia Syra. Muchos tomos de San
Juan Chrisostomo, y de su maestro Diodoro Tarcēse todas sus
obras. Oecumenio, Doroteo, Tyro[2], y Dionysio Alexandrino discipulo de Origines. Serapion en muchos libros, San Justino Martyr
muchas obras, con las de su discipulo Taciano; todos los Theo-
doros, el Antiocheno, el Heracleyta, y el Syro, o Teodorito por
otro nombre, en compañia de Theodolo; los dos Zacharias, el
Obispo de Hierocesarea, y el de Chrisopolis, *Triphon discipulo de
Origines; y Tito Bostrense Arabio.* Tambien estan las obras de
Ticonio y Arnobio, Theophilato Antiocheno: las obras de Theo-
gnosto alabado por San Athanasio, y Theodoto Ancirano, Acacio
discipulo de Eusebio Cesariense, San Alberto Carmelita, Alex-
andro de Capadocia; las obras de Ammonio Alexandrino maestro
de Origines, y las de Amphilochio de Iconio, que tuuo la ciencia

---

[1] Cp. lib. ii. c. 14 "Abdias in vita Apostolorum."
[2] I follow the punctuation of the MS.

reuelada; Anastasio Sinayta, y el Anastasio Antiocheno, y Andreas
el Cretense, y Hierosolimitano, y el Cesariense, Antiocho Monacho,
y Antiocho Ptolemaydo, Antipater Bostrense; los dos Apollinares,
el Junior y el Antiquior; y tambien los dos Aristobolos, el moço y
el viejo, y Aretas Cesariense, *Rodon discipulo de Taciano, Rodul-
pho Agricola, Cayo Mario, Victorino, Catina, Syro, por su nombre
Lepos, esto es, agudo, ingenioso;* Proclo Constantinopolitano,
*Primacio Uticense discipulo de San Augustin, Policronio discipulo
de Diodoro, Phocion, y Pierio Alexandrino, Philon Judio,* del
qual ay mas de trezientos libros, cosa que admiro. Y los Judios de
Egipto, de Arabia, y otras partes se obligā a dar muchos millares
de ducados, solo por que se las dexen trasladar. *Pedro Edesino
discipulo de San Efren, Paulo Emesino, y Patrophilo Palestino,
Pantaleon;* de san *Didimo Alexandrino* ay muchos libros, y
tambien son muchos los *de Egesippo: Oresieso Etiope Monge, que
vivio año* 420; y las obras de *Olimpiodoro* y de san Nilo y
muchas de Nepote Egipcio: Euagrio Antiocheno, y las obras de
Eudoxia Emperatriz muger de Theodosio el menor; Euthalion
Monge, Basilio, Eustachio Antiocheno, y Euthimio y san Metho-
dio, las obras de Melito Sardense, y de San Luciano Antiocheno, y
de *Flauiano Constantinopolitano,* y *Fortunaciano Africano,* y el
glorioso *Fulgencio, Junilio,* y *Julio,* todos *Africanos;* los libros de
*Judas Syro, Isidoro Pelusiota en Egipto, discipulo de San Chriso-
stomo, Isidoro Thesalonicense;* estan las obras *de George Trape-
zuncio,* y de *Gennadio Constantinopolitano; los dos Josephos,*
San Juan Climaco, y Cassiano, *Hisichio Hierosolimitano;* de San
Augustin ay inumerables obras, no solo las que comunmente
andan por las librerias, sin otros muchos libros que nunca se han
impresso: de San Hieronymo, San Ambrosio, San Leon Papa, y
San Gregorio Magno ay algunos libros, aunque muy pocos, porque
de los Dotores Latinos es lo menos que ay. Y aduiertase, que
todos los libros que ay en estas tres salas son en lingua Griega,
Arabiga, Egipcia, Sira, Chaldea, Hebrea, y Abissina: en lingua
Latina no auia ningun libro, sino todas las Decadas de Titoliuio,
que por la Europa no se tenian, y alla estauan oluidadas, que como
no las sabian leer, no hazian caso de ellas. Lo que digo de los
libros de Dotores Latinos, estauan traduzidos en lengua Griega,
como San Hieronymo, Ambrosio, San Augustin en lingua Arabiga.
De los Dotores mas modernos ay algunos, como las partes de
Santo Thomas, y el *Contra Gentes:* las Obras de San Antonino, y

el directorio Inquisitorum, traduzidas en lingua Abissina por
Pedro Abbas Abissin, natural de Etiopia, hombre doctissimo en
lenguas y Theologia Escolastica, traduxo muchas sumas de casos de
conciencia, y cada dia se van traduziendo obras de Latin, Italiano,
Español en el collegio de los Indianos en Roma, para·embiar a la
Etiopia; y al presente se estan traduziendo en lengua Etiopia las
obras deuotas de Fray Luys de Granada. Estan sobra la Sagrada
Escritura todas las translaciones de Origenes, Luciano, Theodosion,
Simacho, Aquila; liciones Griegas, Arabigas, Egipcias, Hebreas,
Chaldeas, Abissinas, en Armenio, y en Persa, tambien esta la
Latina; pero la Vulgata que se cita, y lee, es la Chaldea[1]. De
Astrologia, Matematicas, Medicina, Philosophia, son innumerabiles
los libros que ay escritos en las linguas dichas, Platon, Aristoteles,
Pitagoras, Zenon; de Archimedes, Auicena, Galeno, Hipocrates,
Auerroes, muchos libros, no solo los que comunmente se platican,
sino otros muchos, de los quales no se tiene por aca noticia.
Libros de Poetas como Homero, Pindaro, innumerabiles. De
historias ay gran numero. Basta dezir que los libros que ay son
mas de un million. De Rabinos assi antes de la venida de
Christo, como despues de su santissima muerte, ay muchissimos;
como de Rabi Dauid Kimki, Rabi Moyses Aegyptius, Moyses
Hadarsam, Sahadias, Bengion, Rabi Salomon, Simeon Benjochay,
Simeon Benjoachim, Rabi Abraham, Benesra, Bacaiay, Chischia,
Abraham Parizol, Abraham Saua, Rab. Achaigool, Rabi Ammay,
Rab. Baruchias, Rab. Isaac, Ben Scola, Isaac Karo, Isaac Nathan,
Rab. Ismael, Rab. Leui Bengerson, Rab. Pacieta, y otros muchos.
De la Cabala, y del Talmud de los Judios auia en un aposento mas
de cinco mil tomos. Esta tabla que he puesto en este capitulo es
parte de un indice y aranzel que hizo de todos ellos Antonio
Greco, y Lorenço Cremones, embiados por el Papa Gregorio
decimotercio, a instancia del Cardinal Zarleto: los quales fueron a
la Etiopia solo para reconocer la libreria, en compañia de otros
que eran embiados para lo proprio, y vinieron admirados de ver
tantos libros, que en su vida vieron tantos juntos, y todos de mano
y en pergamino, y todos muy grandes, porque son como libros de
coro, con el pergamino entero, con los estantes de Cedro muy
curioso, y en tan diferentes linguas.

[1] That is the Ethiopic: cf. letter of Gonzalez Roderico to the Jesuits in Goa,
quoted in Purchas lib. vii. c. 8 "I had made my book in Portuguese and it was
necessary to turn it into Chaldee." It is also so named in the *Psalterium in quatuor linguis* of 1518.

Urreta goes on, after this tremendous catalogue, to tell us how all these books got to Abyssinia, beginning with the Queen of Sheba, and working down through various historical persecutions and falls of great cities with subsequent removals of collections of books and the like.

Now what are we to say to all this story?

Is there anything in it and how much? We have noticed already that the suspicions awakened in favour of the genuineness of Purchas' story are not reduced to nothing by reading the accounts of Urreta. There are some things brought to light which betray an actual knowledge of Abyssinia. He tells us, moreover, what, as a member of the Dominican order he ought to know, and which is probably quite correct, that the Roman missionaries were translating various books of doctrine and discipline into Ethiopic, such as the works of Aquinas or S. Luys de Granada. And he says that his lists are taken from catalogues made at the instigation of Sirletus. All of this looks reasonable enough, if it were not for the colossal size of the library and its wonderful inclusiveness. What are we to say to it?

We know what was said by contemporary writers.

Urreta's account was challenged by Godignus in his book *De Abassinorum rebus*, published at Lyons in 1615.

Godignus says (lib. i. cap. xvii.) "Ait in monte Amara, in coenobio sanctae crucis eam (bibliotecam) servari, et ab Regina Sabae accepisse initium, repositos ibi esse libros permultos, quos et tunc Salomon ipsi reginae ab Hierosolymis in patriam discedenti dono dedit: et singulis deinde annis solitus erat ad eandem mittere. Inter reliquos esse quosdam, quos vetustissimus ille Enochus ab Adamo septimus de coelo de elementis etc....

Haec de monstruosa illa biblioteca dixisse satis. Reliqua apud eum videat, qui volet. Duo tamen hic adjungenda quae addit. Unum est, Sirleti Cardinalis rogatu, fuisse a Gregorio xiii Pontifice maximo in Ethiopiam missos Antonium Gricum et Laurentium Cremonensem, ut hanc inspicerent bibliotecam etc....

Haec ille. Sed nullam in monte Amara esse bibliotecam, ex litteris habemus, et narratione eorum, qui loca illa diu coluere. Nonnihil librorum est in eo coenobio, quod Axumum vel Acaxumum dicitur, et a regina Candace ferunt aedificatum in urbe Saba, quae nunc paene euersa, et aequata solo nonnulla retinet antiquae signa pulchritudinis. Quidquid id tamen librorum est, regiae bibliotecae non meretur nomen.

Ita referunt, qui rem perpexere, indubitatae homines fidei."

It may perhaps be thought that Godignus was a little too sweeping in his condemnations; no doubt the Jesuit fathers were not disposed to regard with much confidence the statements of the Friars Preachers with regard to Abyssinia or any other matter. Godignus' contemptuous rejection of Urreta was taken up by Ludolf in his History of Ethiopia, published not long after. I quote the second English edition, which bears the date 1684. Ludolf says:

"Besides sacred books the Habessines have but very few others. For the story of Barratti[1], who chatters of a library containing ten thousand volumes, 'tis altogether vain and frivolous. Some few we had an account of," and he appends the following note:

"Urreta did not think worth while to tell so modest an untruth. The most celebrated Libraries, saith he, that ever had renown were nothing in respect of Presbyter John's: the books are without number, richly and artificially bound; many to which Solomon's and the Patriarchs' names are affixt. Godignus explodes him, l. i. c. 17."

Quétif, the literary historian of the Dominicans, in giving an account of the works of Fr. Luys de Urreta, endeavours to apologize for a description of Abyssinia which he has not courage to defend by suggesting that Urreta was imposed upon by some Ethiopian. He had no intention himself to utter anything that was not truth, but some one played off on him a literary forgery.

"De quibus operibus (sc. Urretae) eruditi alii aliter sentiunt, nos hoc unum contendimus Urretam ab implanatorum falsariorumve crimine immunem esse, nec quid quod verum ipse non putaret edidisse: utrum autem cujusdam Aethiopis agyrtae Joannis Baltazar[2] fraudibus illectus et circumventus fuerit, faciliorisque fidei hominem se praestiterit, ac levioris, id peritorum certe cordatorumque relinquimus arbitrio et criterio."

---

[1] John Nunez Barreti (a Portuguese of the city of Oporto) was appointed Patriarch of Ethiopia by the influence of King John of Portugal and at the instance of Peter the Abyssinian : his life will be found in the second book of Godignus, *De Abassinorum rebus :* cf. Purchas, *Pilgrims,* lib. vii. c. 8.

[2] This John Balthazar Abassinus is alluded to in Godignus lib. ii. c. 18, p, 315. Purchas lib. vii. c. 8 (ed. 1625) speaks of him and his connexion with Urreta in the following decided manner : "One Juan de Baltasar, a pretended Abassine, and Knight of the Militarie Order of Saint Antonie, hath written a Booke in Spanish of that Order, founded (as he saith) by the Prete John, in the daies of Saint Basil, with

But this appeal for mercy leaves us still without an explanation of the way in which the fraud, if it was indeed a fraud, was concocted by the hypothetical Ethiopian. It certainly was no ordinary person that manufactured the catalogue in the first instance. To take a single specimen, we are told that the library contained an account of the events occurring in connexion with the Passion, and subsequently; this evidently means the Gospel of Nicodemus, but the writer goes on to say that it was an account written by the Jews: this arises out of the false prologue to the Nicodemus Gospel which affirms the Hebrew origin of the legends. But the reference implies a writer who had also read carefully the books which be describes. Would an Ethiopic trickster have done it so cleverly as this? Why may not the Acts of Pilate have been extant in Abyssinia?

We will now try to take the enquiry a little further, by pointing out the actual source from which Urreta's lists are derived.

It has occurred to me that perhaps the details may be extracted from the Biblioteca of Sixtus Senensis: and I now propose to shew that this is really the case. The supposition is not an unlikely one, for Sixtus is the great scholar of ·the Dominican order; moreover, there is on the margin of Urreta's book, in one place, a reference to Sixtus. He is describing the works of the Patriarchs who wrote before the Flood, and on the margin are the words

Escrituras hechas antea del diluvio
Sixto Senense lib 4. Bibliothecae.

Our main reason for making this suggestion lies in the fact that Urreta's list has every appearance of being taken from an alphabetically arranged catalogue. For example, we have such conjunctions as:

Tatian: Theodorus Ant.: Theodorus Heracl.: Theodorus Syrus: Theodoritus: Theodoulos:

rules received from him, above seven hundred yeares before any Military Order was in the world. I know not whether his Booke (which I have by me) hath more lies or lines; a man of a leaden braine and a brazen face; seconded, if not exceeded by the Morall, Naturall and Politicall Historie of Ethiopia, the worke of his Scholler Luys d'Urreta, a Spanish Frier and lyer: the said Godignus every where through his first Booke confutes him."

I have examined Baltazar's book, published at Valencia in 1609, entitled *Fundacion, Vida y Regla de la grande orden militar*, and do not see any reason to make him responsible for Urreta in the matter of the Catalogue.

and then after inserting Zacharias of Hierocesarea and Zacharias of Chrysopolis, we go on with Tryphon, Titus of Bostra, and Ticonius and so on.

The list then inserts Arnobius, and returns to the end of the alphabet with Theophylact, and Theognostus.

There is a method in this madness; it is not necessary to spend time in making illustrations of it. Where is the catalogue from which this was taken? Either the books in the library of Prester John were arranged alphabetically, and followed a Western alphabet, or we have here a Western book catalogue from which selections have been made. That the latter is the solution appears at once on consulting Sixtus Senensis.

Let us take one or two extracts from Urreta, and put side by side with them the corresponding parts of the alphabetically arranged catalogue of Sixtus.

Urreta	*Sixtus*
Triphon discipulo de Origenes y Tito Bostrense Arabio. Tambien estan las obras de Ticonio.	Titus Bostrenae ecclesiae in Arabia episcopus. Triphon, Origenis discipulus. Tichonius, natione Afer.
Acacio, discipulo de Eusebio Cesariense, San Alberto Carmelita, Alexandro de Capadocia.	Acacius...Caesariensis Ecclesiae Palestinae episcopus, Eusebii Caesariensis Episcopi discipulus. Albertus Joannis Harlemensis Carmelita.... Alexander, Episcopus Cappadociae.

(The intrusion of the modern writer between the two Church Fathers is very striking.)

Rodon discipulo de Taciano, Rodulpho Agricola,	Rhodon Asianus, Tatiani in scripturis auditor et discipulus, followed by Rodolphus Agricola, Frisius.
Cayo Mario, Victorino,	Caius Marius Victorinus Afer, rhetor sui temporis praestantissimus. And a little later on,
Catina Syro, por su nombre Lepos, esto es, agudo, ingenioso.	Catina Syrus, cognomine Leptos, id est, acutus et ingeniosus...Cuius meminit Hieronymus libro i. comm. in Ezech., referens summatim expositionem illius super visione rotarum et animalium.

Or compare the following:

Oresieso Etiope Monge, que vivio año 420 y las obras de Olimpiodoro.	Oresiesis monachus et eremita, Pachomii et Theodori monachorum in solitudinibus Ægypti commorantium collega...Claruit sub Honorio Aug. anno Dom. 420.... Olympiodorus Monachus.

But we need not occupy more space in proving what is abundantly clear that the list of Urreta is a series of extracts from Sixtus Senensis, and that he follows his authority even in printers' errors[1]. We can hardly interpose another writer between Urreta and Sixtus, and the idea that the catalogue was the fabrication of an Ethiopian monk seems especially improbable.

The only question that remains is whether Urreta has drawn upon the narratives of the Dominican missionaries as well as upon the printed work to which we have tracked him. This is not at all an unlikely supposition, and deserves looking into. But we must first subtract all the information that can fairly be set down to Sixtus: and when this is done, there is very little left. All the lost Gospels are gone, Livy is gone, Abraham, and Noah and

---

[1] The following further coincidences may be noted with passages which we have italicized in Urreta's account.

        Tryphon, Origenis discipulus,
preceded by
        Titus Bostrenae ecclesiae in Arabia episcopus.
and a little earlier
        Tichonius, natione Afer.

        Primasius, Uticensis in Africa episcopus,
          divi Augustini, ut creditur discipulus,
        Pierius, Alexandrinae ecclesiae presbyter...
        Placidus...
        Polychronius...Diodori Tarsensis episcopi
                auditor...
and on an earlier page
        Petrus, Edessenae Ecclesiae presbyter,
          scripsit in morem Sancti Ephrem
          Syro sermone Homilias etc....
and on the previous page
        Paulus, Emesae episcopus,
and a little earlier
        Patrophilus Scythopoleos, Palaestinae episcopus,
and on the previous page
        Pantaleon, magnae Dei ecclesiae diaconus etc.

The reader can also verify a host of other names, both those which we have italicized and most of the others. From Sixtus comes also the table of Rabbis.

Enoch have disappeared, and the crowd of lesser men. Prester John's Library has shrunk to quite an attenuated form, and we are now in danger of expecting nothing from Abyssinia instead of expecting everything. A winter of discontent has followed rapidly on the glorious summer of Urreta's promises. We are reduced from the stately palace of Rasselas to a lodge in a garden of cucumbers. The attitude of despair is, however, as unreasonable as that of extreme hope. The libraries which gave us Enoch and the Book of Jubilees cannot be exhausted. It is not generally known that the English army swept up nearly 1000 MSS. at the capture of Magdala, and left 600 of them behind in a church on their return to the sea-coast[1].

It is much to be regretted that no sufficient band of Ethiopic scholars was attached to the Abyssinian expedition. Were those 600 volumes all prayer-books?

These books from the collection of king Theodore cannot, however, be held to have exhausted the MS. wealth of Abyssinia. And significant rumours have lately been reaching us of discoveries made in an island on one of the great Abyssinian lakes.

Here is a notice from a German paper of March 16, 1894 (*Theol. Lit.-Blatt*): "König Menelek von Abessinien hat, nach der Meldung französischer Blätter, bei einer Expedition nach dem im Süden seines Reiches gelegenen Zuai-See einen werthvollen Fund alt-äthiopischer Manuskripte gemacht. Die Inseln dieses Sees galten immer als 'heilig' und die dortige schwer nahbare Bevölkerung verwahrt trotz ihrer barbarischen Unbildung nach alter Ueberlieferung die äthiopischen Bücher als Heiligthümer. Die auf der Insel Debra-Sina gemachten Funde sind theils liturgischen Inhalts, zum anderen Theil versprechen sie aber werthvollere Ausbeute. Der König beabsichtigt eine Dampferverbindung auf dem See herzustellen, womit der sagenhafte Zauber der heiligen Inseln verschwinden würde."

[1] *Record of the Expedition to Abyssinia*, ii. 396: "On the capture of Magdala a large number of Ethiopian MSS. were found, having been carried there by Theodore from the libraries of Gondar and the central parts of Abyssinia during his late expedition, in which he destroyed very many Christian churches. On finding that Magdala would have to be abandoned to the Gallas, it became necessary to provide for the safety of these volumes, which would otherwise have been destroyed by the Mohammedans. About 900 volumes were taken as far as Chelikot, and there about 600 were delivered to the priests of that church, one of the most important in Abyssinia; 359 books were retained for the purpose of scientific examination."

What makes it practically certain that this is a true report which has reached Europe is that a similar statement with regard to the existence of the books will be found in the Journals of the missionaries Isemberg and Krapf: we find in their account (p. 179) as follows:

"In the lake of Gurague called Suai five islands exist, in which the treasures of the ancient Abyssinian kings are said to have been hidden from Gragne [the Mohammedan desolator of Abyssinia] when he entered Abyssinia. That there are Ethiopic books is confirmed by a man whom the king sent as a spy."

In all probability, then, it is the books mentioned by Isemberg and Krapf that have been brought to light by king Menelek; and one can only hope that before long the contents of this newly-found library may be rendered accessible to Western scholars.

PRESBYTER GAIUS AND THE FOURTH GOSPEL.

*(A Paper read before the Society for Historical Theology,
November 28, 1895.)*

THERE are some learned men whose works it is almost impossible to read with a proper degree of scepticism; their acquaintance with the subjects upon which they write is so wide, the considerations which they bring forward are so varied and new, the collateral information, both relevant and irrelevant, which they furnish is so stupendous, that the critical faculty becomes paralyzed in its most useful members, in its power to doubt and to contradict; and it is often only after long and weary study that we begin at last to realize that these great scholars were just as capable of running down a *cul de sac* as we are ourselves, and that we must resume with regard to them the habit of healthy distrust and apply it to many of their strongest and most elaborate demonstrations.

Such is the temper of mind in which I am trying to read Lightfoot, the writer of all others in our time whose criticisms seem to defy challenge and escape contradiction; and the object of the present paper is to shew in a brief, but I hope conclusive manner, the accumulation of errors for which Lightfoot is responsible in his treatment of a single problem of Church History, and the way in which our progress has been arrested by the erroneous hypothesis which he brought forward and his undue zeal in defending that hypothesis. I am referring to the question of Gaius the Presbyter, a famous third century writer, of whom Eusebius tells us that he wrote or held a dialogue against Proclus the Montanist in the days of Zephyrinus, and that he attacked in this dialogue the Chiliastic views which Cerinthus and others deduced from the Apocalypse, and probably attacked the Apocalypse itself.

As far back as 1868 in an article entitled '*Gaius or Hippolytus*,' published in the *Journal of Philology*, Lightfoot had maintained the theory that Gaius was merely the double of Hippolytus; and he brought forward a number of confirmatory considerations, which were revised and amplified in his *Apostolic Fathers*, a work in which, as I have intimated above, everything has the air of being final and infallible. These considerations were (i) that the historical allusions to Gaius agree exactly with parallel details in the life of Hippolytus; as, for instance, that they both flourished under Zephyrinus, that each was styled presbyter, that they both lived at Rome, that they were both learned men, that they both denied the Pauline authorship of the Epistle to the Hebrews, that each was antimontanistic, and that, more obscurely, the title 'Bishop of the Gentiles,' whatever it may mean, seems to have been applicable to either of them. And (ii) further than these historical allusions there were literary confusions between Gaius and Hippolytus of an extraordinary kind, which were made worse by the modern critics who insisted on referring every anonymous work of Hippolytus to the shadowy Gaius, until at last, as Lightfoot allowed, they overdid the matter by trying to make Gaius the author of the *Philosophumena*. Now since the *Philosophumena* is undoubtedly the work of Hippolytus, and the recognition of its authorship carries also the authorship of a number of lesser works which are in dispute, Gaius would have been a jay stripped of a mass of peacock's feathers and left to us merely as the author of the *Dialogue against Proclus the Montanist*, if it had not happened that Lightfoot ingeniously stuck all the feathers on again by maintaining that Gaius was Hippolytus, and that even the Dialogue against Proclus was due to the latter father. His explanation was that the title of the Dialogue in question ran as follows:

Διάλογος Γαΐου καὶ Πρόκλου
ἢ κατὰ Μοντανιστῶν,

and that Gaius is here either a literary lay-figure, which has given cause to a mass of subsequent misunderstandings, or that it is the actual prænomen of Hippolytus.

Now this was very ingenious; moreover it rid us of the troublesome and perplexing figure of the Higher Critic (for such Gaius certainly was) in the Roman Church; it disposed of a person who was of doubtful orthodoxy (for the fact that Gaius wrote against the Montanists is not a set-off against his attack on the Johannine writings; any stick is good enough to beat a Montanist dog), and it left us a clearer view of the classic form of the great pupil of Irenaeus, who seems to have never been guilty of anything worse than Novatianism, and who in other respects was a genuine *malleus haereticorum*. No doubt there is a certain advantage to be gained from the fact that heretics turn to shades and their works do follow them, while the orthodox defender of the Faith becomes more and more imposing and real, so that we may say, with Homer,

$$ο\mathring{l}ος\ πέπνυται,\ το\mathring{l}\ δὲ\ σκια\mathring{l}\ ἀΐσσουσιν\cdot$$

in no other way could the rule 'quod semper, quod ubique, quod ab omnibus' become verifiable. But, as it happens, in the case which we are studying, the shade has evaded the Charon who had ferried him over, and is back again, as in his last edition Lightfoot admits, in the upper air.

The key to the problem, as in so many modern cases, is of Syrian manufacture.

First of all, we are to set over against the fact of Gaius' attack on the Apocalypse, and the statement on the back of the chair of Hippolytus in the Lateran Museum that Hippolytus wrote a treatise ὑπὲρ τοῦ κατὰ Ἰωάννην εὐαγγελίου καὶ ἀποκαλύψεως the remarkable entry made by the Syriac writer Ebed-jesu at the beginning of the 14th century that Hippolytus, Bishop and Martyr, wrote a treatise called

ܪܫܐ ܕܠܘܩܒܠ ܓܐܝܘܣ

or 'Heads against Gaius.'

This latter entry ought to have been sufficient to prove that Gaius was an antagonist of Hippolytus and not his double; and taken with the first two statements to make it highly probable that Gaius actually attacked both of the Johannine writings, for the defence of Hippolytus is clearly a single work occupied with the Johannine matter in the Canon. But, unfortunately, we have not been in the habit of either studying or trusting Syriac writers in the degree that they deserve.

The second direction from which the Syriac fathers come to our aid is Dr Gwynn's discovery[1] that Dionysius Bar-Ṣalibi in his

---

[1] *Hermathena*, vol. vi. pp. 397—418.

Commentary upon the Apocalypse, of which a copy is extant in the British Museum[1] (of course unpublished), quotes from the very treatise referred to by Ebéd-jesu, giving in a number of instances the substance of the objections made by Gaius to the Apocalypse and the replies of Hippolytus.

The recovery of these passages enabled Dr Gwynn to affirm with certainty the separate identity of Gaius, and to prove that Gaius had rejected the Apocalypse from the Canon on the ground that it contained 'predictions mainly eschatological, irreconcilable with the words of our Lord and the teaching of St Paul'; and these views of Gaius were antagonized by Hippolytus in a treatise whose title was probably 'Heads against Gaius', and we are thus led to conjecture that the complete title was

Κεφάλαια κατὰ Γαΐου ὑπὲρ τοῦ κατὰ Ἰωάννην εὐαγγελίου καὶ ἀποκαλύψεως,

or else that the work of Hippolytus existed also in an Epitome; that is, we equate the title preserved in Syriac with the title on the back of the chair, and so make Gaius to have attacked the canonicity, not merely of the Apocalypse but also of the Fourth Gospel.

But here we are upon new ground, for we have taken a step at which Dr Gwynn hesitated and drew back. For, finding that in replying to Gaius, Hippolytus cites, once at least, from St John's Gospel, he argues that this implies that Gaius accepted the Fourth Gospel. Indeed he says that it seems to follow *with scarcely less certainty* than the preceding conclusions that *Gaius accepted the Fourth Gospel as St John's.* It is this statement into the accuracy of which I propose to enquire.

But before doing so, it is instructive to recall some of the obstacles through which we have threaded our way in the history of the investigation. Lightfoot in his last edition admitted the weight of the new evidence brought forward by Dr Gwynn, but suggested that, although Gaius may be come to life again, it may be some other Gaius. He clung to the theory which he had carefully elaborated, and was unwilling to abandon it. I think this tenacity is to be regretted; it would have been better to have been more Saturnian with one's offspring. But Lightfoot, of course, granted at once that Gaius had written against the Apo-

---

[1] Rich, 7185.

calypse, and from this it follows that the remarks which Gaius makes about Cerinthus and the sensuous millennium which he proclaimed in the name of a great Apostle, must be understood as a criticism of the Apocalypse and the Chiliastic interpretations of it. In the light of which recently acquired knowledge it is interesting to compare the misunderstanding of the situation involved in the following sentence from Lightfoot (*Apost. Fathers*, Pt. I. vol. ii. p. 386), "It is difficult to see how an intelligent person should represent the Apocalypse as teaching that in the kingdom of Christ ' men should live in the flesh in Jerusalem and be the slaves of lusts and pleasures;' and again 'that a thousand years should be spent in marriage festivities.'" Amongst the people of ecclesiastical rank and dignity who held the view involved, though somewhat caricatured, in these words were Papias, Irenaeus, Nepos and Victorinus of Pettau. They certainly were not all of them idiots, though perhaps we may allow Papias the title of σφόδρα σμικρὸς τὸν νοῦν. The fact is that Lightfoot did not do justice to the Chiliastic movement.

Dr Gwynn is in the same case; in order to save the credit of the Apocalypse he ventures to suggest that Cerinthus "may have written a pseudo-Apocalypse, containing previsions of a millennium of carnal pleasures, and that Gaius, in his anti-millenarian over-zeal, may have rejected both Apocalypses, the genuine and the spurious alike." But since Cerinthus is credited with nothing worse than the rest of the Chiliastic succession, we have no reason to make him the author of a further Apocalypse, which would not also apply to the other fathers who are named, all of whom hold what their opponents call the 'sensuous millennium.' We must not multiply Apocalypses: the one which is certainly involved in the phenomena is sufficient for the explanation of the phenomena.

And now for our problem; did Gaius write against the Fourth Gospel, yea or nay?

The answer will come from the same quarter as before, for the Syrian Church holds the keys of all the problems. Suppose we turn to Dionysius Bar-Ṣalibi's Commentary upon St John, of which a Latin translation is preserved in the Bodleian Library[1], made by Dudley Loftus from a MS. now in the Library of Trinity College, Dublin. We find the following sentence, which I give in Loftus' own words:

[1] *Fell MSS.* 6 and 7.

Gaius haereticus reprehendat Johannem quia non concors fuit cum sociis, dicentibus[1], quod post baptismum abiit in Galilaeam, et fecit miraculum vini in Katna. *Sanctus Hypolitus e contrario* (l. adversus eum) scilicet, Christus postquam baptizatus fuerat, abiit in desertum, et quando inquisitio facta erat de illo per discipulos Johannis et per populum, quaerebant eum et non inveniebant eum, quia in deserto erat, cum vero finita fuisset tentatio et rediisset, venit in partes habitatas non ut baptizaretur, baptizatus enim jam fuerat, sed ut monstraretur a Johanne qui dixit intuens eum, ecce **Agnus Dei**! baptizatus igitur fuit et abiit in desertum dum exquirerent eum, et quod vidissent eum bene persuasi erant, quis fuit, sed quo abiisset non sciverant, sed quando rediisset persuasit eis ex quo quod monstratus fuit a Johanne, *crastino die vidit eum Johannes et dixit ecce agnus Dei!* istos quadraginta dies exquisiverunt eum et non viderunt eum; peractis vero diebus tentationis, cum venisset et visus esset venit in Galilaeam; quapropter inter se conveniunt Evangelistae quia postquam rediisset Dominus noster a deserto eumque monstrasset Johannes, illi, qui vidissent eum baptizatum, apprehendissent patrem clamantem, non viderunt eum amplius, quia abiit in desertum, necesse habuit Johannes ut iterum testimonium hujusmodi perhiberet de eo, quod hic est quam quaeritis *et illinc* abiit in Galilaeam virtute spiritus.

Now this extract at first sight seems to dispose completely of Dr Gwynn's statement as to the acceptance of the Fourth Gospel by Gaius. There is, however, a textual difficulty. On comparing Loftus' rendering with two MSS. in the British Museum (Codd. Add. 7184 and 12,143), I find reason to suspect that the name of Gaius was not in the primitive draft of the Commentary. For example the MS. Add. 7184 begins as follows:

ܐܢܫ ܐܝܪܛܝܩܘܣ ܗܘܐ ܐܩܒܠ ܝܘܚܢܢ

'A certain heretic had accused John &c.'

and a later hand adds above the line the word ܩܐܝܣܐ. On the other hand this addition is wholly wanting in the MS. Add. 12,143, and as we can see no reason for the omission of the name of Gaius in these two copies, we suspect that it has come in by editorial correction. Indeed the opening words which answer to the Greek αἱρετικός τις would of themselves suggest the absence

---

[1] We should probably correct the Syriac text and read *dicentem*.

of the name of the heretic. The question is whether the name is rightly added by way of identification. And to this I think we may answer in the affirmative; for the description of Hippolytus' reply which follows

ܕܩܕܝܫܐ ܐܦܘܠܝܛܘܣ ܠܘܩܒܠܗ

'Of the holy Hippolytus against him,'

immediately recalls the title 'Heads against Gaius.' And indeed there is no other candidate for the honour of the place of opposition. It is, moreover, interesting to compare the way in which the quotations are introduced with the passages quoted by Bar-Ṣalibi in his commentary on the Apocalypse.

The five cases given by Dr Gwynn are introduced as follows:

(i) ܓܐܝܘܣ ܐܪܣܝܘܛܐ ܕܠܩܒܠ ܗܢܐ ܓܠܝܢܐ
ܘܐܡܪ:

ܐܦܘܠܝܛܘܣ ܕܪܘܡܝ ܐܟܣܗ ܘܐܡܪ

i.e. 'Gaius the heretic, who objected to this Revelation and said ... Hippolytus of Rome refuted him and said'

(ii) ܓܐܝܘܣ ܐܡܪ:

ܘܐܡܪ ܐܦܘܠܝܛܘܣ ܠܘܩܒܠ ܗܕܐ ܣܩܘܒܠܝܘܬܐ
ܕܐܪܣܝܘܛܐ.

i.e. Gaius said:
and Hippolytus said in reply to this objection of the heretic:

(iii) ܗܪܟܐ ܣܩܒܠ ܓܐܝܘܣ:

ܘܐܦܘܠܝܛܘܣ ܟܣܐ ܠܗ ܘܐܡܪ

i.e. Here Gaius objected...
and Hippolytus refuted him and said:

(iv) ܓܐܝܘܣ:

ܐܦܘܠܝܛܘܣ ܠܘܩܒܠܗ.

i.e. Gaius:
Hippolytus against him...

(v) ܓܐܝܘܣ ܗܪܣܝܘܛܐ ܐܣܩܒܠ:

ܐܦܘܠܝܛܘܣ ܐܟܣܗ ܠܗܕܐ ܘܐܡܪ:

i.e. Gaius the heretic objected...
Hippolytus refuted this and said.

and these prefaces are so closely parallel to the passage which we
have quoted from Bar-Salibi's Commentary on the Fourth Gospel,
that we need have no hesitation in saying that if the name of
Gaius was wanting in the first copy, it has been rightly suggested
by later readers. And if this be so, we can only regard as a
serious misstatement Dr Gwynn's remark that it follows with
hardly less certainty than the fact that Gaius lived and opposed
the canonicity of the Apocalypse that the said Gaius accepted the
Fourth Gospel.

But in order that the matter should be put outside of doubt,
we will take the argument a little further and examine what
Epiphanius brings forward in his treatment of the 51st Heresy,
that of the people whom he calls the *Alogi*. It is commonly
supposed that this title is an invention of Epiphanius to describe
the people who did not believe in the Johannine writings, which
contain the Doctrine of the Logos. And Epiphanius actually says
in c. 3 Τί φάσκουσιν τοίνυν οἱ Ἄλογοι; Ταύτην γὰρ αὐτοῖς
τίθημι τὴν ἐπωνυμίαν· ἀπὸ γὰρ τῆς δεῦρο οὕτως κληθήσονται, καὶ
οὕτως, ἀγαπητοί, ἐπιθῶμεν αὐτοῖς ὄνομα, τουτέστιν Ἄλογοι. And
he speaks with the same air of originality in c. 28, in the words,
Ἠλέγχθησαν καὶ οἱ ἀποβαλλόμενοι τὸ κατὰ Ἰωάννην εὐαγγέλιον,
οὓς δικαίως Ἀλόγους καλέσομαι, ἐπειδὴ τὸν λόγον τοῦ θεοῦ ἀπο-
βάλλονται, τὸν διὰ Ἰωάννην κηρυχθέντα κτέ. There is, however,
a curious feature in the title of the refutation of this heresy which
suggests that this originality is an illusion. For the title runs as
follows: Κατὰ τῆς αἱρέσεως τῆς μὴ δεχομένης τὸ κατὰ Ἰωάννην
εὐαγγέλιον καὶ τὴν Ἀποκάλυψιν, ἣν ἐκάλεσεν Ἀνοήτων, τρια-
κοστὴ πρώτη, ἡ καὶ πεντηκοστὴ πρώτη. Here the obvious
suggestion is to restore Ἀλόγων for Ἀνοήτων in harmony with
the passages quoted above. But how did the error arise? The
answer is, I think, as follows: the title must have been confused
with the title of another heresy, viz. the heresy of Noetus, to
whom the appellation of Ἀνόητος would be peculiarly applicable.
And when we turn to the heresy in question, which is the 57th in
Epiphanius' list, we find him using this very play upon the name,
though it does not appear in the title prefixed to the heresy. For
example in c. 4 he says καὶ διέπεσεν ἐκ πανταχόθεν ὁ τῆς
ἀνοησίας σου λόγος, ὦ ἀνόητε. It is to this heresy then that
the name applies. We may also compare c. 6 οὗτος καὶ ὁ ἀπ᾽
αὐτοῦ Νοητοῦ ἔχων ὄνομα ἀνόητος ὑπάρχει καὶ οἱ ἐξ αὐτοῦ ἀνοη-

τοῦντες, also c. 8 Τί οὖν ἐρεῖ Νοητὸς ἐν τῇ αὐτοῦ ἀνοησίᾳ; etc. etc. Now when we turn to the heresy of the Noetians as described by Philaster (Haer. 53) we find that the same play upon words occurs, as the following sentence will shew:

alii autem Noetiani *insensati* cuiusdam nomine Noëti, qui dicebat patrem omnipotentem ipsum esse Christum;

and here, as Lipsius shews, the word *insensati* stands for ἀνοήτου. And a comparison with the language of Hippolytus *contra Noetum* shews that Philaster is following Hippolytus closely; so that we reasonably infer that the play upon the name began originally with Hippolytus, and this inference is fully confirmed by an examination of Hippolytus' treatment of the subject. For not only does Hippolytus shew an acquaintance with the joke, but we can see the way in which he was led to it. He compares the theological system of Noetus with that of Heraclitus, in which all contraries are harmonized so that crooked things are the same as straight things, mortal and immortal are equivalent terms, and God is at once 'summer and winter, peace and war, satiety and famine.' What wonder then if he should apply the same reasoning to the name of Noetus, who should turn out to be Anoetus! And that he does so reason will appear from *Ref. Haer.* ix. 10, where he follows the sentence Ὁ θεὸς...πόλεμος, εἰρήνη, κόρος, λιμός by saying Τἀναντία ἅπαντα. οὗτος (*l.* οὕτως) ὁ νοῦς.... Φανερὸν δὲ πᾶσι τοὺς νοητοὺς (*l.* ἀνοήτους) Νοητοῦ διαδόχους καὶ τῆς αἱρέσεως προστάτας, εἰ καὶ Ἡρακλείτου λέγοισαν ἑαυτοὺς μὴ γεγονέναι ἀκροατὰς, ἀλλά γε τὰ τῷ Νοητῷ δόξαντα αἱρουμένους ἀναφανδὸν, ταῦτα ὁμολογεῖν. For, as he continues, they hold the doctrine of contraries in regard to the Divine Nature. It was reasonable, then, that they should furnish a parallel to it in themselves.

But if this title is derived primarily from the wit of Hippolytus it is not unreasonable to suppose that the title Ἄλογος which it has displaced in the text of Epiphanius comes from the same mint. For Epiphanius does not, apparently, use the title Ἀνόητοι at the head of his treatment of the heresy of Noetus, however much it is involved in the text: yet it must have stood in the list of heresies, in order that a transcriptional confusion should arise between the *Alogi* and the *Anoeti*. We infer, therefore, that the presence of the title *Alogi* is probable in the book or table of heresies upon which Epiphanius is working. And with this Lightfoot agrees (*S. Clement of Rome*, ii. 394), for he says, " We may suspect that Epiphanius borrowed the name ἄλογοι, 'the irrational ones,' from Hippolytus; for these jokes are very much in his way; e.g. νοητός, ἀνόητος, and δοκός, δοκεῖν, δοκηταί." We may also add the heresy which Epiphanius describes as Κηριν-θιανοὶ ἤτοι Μηρινθιανοί[1] to our list, and here Epiphanius has failed to see the Hippolytean joke (Μήρινθος = a noose) and discusses whether it is one person or two that is meant.

So much for the title of the 51st Heresy: it suggests the use of Hippolytean material; and now let us turn to the text of the section. It is mainly made up of two separable defences, that of the Fourth Gospel and that of the Apocalypse. For aught Epiphanius knows (τάχα), the Alogi may have also rejected the Johannine Epistles which confirm the authenticity of the other two books, but he is concerned only with material furnished by the attacks upon the greater Johannine writings. He deals accordingly with selected objections. And amongst the refutations which he makes of the attacks on the Apocalypse there is, as Dr Gwynn has pointed out, one which is closely parallel to one of the instances in the Bar-Ṣalibi extracts from the Heads against Gaius. For convenience we will print the text of Epiphanius side by side with the Gwynn-Gaius fragment:

Epiph. Haer. li. c. 34.	*Gaius.*
καί φασιν ὅτι, Εἶδον, καὶ εἶπε τῷ ἀγγέλῳ, Λῦσον τοὺς τέσσαρας ἀγγέλους τοὺς ἐπὶ τοῦ Εὐφράτου· καὶ ἤκουσα τὸν ἀριθμὸν τοῦ στρατοῦ, μύριαι μυριάδες καὶ χίλιαι χιλιάδες, καὶ ἦσαν ἐνδεδυμένοι θώρακας πυρίνους καὶ θειώδεις καὶ ὑακινθίνους. Ἐνόμισαν γὰρ οἱ τοιοῦτοι, μή πη ἄρα γελοῖόν ἐστιν ἡ ἀλήθεια· ἐὰν γὰρ λέγῃ τοὺς τέσσαρας ἀγγέλους τοὺς ἐν τῷ Εὐφράτῃ καθε-ζομένους, ἵνα δείξῃ τὰς τέσσαρας διαφορὰς τῶν ἐκεῖσε ἐθνῶν καθεζομένων ἐπὶ τὸν Εὐφράτην, οἵτινές εἰσιν Ἀσσύριοι, Βαβυλώνιοι, Μῆδοι καὶ Πέρσαι. Αὗται γὰρ αἱ τέσσαρες βασιλεῖαι κατὰ διαδοχὴν ἐν τῷ Δανιὴλ ἐμφέρονται, ὡς πρῶτοι Ἀσσύριοι ἐβασίλευον, καὶ Βαβυλώνιοι ἐν χρόνοις αὐτοῦ, Μῆδοι δὲ διεδέξαντο, μετ' αὐτοὺς δὲ Πέρσαι, ὧν πρῶτος γέγονε Κῦρος ὁ βασιλεύς. Τὰ γὰρ ἔθνη ὑπὸ ἀγγέλους τεταγμένα εἰσίν, ὡς	*And the angels were loosed, which were prepared for seasons and for days to slay the third part of men* (Rev. ix. 15). On this Caius says : It is not written that angels are to make war, nor that a third part of men is to perish : but that *nation shall rise against nation* (Matt. xxiv. 7). Hippolytus in reply to him : It is not of angels he says they are to go to war, but that four nations are to arise out of the region which is *by Euphrates* and to come against the earth and

[1] See Lightfoot, *Lectures on St John.*

ἐπιμαρτυρεῖ μοι Μωϋσῆς ὁ ἅγιος τοῦ Θεοῦ θερά-
πων, τὸν λόγον κατὰ ἀκολουθίαν ἑρμηνεύων καὶ
λέγων, 'Επερώτησον τὸν πατέρα σου καὶ ἀγγελεῖ
σοι, τοὺς πρεσβυτέρους καὶ ἐροῦσί σοι· "Οτε
διεμέριζεν ὁ ὕψιστος ἔθνη, ὡς διέσπειρεν υἱοὺς
'Αδάμ, ἔστησεν ὅρια ἐθνῶν κατὰ ἀριθμὸν ἀγγέλων
Θεοῦ· καὶ ἐγενήθη μερὶς κυρίου λαὸς αὐτοῦ
'Ιακώβ, σχοίνισμα κληρονομίας αὐτοῦ 'Ισραήλ.
Εἰ οὖν τὰ ἔθνη ὑπὸ ἀγγέλους εἰσὶ τεταγμένα,
δικαίως εἶπε, Λῦσον τοὺς τέσσαρας ἀγγέλους
τοὺς ἐν τῷ Εὐφράτῃ καθεζομένους καὶ ἐπεχομέ-
νους ἐπιτρέπειν τοῖς ἔθνεσιν εἰς πόλεμον, ἕως
καιροῦ μακροθυμίας κυρίου, ἕως προστάξει δι'
αὐτῶν ἐκδικίαν γενέσθαι τῶν αὐτοῦ ἁγίων. 'Εκρα-
τοῦντο γὰρ οἱ ἐπιτεταγμένοι ἄγγελοι ὑπὸ τοῦ
πνεύματος μὴ ἔχοντες καιρὸν ἐπιδρομῆς, διὰ τὸ
μήπω λύειν αὐτοῖς τὴν δίκην, τοῦ τὰ λοιπὰ ἔθνη
λύεσθαι ἕνεκεν τῆς πρὸς τοὺς ἁγίους ὕβρεως.
Λύονται δὲ οἱ τοιοῦτοι καὶ ἐπέρχονται τῇ γῇ ὡς
'Ιωάννης προφητεύει καὶ οἱ λοιποὶ προφῆται.
Καὶ γὰρ κινούμενοι οἱ ἄγγελοι κινοῦσι τὰ ἔθνη εἰς
ὁρμὴν ἐκδικίας. "Οτι δὲ πυρίνους καὶ θειώδεις
καὶ ὑακινθίνους θώρακας σημαίνει, οὐδεὶς ἀμφι-
βάλλει. 'Εκεῖνα γὰρ τὰ ἔθνη ἀπὸ τῆς τοιαύτης
χρόας ἔχει τὴν ἀμφίασιν. Τὰ μὲν γὰρ θειώδη
ἱμάτια χρόα τίς ἐστι μηλίνη οὕτω καλουμένη
ἐρέα. τὰ δὲ πύρινα, ἵνα εἴπῃ τὰ κοκκηρὰ ἐνδύ-
ματα, καὶ ὑακίνθινα, ἵνα δείξῃ τὴν καλλαΐνην
ἐρέαν.

to war with mankind. But this that he says, *four angels* is not alien from Scripture. Moses said, *When He dispersed the sons of Adam, He set the boundary of the nations according to the number of the angels of God* (Deut. xxxii. 8). Since therefore nations have been assigned to angels, and each nation pertains to one angel, John rightly declared by the Revelation a loosing for those four angels: who are the Persians and the Medes and the Babylonians and the Assyrians. Since then those angels who have been appointed over the nations have not been commanded to stir up those who have been assigned to them, a certain bond of the power of the word is indicated which restrains them until the day shall arrive and the Lord of all shall command. And this then is to happen when Antichrist shall come.

The parallelism between the two lines of defence is so striking that it betrays a common origin, and this must be the work of Hippolytus, which has been rehandled by Epiphanius, and which appears, perhaps in an abbreviated form, in the extracts of Bar-Salibi. Such an abbreviation might be due to Bar-Salibi himself, or to the fact that the *Heads against Gaius* is a summary of a larger work.

But if this be the case, that we are dealing with lost Hippolytean and Gaian matter, we cannot limit ourselves to the single passage in which Epiphanius and Bar-Salibi agree. We must group together all the extracts in the two writers which defend the Apocalypse, and regard them as the residue of a single lost work; after which we must make a similar investigation with regard to the Fourth Gospel.

We thus learn, over and above what Bar-Salibi tells us, that

the Alogi objected to the machinery of the Apocalypse, especially
to the Angels and Trumpets; and that they criticised the Epistle
to Thyatira, on the ground that no Church existed in Thyatira in
St John's day.

And the same method of enquiry holds with regard to the
relation of Gaius to the Fourth Gospel: for we find Epiphanius
dealing with a series of objections made to the Chronology of the
Fourth Gospel and to special disagreements between St John and
the Synoptics, and we shall see that under both these heads he is
dealing with Hippolytean matter; the replies are the replies of
Hippolytus, rehandled by Epiphanius, and the Chronology is the
Hippolytean modification of the work of Julius Africanus.

We have shewn from Bar-Ṣalibi a single instance of a Gaian
objection to the Fourth Gospel, viz. the discordant accounts of the
events connected with the Baptism. And when we turn to
Epiphanius we find that the very first objection of the Alogi
which he refutes is this very difficulty. Φάσκουσι γὰρ καθ᾽
ἑαυτῶν, οὐ γὰρ εἴποιμι κατὰ τῆς ἀληθείας, ὅτι οὐ συμφωνεῖ τὰ
αὐτοῦ βιβλία τοῖς λοιποῖς ἀποστόλοις. Here Epiphanius is
working on a text which read ἑτέροις for which he gives λοιποῖς;
for we find the equivalent sentence in Bar-Ṣalibi:

> quia non concors fuit cum *sociis* (i.e. ἑταίροις).

The form of the objection turns upon the quotation of a
number of verses from the beginning of the Gospel, such as:
Ὁ Ἰωάννης μαρτυρεῖ, καὶ κέκραγε, λέγων ὅτι, οὗτός ἐστιν ὃν
εἶπον ὑμῖν· καὶ ὅτι, Οὗτός ἐστιν ὁ ἀμνὸς τοῦ θεοῦ, ὁ αἴρων τὴν
ἁμαρτίαν τοῦ κόσμου· καὶ καθεξῆς φησι, Καὶ εἶπον αὐτῷ οἱ
ἀκούσαντες, Ῥαββὶ, ποῦ μενεῖς; ἅμα δὲ ἐν ταυτῷ, Τῇ ἐπαύριον,
φησὶν, ἠθέλησεν ἐξελθεῖν εἰς τὴν Γαλιλαίαν καὶ εὑρίσκει Φίλιππον,
καὶ λέγει αὐτῷ ὁ Ἰησοῦς, Ἀκολούθει μοι. Καὶ μετὰ τοῦτο ὀλίγῳ
πρόσθεν φησὶ, Καὶ μετὰ τρεῖς ἡμέρας γάμος ἐγένετο ἐν Κανᾷ τῆς
Γαλιλαίας κτέ.

Epiphanius' reply is long and diffuse; he begins by pointing
out that the same method of criticism might be applied to the
internal disagreements of the Synoptics; how, for example, are
we to piece together the infancy accounts in Matthew and Luke;
and how are we to place the visit of the Magi and the flight into
Egypt, so as to be in harmony with the presentation of Christ
in the Temple etc. The criticism of the Alogi who accepted the

Synoptics could thus be easily directed against themselves. When at length Epiphanius comes to the discussion of the Johannine passage, he explains that the Lord, after his baptism, went into the wilderness, returned to Nazareth, and afterwards came back again to the Jordan where John was baptizing : ἵνα δείξῃ μετὰ τὰς τεσσαράκοντα ἡμέρας τοῦ πειρασμοῦ, καὶ μετὰ τὴν ἀπ᾽ αὐτοῦ τοῦ πειρασμοῦ ἐπάνοδον καὶ ὁρμὴν τὴν ἐπὶ Ναζαρὲτ καὶ Γαλιλαίαν, ὡς οἱ ἄλλοι τρεῖς εὐαγγελισταὶ ἔφησαν, πάλιν ἐπὶ τὸν Ἰορδάνην αὐτὸν ἡκέναι κτὲ.

And this is substantially the same as we find in the passage in Bar-Ṣalibi, so that we may claim again the recognition of Hippolytean matter.

The second difficulty which he undertakes to handle is the question of the number of passovers in our Lord's ministry. According to the Alogi, John mentions two passovers in our Lord's ministry, the Synoptics only one. Epiphanius adds the accounts together and argues, reasonably enough, for three passovers. But he is evidently falling foul of the belief of the early Church that our Lord's ministry was confined to a single year, an opinion which was based upon or confirmed by the words of Isaiah that he came to preach *the acceptable year of the Lord.* Accordingly Epiphanius, who is working at the data of some Chronographer, that our Lord was born on the 11th of the Egyptian month Tybi, and that he was baptized in his 30th year on the 12th of the Egyptian month Athyr proceeds to the question of the acceptable year in the following words ; καὶ ἀπεντεῦθεν ἀπὸ Ἀθὺρ δωδεκάτης κηρύττοντος αὐτοῦ τὸν δεκτὸν ἐνιαυτὸν κυρίου κτέ. And certainly he argues, the Lord did preach the acceptable year, because for the first year of his ministry he met with general acceptance, but after that with opposition ! This ingenious argument shews that Epiphanius is trying to get rid of the theory of a single year of the ministry, which he found in his sources.

Now it would be very interesting if we could compare the Chronology which Epiphanius gives with that of Hippolytus either as it existed in the *Chronica* or as we are entitled to assume that it must have existed in the defence of the Fourth Gospel and the Apocalypse (for certainly Hippolytus must have dealt with the objection made by the Alogi on the subject of the Passovers).

But unfortunately we are dealing here with lost documents. What does seem clear is that Epiphanius has been tinkering the data before him; for he alters the date of Christ's death, which in the Hippolytean tradition is usually the consulate of the two Gemini, and makes it two years later, by assuming in the life of our Lord two further consulates, of which the first is that of Rufus (Fufius) and Rubellio (*who are in fact the Gemini over again*); and the second is the consulate of Vinicius and Longinus Cassius. It is clear that such a confusion as this cannot be due to Hippolytus, and we suspect that some one has been trying to add a couple of years to the tale.

But in the next place when we compare the list of consuls given by Epiphanius for the first thirty years of our Lord's life with the table in the Chronographer of 354 which is taken from the Hippolytean table of 234, we find that Epiphanius has placed the birth of Christ two consulates earlier than the Chronographer; and this again suggests an attempt to gain two years in our Lord's life by some one who was working on a chronicle of 31 years which he was trying to turn into one of 33 years. Now whether all of this confusion is due to Epiphanius, or whether part of it is due to Hippolytus who has emended the 31 year life of Christ which appears in his paschal cycle into some system more consistent with the Gospels, I am not at present prepared to say; it is possible that the correction is due to more than a single reformer.

At all events, we may be confident that Hippolytus in dealing with Gaius must have had to face the difficulty of the Chronology, and if he did not succeed in abandoning the theory of the acceptable year, Epiphanius must have done it for him, and done it with much blundering. But behind all these confused data of Epiphanius there must lie the Hippolytean tables as they were taken from Africanus. And perhaps some day we may be able to say how much of the work of Africanus has escaped mutilation at the hands of those who worked him over. We have shewn, then, that Epiphanius in his 51st heresy, that of the Alogi, is using material which was taken in part at least from the reply of Hippolytus to Gaius in defence of the fourth Gospel and the Apocalypse. And it is clear, since Hippolytus would not have been defending what no one was attacking, that objections were still current at Rome in the early part of the third century to

the canonicity of the fourth Gospel. How much is involved in
this admission as regards the existence of a previous succession of
adverse Higher Critics, is difficult to say. In the case of the
Apocalypse the objection taken can easily be seen to be early and
constant and widely diffused. Whether criticism of the same
intensity was applied to the fourth Gospel, we have no means of
determining: but it is a fixed point gained to have restored, as
Dr Gwynn has done, the personality of Gaius: and to have defined,
as we hope to have done, his position as a critic.

An Extract from the Commentary of Dionysius Bar-Salibi on the Gospel of John (c. ii. v. 1).

From (A) *Cod. Mus. Britt. Add.* 7184, *f.* 2432 *with some variants from* (B) *Cod. Mus. Britt. Add.* 12,143.

ܕܡܕܢܚܐ ܐܘܢܓܠܝܣܛܗ ܕܝܘܚܢܢ:

ܝܘܡܐ ܩܕܡܝܐ ܕܒܗ ܫܐܠܘ ܦܪ̈ܝܫܐ ܠܝܘܚܢܢ ܕܡܢ

ܐܢܬ. ܘܝܘܡܐ ܬܪܝܢܐ ܗܘ ܕܒܗ ܚܙܐ ܡܪܢ ܘܡܫܝܚܐ

ܐܙܠ ܠܡܕܒܪܐ. ܘܒܬܪ ܐܪܒܥܝܢ ܝܘ̈ܡܝܢ ܘܗܘ ܗܦܟ.

ܝܘܡܐ ܩܕܡܝܐ ܕܒ ܚܕ ܒܫܒܐ ܕܬܠܡܝܕܘܗܝ[1].

ܘܢܦܩܘܗܝ ܬܪܝܢ ܬܠܡܝ̈ܕܐ. ܝܘܡܐ ܬܪܝܢܐ ܗܘ ܕܒܗ

ܢܦܩ ܠܓܠܝܠܐ. ܝܘܡܐ ܕܬܠܬܐ ܗܢܐ[2] ܕܡܫܬܘܬܐ

ܐܝܟ ܐܘܣܒܝܘܣ ܕܡܦܪܫ[3] ܗܘܐ ܠܝܘܚܢܢ ܕܠܐ

ܥܠܡ ܗܘܐ ܠܐܘܢܓܠܝܣܛܐ ܚܒܪ̈ܘܗܝ. ܕܐܡܪܝܢ ܕܒܬܪ

ܕܡܬܐ ܐܙܠ ܠܓܠܝܠܐ: ܘܗܕܪ ܒܡܦܩܢܐ ܠܐܬܪܐ ܕܫܡܪܝܐ.

ܕܡܕܢܚܐ ܐܘܢܓܠܝܣܛܗ ܠܝܘܚܢܢ.

[1] A (not B) adds on marg. in a late hand:

ܘܐܡܪ ܗܐ ܐܡܪܗ ܕܐܠܗܐ ܗܘ ܕܫܩܠ ܚܛܝܬܗ

ܕܥܠܡܐ.

[2] A (not B) adds on marg. in a late hand: ܗܘܐ ܕܝܢ ܡܫܬܘܬܐ

[3] A (not B) adds over line in a late hand ܠܐܝܘܣ

ܡܫܝܚܐ ܒܬܪ ܕܡܥܡܕ ܢܦܩ ܠܡܕܒܪܐ. ܘܡܚܕ ܗܘܬ
ܒܬܐ ܡܫܬܠܬܗ ܡܢ ܬܠܡܝܕܘܗܝ ܕܝܘܚܢܢ ܘܡܢ ܒܬܪܐ
ܘܒܬܪܟܢ ܗܘܘ ܠܗ ܠܐ ܐܢܣܝܘܗܝ. ܒܗܝ ܕܒܡܕܒܪܐ
ܗܘܐ. ܟܕ ܕܝܢ ܫܠܡ ܠܢܣܝܘܢܐ ܘܗܦܟ ܐܬܐ ܠܢܬܟܐ
ܠܗ ܕܢܚܕܐ. ܒܡܚܕ ܗܘܐ ܓܝܪ. ܐܠܐ ܕܢܬܚܘܐ ܡܢ
ܝܘܚܢܢ. ܠܗܘ ܕܗܕܐ ܚܙܝܗ ܐܡܪ. ܕܗܐ ܐܡܪܗ ܕܐܠܗܐ.
ܡܕܝܢ ܒܡܕܐ ܘܐܙܠ ܠܡܕܒܪܐ ܟܕ ܡܬܒܣܡܝܢ ܗܘܘ ܒܠܗܘܢ.
ܘܕܚܙܐܘܗܝ ܡܬܦܫܝܢ ܗܘܘ. ܗܝ ܕܡܢ ܐܬܚܙܝܘܗܝ ܗܘܐ.
ܘܠܐܝܟܐ ܐܙܠ ܠܐ ܝܕܥܝܢ ܗܘܘ. ܘܟܕ ܗܦܟ ܐܦܫ
ܐܝܟ. ܒܝ ܕܐܬܚܙܝ ܡܢ ܝܘܚܢܢ. ܠܝܘܡܐ ܕܚܕܪ
ܚܙܝܗ ܝܘܚܢܢ ܘܐܡܪ. ܗܘ ܐܡܪܗ ܕܐܠܗܐ. ܒܗܠܝܢ
ܐܪܒܥܝܢ ܝܘܡܝܢ ܒܟܐܒܘܗܝ ܘܠܐ ܚܙܐܘܗܝ. ܘܒܬܪ ܗܠܝܢ
ܕܢܣܝܘܢܐ ܟܕ ܐܬܐ ܘܐܬܚܙܝ ܐܬܐ ܠܓܠܝܠܐ. ܡܕܝܢ
ܫܠܝܡ ܐܘܢܓܠܝܣܛܐ ܠܫܪܒܐ. ܡܛܠ ܕܒܬܪ ܕܗܦܟ
ܡܢ ܡܕܒܪܐ. ܘܫܘܚܠܦ ܝܘܚܢܢ ܠܗܘܢ ܕܝܫܘ
ܕܒܡܕܒܪ. ܘܠܐܟܐ ܕܗܘܐ ܘܠܐ ܚܙܐܘܗܝ ܬܘܒ. ܡܛܠ
ܕܠܐ ܠܡܕܒܪܐ. ܐܫܬܥܝ ܝܘܚܢܢ ܕܢܦܩ ܒܠܗܘܢ.
ܬܫܘܥܬܐ: ܒܗܝ ܕܗܘܐ ܕܟܕܝܢ ܐܬܝܬܘܢ. ܘܡܢ ܬܡܢ ܐܙܠ
ܠܓܠܝܠܐ ܒܚܝܠܐ ܕܪܘܚܐ

EUTHALIUS AND EUSEBIUS.

By the publication of his researches into the problems associated with the name of Euthalius of Alexandria, Prof. Robinson has laid all New Testament scholars under a great debt of gratitude. If his *Euthaliana* had done nothing more than restore to us a number of pages of the famous Codex H of the Pauline Epistles by the simple process of reading the impress of the ink of the perished pages upon the pages which remain, it would have been a distinct paleographical triumph. For it must be remembered that this MS. of which the extant leaves are scattered over the libraries of Paris, St Petersburg, Moscow, Kieff, Turin and Mt Athos, has been the object of study of a great many pairs of eyes that are usually in the habit of seeing. Dr Gregory, acting as literary executor to Tischendorf, had certainly planned an edition of the H-fragments, and made preparation for that edition, yet he does not seem to have suspected that the worn and stained pages had a double tale to tell, and could furnish the text of leaves lost as well as of leaves preserved. We also made a careful study of this Codex, so far as its Paris fragments are concerned, yet it never dawned upon our minds that the set-off on the pages belonged to a different set of pages than those which were extant; nor did the thought occur to us when, not long since, we were examining the Athos fragments. These Athos leaves were also examined by Duchesne[1], but neither does he appear to have suspected that there was any supplementary evidence forthcoming from the manuscript.

More curious still, M. Omont in publishing an edition of the St Petersburg leaves, actually read a lost page of the MS. by the

[1] *Archives des Missions scientifiques et littéraires*, ser. 3, vol. 3. Paris, 1876.

reversed writing, but does not seem to have applied his method to any further leaves either at Paris or St Petersburg. It is, therefore, a distinct triumph and a very welcome increase to our knowledge that Prof. Robinson, working independent of us all, has been able to read, without serious lacunae, sixteen fresh pages of this valuable text.

But, valuable as this increment to our knowledge is, it is only a small part of Mr Robinson's services to the critic who occupies himself with the supposed Euthalian text of the Epistles and the shadowy editor of that text. He has passed under review almost the whole of the literature of the subject from Zacagni onwards, with the view of determining all that can be known with regard to the person and work of Euthalius. And in so doing he has shewn a remarkable grasp of critical methods, far beyond what one is used to look for in English work. Nor is the study the less interesting because the author displays such evident delight in knocking down all the ninepins which recent students of Euthalius had set up, including Ehrhard, Dobschütz, Conybeare and myself. 'The scholar's melancholy,' as Shakespeare says, 'is emulation.' We have sometimes a touch of the complaint ourselves, and Prof. Robinson will not be angry if we indulge the hope that, as far as our own ninepins are concerned, we may be able to set some of them up again. At least that is the object of the following pages. But whether we succeed in our attempt or not, we have a good hope that we shall not leave the subject without adding to our knowledge something which will be of permanent value.

This is the third time, I think, that I have approached the Euthalian problems. The first occasion was when in connexion with the study of the Stichometry of ancient MSS. I came across the collection of Euthalian and Ps.-Euthalian data which Zacagni had amassed in his *Collectanea Monumentorum Veterum*, and undertook to prove, as against the traditional view held by Scholz, Scrivener and others, that the lines numbered by Euthalius were not sense-lines (*cola* and *commata* as they are sometimes called) but space-lines of which the unit of measurement is a 16-syllabled hexameter. There has been no exception taken to this demonstration (nor is it easy to see how any exception was possible, for the investigation was self-verifying); but a new point has been raised by Prof. Robinson who questions with great propriety why we should attribute to Euthalius at once the art of writing the

N.T. in sense-lines, and the counting of the N.T. and attached matter in space-lines. He proposes, therefore, to divide the Euthalian materials, speaking roughly, between two artists of whom one, Euthalius, should write the Acts and Epistles in *cola*, and add certain prologues, while the other, whom he identifies with an Evagrius who appears in the subscription to certain Euthalian MSS. (notably in Cod. H, as recent investigations have shewn) should publish an *editio minor* of the Euthalian text and materials and be responsible for the stichometry, properly so called, of the text and prologues. This suggestion has a great air of probability about it. For the present we leave it on one side, as we hope to re-open the investigation from a fresh quarter. Most of what we had said upon the interpretation of the Euthalian lines will be found reprinted in the little volume *Stichometry*[1].

The second attack which we made upon the Euthalian problem dealt with the obscure personalities of the writer and of the person to whom the work was dedicated. It is well known that there is a great air of uncertainty about the titles prefixed to the works attributed to Euthalius. The MSS. speak, but by no means uniformly, of Euthalius of Sulci, but no one knows where Sulci is, not even Prof. Robinson, for it is almost impossible to refer the work to Sardinia, where a place of that name is known; they make Euthalius a bishop, but we cannot identify either him or his diocese. His first work, that on the Pauline Epistles, is based upon the previous work of a pious father whom he does not name, though he speaks of him flatteringly enough, and the influence has not been an unnatural one that the father in question was not exactly in the very odour of sanctity; and internal evidence has been produced which suggested that the great nameless one might perhaps be Theodore of Mopsuestia. In the second part of his work, that which deals with the Acts and the Catholic Epistles, Euthalius (whoever he was) expressly addresses in his prologues a father of the name of Athanasius; but here, too, the critic found a difficulty, for of the actual dates found in the Euthalian prefaces one (A.D. 396) was too late for Athanasius the Great, and the other (A.D. 458), which might seem to refer the work to the time of the second Athanasius, appeared not to be due to the hand of the original author of the Prologues.

---

[1] *Stichometry*, Cambridge University Press Warehouse, 1893.

At this point I took up the matter with the object of proving that the name of Athanasius which occurs in the Prologues to the Acts and Catholic Epistles is an orthodox substitute for an unorthodox name which has disappeared; and, guided by what seemed to me an obvious and repeated play upon words in the Euthalian text, where there were frequent and significant allusions to Μελέτη or study, I maintained that the work was originally dedicated to a father of the name of Meletius upon whose name Euthalius was playing, and that its true title was Εὐθαλίου πρὸς Μελέτιον.

The subordinate question, as to which of the possible Meletii of doubtful ecclesiastical repute was the one to whom the book was dedicated was decided, perhaps too rapidly, in favour of Meletius of Mopsuestia, the pupil and successor of the great Theodore. In making this identification, I was, of course, influenced by the first of the two dates (A.D. 396) found amongst the Euthalian matter, which I took to be the true date of Euthalius.

But to all this Prof. Robinson takes exception: according to him the date 396 is not the date of Euthalius, but of his successor Evagrius, and consequently we have no chronological difficulty to get over in accepting the ascription of certain MSS. and of the text itself to Athanasius; while, as to the supposed play upon a name, while not entirely denying that there is something of the kind involved, he thinks that it is merely a play upon a word capable of two senses, because Μελέτη, which I take to be the key-word to the understanding of the prologues, is a word which may mean either *study* or *training* in the athletic sense: according to which interpretation, since the word *training* is susceptible of a double sense even amongst ourselves, we are to understand Euthalius as saying 'I recommend to you my foster-sister and friend, the appropriately named lady, Madam Training.' And Prof. Robinson concludes by saying, 'I cannot myself think that a case is made out for any deletion of the name Meletius at all.' With which observation he finally knocked over my ninepin!

Now, as far as I am concerned, I have no special objection to be put in the wrong, but inasmuch as we are obliged by Euthalius to sing the praises of Mistress Study, whoever she was, and the praise ought not to be mere superficial adulation, it might be as well to make the examination a little more closely concerning these

two points, the question of the supposed Meletius whom I maintain
to have been erased, and the subordinate issue as to the date of
Euthalius. The latter question can, indeed, be treated indepen-
dently of the former; for, as Mr Robinson allows, if A.D. 396 is
the date of Evagrius and not of Euthalius, there is at least one
other Meletius of an earlier date, viz. Meletius of Antioch, who
might be a candidate at once for ecclesiastical disgrace and the
hand of Melete; but I shall not abandon the date 396 for Euthalius without applying to the subject some more of the sleepless
discipline which Euthalius praises; and as for Melete, who has
engaged me as well as the pious father of antiquity in her toils, if
I find her fallacious, she shall be burnt for a witch.

And so we come to our third contribution to the Euthalian
problem, which is *the relation of the prologues of Euthalius to the
text of Eusebius.* According to Robinson (and the impression is
not an unnatural one), Euthalius is a very original writer, with a
'great wealth of expression,' a person who can not only talk in
high-sounding Greek, but who would also not sully his style by
'repeating his own language in a slavish manner': in other words
a literary artist of some eminence whose commodity of words and
of ideas (which words are meant either to express or to conceal) is
something more than

A beggarly array of empty boxes,
Of musty packthread and old cakes of roses.

I will confess that, until recently, I shared with Mr Robinson
this idea of Euthalius; he was one of the writers who drove one
to the dictionary, and such we always respect—and hate. But I
hope to be able to shew that this grandeur of style is only
apparent, and that, in reality, one of the main uses of the swollen
speech of Euthalius is to furnish various readings for the text of
Eusebius!

In the first place, then, we observe that Euthalius himself has
directed us to Eusebius as one of his sources: he tells us, in his
Prologue to the Pauline Epistles (Zacagni, p. 531) as follows:

Εὐσέβιος δὲ, τοὺς μετέπειτα χρόνους ἀκριβῶς περιεργασάμενος,
ἱστόρησεν ἡμῖν καὶ ἐν τῷ δευτέρῳ τόμῳ τῆς Ἐκκλησιαστικῆς
ἱστορίας τούτου καὶ τὸ μαρτύριον· καί φησι τὸν Παῦλον ἄνετον
διατρίψαι καὶ τὸν τοῦ Θεοῦ λόγον ἀκωλύτως κηρύξαι ἐπισημηνάμενος. Τότε μὲν οὖν ἐπὶ Νέρωνος ἀπολογησάμενον τὸν Παῦλον
αὖθις ἐπὶ τὴν τοῦ κηρύγματος διακονίαν λόγος ἔχει στείλασθαι.

The passage, to which we shall presently have to refer more at
length, is taken from Euseb. *H. E.* ii. 22, where Eusebius is
relating what *St Luke* says about Paul's first imprisonment and
what *report* says about the second imprisonment. As it stands in
Euthalius the structure of the sentence is harsh enough : but it
all becomes clear when we refer to the History which tells us :

Καὶ Λουκᾶς δὲ ὁ τὰς πράξεις τῶν ἀποστόλων γραφῇ παραδούς,
ἐν τούτοις κατέλυσε τὴν ἱστορίαν, διετίαν ὅλην ἐπὶ τῆς Ῥώμης
τὸν Παῦλον ἄνετον διατρίψαι καὶ τὸν τοῦ Θεοῦ λόγον ἀκωλύτως κηρύξαι ἐπισημηνάμενος. Τότε μὲν οὖν ἀπολογησάμενον
αὖθις ἐπὶ τὴν τοῦ κηρύγματος διακονίαν λόγος ἔχει στείλασθαι
τὸν ἀπόστολον.

We see then the way in which Euthalius appropriates his
author, and we could easily extend our recognition of the matter
borrowed from Eusebius by examination of the immediate context.
But, for the present, let it suffice to shew that *the Ecclesiastical
History of Eusebius is one of the sources of Euthalius.* A second
source may be identified by a reference to c. 3 of the Pauline
prologue (Z. p. 529) where Euthalius tells us as follows :

Ἀναγκαῖον δὲ ἡγησάμην ἐν βραχεῖ καὶ τὸν χρόνον ἐπισημειώσασθαι τοῦ κηρύγματος Παυλοῦ ἐκ τῶν χρονικῶν κανόνων
Εὐσεβίου τοῦ Παμφίλου τὴν ἀνακεφαλαίωσιν ποιούμενος. ἔνθα
δὴ τὴν βίβλον μετὰ χεῖρας εἰληφώς κτέ., where from the very
language we are led to expect that quotations are coming, or at
all events, statements which are the equivalent of quotations.
And we shall shew that Euthalius actually had the Chronicon
open before him, as well as the History to which, as we have
already pointed out, he refers on a subsequent page.

He begins his extracts by saying that the Passion of our Lord
occurred in the 18th year of Tiberius. The passage of the
Chronicon from which this is taken is preserved in Syncellus
(614. 7) :

Ἰησοῦς ὁ Χριστὸς ὁ υἱὸς τοῦ θεοῦ ὁ κύριος ἡμῶν κατὰ τὰς
περὶ αὐτοῦ προφητείας ἐπὶ τὸ πάθος προῄει ἔτους ιθ' τῆς Τιβερίου
βασιλείας.

The Hieronymian version of the Chronicon gives the xviiith
year, the Armenian agrees with Syncellus in giving the xixth
year.

Euthalius then alludes to the election of the seven deacons,
and in particular of Stephen, in the following terms :

καὶ μεθ᾽ ἡμέρας τινὰς ὀλίγας εἶδον ἐκεῖ προχειριζομένους τοὺς Ἀποστόλους εἰς διακονίαν τὸν αὐτοφερώνυμον Στέφανον καὶ τοὺς ἀμφὶ αὐτόν.

Of this we find, in spite of Euthalius' express statement, no trace in the Chronicon, but on looking into the History (*H. E.* ii. 1) we find

καθίστανται...εἰς διακονίαν...ἄνδρες δεδοκιμασμένοι τὸν ἀριθμὸν ἑπτὰ οἱ ἀμφὶ τὸν Στέφανον, where the coincidences in language will be noticed, and then a little lower Eusebius speaks of Stephen as follows:

πρῶτος τὸν αὐτῷ φερώνυμον τῶν ἀξιονίκων τοῦ Χριστοῦ μαρτύρων ἀποφέρεται στέφανον[1].

And here a curious fact comes to light, viz. that Euthalius has failed to understand Eusebius' language.

Eusebius speaks of Stephen as bearing away the martyr's crown, which is appropriately named (στέφανος) for him. Here the play upon words has taken Euthalius' fancy, but he has blunderingly carried off αὐτῷ φερώνυμον and applied it to Stephen, without mentioning the crown to complete the parallel. He might have contented himself with calling Stephen φερώνυμος and leaving his readers to see the obvious play upon the name; but he was appropriating from Eusebius, and not 'mixing his paints with brains,' and so we have the impossible reading which appears in Cod. Boeclerianus as αὐτῷ φερώνυμον, in other MSS. as a single impossible word αὐτοφερώνυμον, in Cod. Lollinianus by emendation as πάνυ φερώνυμον[2].

And lest there should be any doubt about the fact that Euthalius has been appropriating Eusebian language, we can compare with the foregoing passage from Eusebius the language in which Euthalius speaks of the martyrdom of Paul (Z. 522):

τῷ τῶν ἱερονίκων Χριστοῦ μαρτύρων στεφάνῳ κατεκοσμήθη.

Cf. also Euseb. *Mart. Pal.* 3 τὸν τῶν ἱερονίκων τῆς θεοσεβείας ἀθλητῶν στέφανον ἀπηνέγκατο,

and *Mart. Pal.* 9 θείῳ κατεκοσμήθη μαρτυρίῳ etc.

Euthalius continues his discussion of the Pauline chronology, and presently he makes the statement that Paul continued

---

[1] With this compare Syncellus, 621. 4: Ἑπτὰ τὸν ἀριθμὸν, δοκεῖ μοι, πρὸς ὑπηρεσίαν τῶν ἀδελφῶν ὑπὸ τῶν ἀποστόλων κατεστάθησαν· ὧν πρῶτος ἦν Στέφανος ὁ πρῶτος μετὰ τὸν σωτῆρα παρὰ τῶν κυριοκτόνων λιθοβοληθεὶς καὶ τὸν φερώνυμον ἀξίως ὑπενεγκάμενος στέφανον ὑπὲρ αὐτοῦ.

[2] I was wrong in defending this last reading; let the barbarism stand.

preaching from the 19th year of Tiberius to the 13th year of Claudius, ἡγεμονεύοντος τότε τῆς Ἰουδαίας Φήλικος ἐφ᾽ οὗ κατηγορηθεὶς ὑπὸ Ἰουδαίων τὴν ἀπολογίαν ἐποιήσατο Παῦλος.

Turning to the Chronicon we find the following entries from Syncellus:

(629. 3) Κλαύδιος Φήλικα τῆς Ἰουδαίας ἡγεμόνα ἐξεπέμψε.

(632. 17) ἐπὶ αὐτοῦ Παῦλος ὑπὸ Ἰουδαίων κατηγορηθεὶς τὴν ἀπολογίαν πεποίηται.

After describing Paul's appeal to Rome, Euthalius continues (Z. 531):

συνῆν δὲ αὐτῷ καὶ Ἀρίσταρχος ὃν καὶ εἰκότως συναιχμάλωτόν που τῶν ἐπιστολῶν ἀποκαλεῖ, καὶ Λουκᾶς ὁ τὰς πράξεις τῶν Ἀποστόλων γραφῇ παραδούς.

But this is taken, word for word, from the History (*H. E.* ii. 22): and shortly after this the quotation from the History is continued in language which we transcribed above.

A little lower down Euthalius tells us, against which we will set the Eusebian parallels, as follows:

Euthal. (Z. 532).	Euseb. *H. E.* ii. 25.
ἀνεῖλεν μὲν Ἀγριππίναν πρῶτα τὴν ἰδίαν μητέρα, ἔτι δὲ καὶ τὴν ἀδελφὴν τοῦ πατρὸς, καὶ Ὀκταουίαν τὴν ἑαυτῷ γυναῖκα καὶ ἄλλους μυρίους τῷ γένει προσήκοντας.	μητέρα δὲ ὁμοίως καὶ ἀδελφοὺς καὶ γυναῖκα σὺν καὶ ἄλλοις μυρίοις τῷ γένει προσήκουσι....
	Euseb. *Chron.* ap. Syncell. 636. 8.
	Νέρων ἀνεῖλε τὴν ἑαυτοῦ μητέρα Ἀγριππίναν καὶ τὴν τοῦ πατρὸς ἀδελφήν.
	Euseb. *Chron. Armen.*
	Neron cum aliis viris illustribus et Hochtabiam uxorem suam interfecit.
	Euseb. *Chron.* ap. Cedrenum 360. 17.
	καὶ ἄλλους μυρίους τῷ γένει προσήκοντας.
Euthalius continues :	Euseb. *H. E.* ii. 25.
μετέπειτα δὲ καθολικὸν ἐκίνησε διωγμὸν κατὰ τῶν Χριστιανῶν, καὶ οὕτως ἐπὶ τὰς κατὰ τῶν Ἀποστόλων ἐπήρθη σφαγάς.	ταύτῃ γοῦν οὗτος θεομάχος ἐν τοῖς μάλιστα πρῶτος ἀνακηρυχθείς, ἐπὶ τὰς κατὰ τῶν Ἀποστόλων ἐπήρθη σφαγάς·
	and cf. *Chron.* ap. Syncell. 644. 2.
	ἐπὶ πᾶσι δ᾽ αὐτοῦ τοῖς ἀτυχήμασι καὶ τὸν πρῶτον κατὰ Χριστιανῶν ἐνεδείξατο διωγμόν...
	ἐπὶ πᾶσι δ᾽ αὐτοῦ ἀδικήμασι καὶ τὸν πρῶτον κατὰ Χριστιανῶν ἐνεδείξατο διωγμόν, ἡνίκα Πέτρος καὶ Παῦλος κτέ.

After calculating the years from the Passion to the Martyrdom of Paul (which is evidently reckoned by the aid of the Chronicon), we find that he has turned back to *H. E.* ii. 22 and is working very literally:

Euthalius (Z. 533)

περὶ μὲν τῆς πρώτης αὐτοῦ ἀπολογίας φάσκων τάδε· ἐν τῇ πρώτῃ μου ἀπολογίᾳ¹...ἐκ στόματος λέοντος, τοῦτον τὸν Νέρωνα εἶναι λέγων· περὶ δὲ τῆς δευτέρας ἐν ᾗ καὶ τελειοῦται τῷ κατ᾽ αὐτὸν μαρτυρίῳ, φησὶν, τὴν καλήν διακονίαν σου πληροφόρησον. ἐγὼ γὰρ ἤδη σπένδομαι²...ἐφέστηκε. καὶ ὅτι Λουκᾶς ἦν πάλιν σὺν αὐτῷ κτέ,

with which we may compare

Euseb. H. E. ii. 22

ἐν τῇ πρώτῃ μου, φησὶν, ἀπολογίᾳ...λέοντος, τὸν Νέρωνα ταύτῃ, ὡς ἔοικε, διὰ τὸ ὠμόθυμον προσειπών...ἐν τῇ αὐτῇ προλέγει γραφῇ φάσκων· ἐγὼ γὰρ ἤδη σπένδομαι...ἐφέστηκεν.

But enough has been said to shew that Euthalius is for the most of his time a plagiarist, as well as sometimes a blunderer. Will it be said in reply that it was quite natural that he should use the Chronicon· and the History in writing the life of the Apostle Paul, and that, at all events, he has confessed to borrowing? It usually happens that debts confessed are only a fraction of those contracted, and an examination of the rest of Euthalius' work will confirm that proposition. If he should be original anywhere, it ought to be in his opening remarks, where he explains the scope of the work which he has undertaken and is untrammelled by history or by chronology. But is it so? Let us turn to the prologue to the Acts (Z. p. 404), and see whether it reads like the work of an original and fecund mind. We find him telling us of the new and difficult path that he has to tread in making his edition of the Acts: οἷά τις πῶλος ἀβαδὴς ἢ νέος ἀμαθὴς ἐρήμην ὁδὸν καὶ ἀτριβῆ ἰέναι προστεταγμένος. οὐδένα γάρ που τῶν ὅσοι τὸν θεῖον ἐπρεσβεύσαντο λόγον εἰς δεῦρο διέγνων περὶ τούτο τῆς γραφῆς ταύτης εἰς σπουδὴν πεποιημένον τὸ σχῆμα.

---

¹ 2 Tim. iv. 16.   ² 2 Tim. iv. 5.

But when we turn to the opening chapter of the Ecclesiastical History, the secret is out, for here we find

ἐπεὶ καὶ πρῶτοι νῦν τῆς ὑποθέσεως ἐπιβάντες οἷά τινα ἐρήμην καὶ ἀτριβῆ ἰέναι ὁδὸν ἐγχειροῦμεν,

and somewhat further on

Ἀναγκαιότατα δέ μοι πονεῖσθαι τὴν ὑπόθεσιν ἡγοῦμαι ὅτι μηδένα πω εἰς δεῦρο τῶν ἐκκλησιαστικῶν συγγραφέων διέγνων περὶ τοῦτο τῆς γραφῆς σπουδὴν πεποιημένον τὸ μέρος.

Further the expression ὅσοι τὸν θεῖον ἐπρεσβεύσαντο λόγον may be compared with the opening sentences of Eusebius ὅσοι τε κατὰ γενεὰν ἑκάστην ἀγράφως ἢ καὶ διὰ συγγραμμάτων τὸν θεῖον ἐπρέσβευσαν λόγον κτέ.

Other coincidences in thought and expression may be noted[1], and it follows that the loans which Euthalius makes on Eusebius are not limited to a single section, but that he is a systematic plagiarist.

It will be admitted, I think, that the dependence of Euthalius upon Eusebius is established: but it may well be questioned whether it does not go much further than our identifications, and whether it does not involve other authors beside Eusebius.

Take, for example, the Pauline prologue in which Euthalius speaks in such choice language of the reasons which led him to his task, and of his own ecclesiastical obedience to the superiors who set him at the work. At first sight these sentences appear to be the most original in the whole document and to have the flavour of real history. No one would suspect, at the first reading of these personal statements on the part of Euthalius, that they constitute a conventional opening to a new book. But that such is the case will, I think, be clear by comparing with the language of Euthalius the opening sentences of the Armenian historian, Lazarus of Pharbi.

---

[1] e.g. (Z. 405) συγγνώμην γε πλείστην αἰτῶν ἐπ' ἀμφοῖν, τόλμης ὁμοῦ καὶ προπετείας τῆς ἐμῆς.

Euseb. H. E. i. 1 ἀλλὰ μοι συγγνώμην ἤδη εὐγνωμόνων ἐντεῦθεν ὁ λόγος αἰτεῖ, with which cf. H. E. vi. 20 τὴν περὶ τὸ συντάττειν καινὰς γραφὰς προπέτειάν τε καὶ τόλμαν ἐπιστομίζων.

The pilfering runs through the prologue to the Acts. Cf. (Z. 410) Ἀντιοχεὺς γὰρ οὗτος ὑπάρχων τὸ γένος, ἰατρός τε τὴν ἐπιστήμην, πρὸς Παύλου μαθητευθείς, with Euseb. H. E. iii. 4 Λουκᾶς δὲ τὸ μὲν γένος ὢν τῶν ἀπ' Ἀντιοχείας, τὴν δὲ ἐπιστήμην ἰατρός, τὰ πλεῖστα συγγεγονὼς τῷ Παύλῳ....

Euthalius.

Prol. in Epp. Paul.

Τὸ φιλομαθὲς καὶ σπουδαῖον ἀγάμενος
τῆς σῆς ἀγάπης, Πάτερ τιμιώτατε, αἰδοῖ
τε καὶ πειθοῖ εἴκων, στενωπῷ τινι καὶ
παρεισδύσει τῆς ἱστορίας ἐμαυτὸν ἐπα-
φῆκα, τονδὲ τὸν πρόλογον τοῦ Παύλου
πραγματείας συγγράψαι· καὶ πολὺ μεῖ-
ζον ἢ καθ᾽ ἡμᾶς ἔργον ἀνεδεξάμην δέει
τῆς παρακοῆς· ἔγνων γὰρ ἐν παροιμίαις
τὸ λαλούμενον, ὅτι δὴ υἱὸς ἀνήκοος ἐν
ἀπωλείᾳ ἔσται, ὁ δὲ ὑπήκοος ἔσται
ταύτης ἐκτός (cf. Prov. 13. 1).

Lazarus of Pharbi.
History of Armenia.

Written at the request of Vahan,
general and marzban of Armenia.

(Translation of Victor Langlois.)

Le présent ouvrage, œuvre de
notre faiblesse, va former comme la
troisième partie de ces annales. Nous
sommes forcé d' [entreprendre] un
semblable travail par ordre des princes
et sur les exhortations des saints
docteurs, n'osant pas nous opposer,
en nous rappelant les menaces que
la saint Écriture fait aux enfants
désobéissants et de l'indulgence
[qu'elle] montre vis-à-vis de ceux
qui sont soumis et dociles.

Here the same idea is seen to underlie both authors, viz. the
fear of disobedience to superiors, based on the warning of the
Scriptures against disobedient children. The passage which Euthalius quotes from the Proverbs underlies the prologue of Lazarus.
Each writer suggests by antithesis, in the manner of the Proverbs,
the well-being which is the portion of the obedient. Each of
them speaks modestly of his own powers, Lazarus calling the task
one that is 'the work of his weakness,' and Euthalius 'a work
that is too great for me.'

Euthalius further describes his work by saying that he has
rushed into 'the narrows and straits of history' in writing the
present prologue to St Paul.

Surely the natural suggestion is that both writers are using
conventional openings, and Euthalius' language suggests further
that he has borrowed from the prologue *to a history*.

Lazarus wrote his History not earlier than A.D. 485 as a sequel
to the works of Agathangelus and Faustus of Byzantium. Euthalius cannot have imitated him, both by reason of the date, as well
as because the work is written in Armenian. Will it be said that
Lazarus has imitated the Euthalian prologue? this is extremely
unlikely, for Lazarus was well acquainted with Greek literature
and was hardly likely to select for a model of style so trifling a
piece as Euthalius' prologue. Moreover when we take into
account the proved borrowing of Euthalius from Eusebius and the

suspicious statement about the 'narrows and straits of history' we are led to infer that both writers are drawing upon some classic opening in which the work of a historical writer is compared to the course of a ship navigated in difficult and narrow seas. And this supposition is not an unnatural one. It will be found to be the main idea of the prologue to the history of Agathangelus, who tells us (Langlois, p. 106) "Pour nous, ce n'est pas une orgueilleuse résolution qui nous pousse à entreprendre témérairement ce travail; mais nous sommes contraint malgré nous, par les ordres formels des princes, à naviguer sur la mer des lettres." And a reference of the prologue of Euthalius to the Catholic Epistles shews the same comparison of the literary artist to the tempest-tossed voyager in a tiny skiff.

We say, then, that the evidence favours a belief that Euthalius found a literary model for his prologue to the Pauline Epistles in the proem of some well-known historical work; and from the suspicious use of a quotation from the Proverbs we suspect that it was the work of a Christian historian. And certainly we do not think any one will have anything further to say in defence of the originality of Euthalius or in praise of his copious vocabulary.

Having now proved the dependence of Euthalius upon Eusebius and others we are in a better position to determine the text of Euthalius in doubtful cases and the interpretation where the meaning is obscure.

For example, in a passage quoted above (Z. 532) the printed text of Euthalius reads ἀνεῖλεν μὲν 'Αγριππίναν πρῶτα τὴν ἰδίαν μητέρα where Cod. Vat. 761 has τὴν ἑαυτοῦ μητέρα. A reference to the Eusebian text shews that this latter reading is probably correct.

On the same page Euthalius has συνῆλθε δὲ πάλιν ὁ Λουκᾶς αὐτῷ, but Cod. Vat. 761 and Cod. Boeclerianus read συνῆν. A reference to the text of Eusebius shews that he constantly, and in this very connection reads συνῆν. Conversely, where the text of Eusebius is doubtful, we have reason to believe that the Euthalian extracts furnish fresh material for its elucidation.

Coming now to the question of interpretation, we have a right to assume as a general principle that when Euthalius uses Eusebian language he uses it in the Eusebian sense; he may sometimes misunderstand, but even a stupid transcriber will, in the majority of cases, take the words in their proper sense. Let us then turn to the disputed passage in which I claim to have detected a deletion of the unorthodox name Meletius and the insertion of the orthodox Athanasius, and in which Mr Robinson thinks no case has been made out for any tampering with the text.

The principal sentences which need interpretation are as follows:

(Z. 406) ἐγὼ δὲ δικαιώτατα, καὶ μάλα γε ὀρθῶς, σύντροφόν τε καὶ φιλὴν ἐπιφημίσαιμ᾽ ἄν σοι, καὶ καταλέξω τὴν εὐπροσήγορον, τὴν πάνυ φερώνυμον, τὴν τῶν θείων λογίων ἐμφιλόσοφόν φημι μελέτην, ὑφ᾽ ἣν γεγωνὼς, φιλόχριστε, καὶ εἴσωγέ τοι τῶν δικτύων αὐτῆς ὑπάρχων, καὶ τὴν ἐράσμιον αὐτῆς προσηγορίαν ἐγκαταπραγματευόμενος συχναῖς τε ἀεὶ καὶ ἀκοιμήτοις γυμνασίαις ἀκουόμενος (l. ἀσκούμενος) εὐθαλεστάτην κατέστησας.

Starting from the known fact that Euthalius is a careful student of Eusebius, we naturally ask the question whether Eusebius uses the word φερώνυμος, which is a little difficult of interpretation, and what meaning he attaches to it.

We have already given one instance in which Euthalius plays on the name of Stephen, and the crown, φερώνυμος αὐτῷ, that is involved in that name, and have shewn that the word-play was based upon a similar one in the text of Eusebius, which Euthalius has blunderingly appropriated.

But it is when we come to look into the text of Eusebius generally that we find the meaning of the disputed word and discover that it is one of the commonest literary artifices of Eusebius to indulge in an etymological subtlety over the names of the people whom he describes. Let us take some cases.

H. E. iv. 16. Eusebius describes the philosophy of Crescens the opponent of Justin by saying τὸν φερώνυμον δὲ οὗτος τῇ Κυνικῇ προσηγορίᾳ βίον τε καὶ τρόπον ἐζήλου.

The mode of life of Crescens was appropriately named after the Cynic or Canine philosophy.

H. E. v. 24 (which, I see, Prof. Robinson also refers to) Καὶ ὁ μὲν Εἰρηναῖος, φερώνυμός τις ὢν τῇ προσηγορίᾳ, αὐτῷ τε τῷ τρόπῳ εἰρηνοποιός, τοιαῦτα ὑπὲρ τῆς τῶν ἐκκλησιῶν εἰρήνης παρεκάλει, where the meaning is sufficiently clear.

H. E. vii. 32 describing the bishop Theodotos, Eusebius speaks of him as πράγμασιν αὐτοῖς ἀνὴρ καὶ τὸ κύριον ὄνομα καὶ τὸν ἐπίσκοπον ἐπαληθεύσας, a man who verified by his actions his proper name (i.e. as involved in the interpretation of Theodotos, or God-bestowed) and the name of bishop.

H. E. ix. 2. In the same way Theotecnos, the persecutor, is spoken of as δεινὸς καὶ γόης καὶ πονηρὸς ἀνὴρ καὶ τῆς προσωνυμίας ἀλλότριος. No child of God he! Somewhat more obscure is the passage *Mart. Pal.* 8, in which Eusebius speaks of the martyrs in the Porphyritic mine in the Thebaid: εἶχε μὲν πρὸ τούτου τὸ καλούμενον ἐν Θηβαΐδι φερωνύμως οὗ γεννᾶται Πορφυρίτου λίθου μέταλλον πλείστην ὅσην πληθὺν τῶν τῆς θεοσεβείας ὁμολογητῶν : a sentence which the contemporary Syriac version interprets as follows : " great multitudes of confessors were in the mines that are called Porphyrites, in the country of Thebais, which is on one side of Egypt: and on account of the purple marble which is in that land the name of Porphyrites has also been given to those who were employed in cutting it."

There is no doubt Eusebius is playing upon the name Πορφυρίτης, but whether we have the Greek sentence in its original form is a little doubtful.

A still more difficult case to interpret is *Mart. Pal.* 9, where a persecutor is spoken of, Μάξυς ὄνομα, χείρων τῆς προσηγορίας ἄνθρωπος. The word Μάξυς does not seem to be Greek, and an attempt has been made, not very successfully, to give it a Syriac etymology (see Ruinart, *Act. Sinc.* p. 287).

The word φερωνύμως is used also with reference to the name of a disease, which, for the present investigation, is much the same as a proper name, and Eusebius says, in describing a pestilence that had broken out, *H. E.* ix. 8 ἕλκος δὲ ἦν φερωνύμως τοῦ πυρώδους ἕνεκεν ἄνθραξ προσαγορευόμενον, ' there was a sore that was rightly called *carbuncle* on account of its inflammatory nature.'

Very similar is the way in which Eusebius plays upon the name of the heretic Manes, whom he describes, *H. E.* vii. 31, as ὁ μανεὶς τὰς φρένας, ἐπώνυμός τε τῆς δαιμονώσης αἱρέσεως...δαιμονικός τις ὢν καὶ μανιώδης...τυφούμενος ἐπὶ τῇ μανίᾳ[1].

But perhaps most striking of all is the way in which he plays with the name of *Meletius* the bishop of the churches in Pontus (*H. E.* vii. 32) : ὁ δὲ Μελέτιος (τὸ μέλι τῆς Ἀττικῆς ἐκάλουν αὐτὸν

---

[1] Similarly Titus Bostrensis adv. *Manichaeos*, Prol. : ὁ δὲ Μαντῆς ἐκ βαρβάρων καὶ τῆς μανίας αὐτῆς ἐπώνυμος.

οἱ ἀπὸ παιδείας) τοιοῦτος ἦν οἷον ἂν γράψειέ τις τῶν κατὰ πάντα λόγων ἕνεκα τελεώτατον.

There can be no reason to doubt, then, from the cases of word-play which we find applied in Eusebius to proper names, that Euthalius has been imitating a literary peculiarity of the Ecclesiastical History: and in the case of the play upon the name of Stephen, he was found guilty of the theft, *flagrante delicto*.

And it follows from this that when we read his description of the attractive Melete who ensnares holy fathers in her net, and calls her φερώνυμος, we are to expect a pun. Moreover when in Eusebius we find that he uses in connection with his φερωνύμως, the expression φερώνυμος τῇ προσηγορίᾳ, we can scarcely doubt that when Euthalius describes Miss Melete as τὴν εὐπροσήγορον, τὴν πάνυ φερώνυμον, he means, not that she is *affable*, or *easy of access*, but that she is *rightly named*: so that the repetition of two almost equivalent expressions accentuates the belief that there is some play upon the word[1]. The only thing left to determine is what the word-play consists in. According to Prof. Robinson it is nothing more than a play upon the alternative meanings of Study and Training: in support of which it might be pointed out that Eusebius, whose cast-off garments furnish Euthalius' wardrobe, uses the word in both senses. So much might be readily admitted.

But to this explanation there are objections from every quarter: Eusebius in the cases which we have quoted plays almost exclusively upon titles and proper names, such as Cynic, Irenaeus, Theodotos, Theotecnos, Porphyrite, Maxys, Manes, and Meletius. The only exception, and that is more apparent than real, is when he describes the disease called Anthrax and says it was rightly named.

Euthalius also in three cases (Stephen, Saul, and Paul) expounds proper names; and the presumption, therefore, is that something of the same kind is involved in the description of Melete as φερώνυμος and εὐπροσήγορος. The conditions are perfectly satisfied by the assumption that the person addressed is named Meletius. Euthalius might, to be sure, have called Meletius φερώνυμος and left us to imagine what he meant, but it answered

---

[1] With which previous explanation of mine, I see Mr Robinson agrees.

his purpose just as well to call Melete φερα'νυμος, the father Meletius having been already mentioned in the context. On Prof. Robinson's supposition, we have a play upon words which is (i) obscure, and (ii) not of sufficient importance in view of the space which is occupied by the praises of Melete. From the very beginning of the prologue to the Acts the play upon the word betrays itself, and the allusions to Study are kept up almost to the end of the prologue. It is evidently the nucleus of the composition. Is it possible that one doubtful oscillation between the senses of Study and Training could have exercised such an influence upon the mind of Euthalius as to colour the whole of the dedication of his work?

But this is not all: we are able to shew that the name of Meletius was a name that was commonly played with. When I first announced that I believed there were traces of the erasure of this name in the Euthalian prologue, it never occurred to me that a parallel instance could be found of the literary trick which I had, as I supposed, unearthed. I simply saw that Euthalius made puns (often bad ones[1]), and suggested that he had made one more than the three of which he was proved to be guilty. But I discovered subsequently, and added a note to that effect, that Gregory of Nazianzus had called Meletius of Antioch his 'honey-sweet' friend, in the following lines:

Carm. xi. 1521 τὸν ὄνθ' ὅπερ κέκλητο καὶ καλούμενον

ὃ ἦν· Μέλιτος γὰρ τρόπος καὶ τοὔνομα.

If Gregory of Nazianzus played with the name of his Meletius, there was certainly nothing against the supposition that Euthalius might have treated one of his friends in a similar manner.

But surely the case is immensely strengthened when we find amongst the names upon which Eusebius plays *the very name of Meletius;* for we have shewn conclusively that Euthalius appropriates the ideas and language of Eusebius freely, and that he imitates him in playing upon the name of Stephen. Why then should there be any difficulty in the supposition that Euthalius has also borrowed from Eusebius the idea of playing upon the name of Meletius? And is not this hypothesis further strengthened

---

[1] I refuse to credit Eusebius with Σαῦλος ὅτι ἐσάλευεν or with Παῦλος ὅτι πέπαυται.

by the fact that in the very same sentence, as Mr Robinson admits, Euthalius plays upon his own name? I consider, then, that my case, so far from having been rendered hopeless, or reduced to an unnecessary piece of ingenuity in the face of Prof. Robinson's investigations, is in reality very much stronger than I had at first imagined it to be[1].

A further test of the accuracy of the solution will lie in the fact that it helps us to clear up some of the remaining obscurities in the text of Euthalius.

For instance in the opening sentences of the prologue to the Acts, we are told of students of the Scripture in quest of immortality, who seek to realize the blessing of the first Psalm,

τοὺς περὶ τοῦ θείου λόγου λόγους ἐμμελέτημα νύκτωρ τε καὶ μεθ᾽ ἡμέραν, τῇ σφῶν αὐτῶν τέθεινται ψυχῇ, ἀληθῶς τὸ τῆς ἀγλαοφεγγοῦς καὶ μακαρίας ταύτης [τροφῆς] ἡμεροτρωθέντες, καὶ τῶν ἐναρέτων αὐτῆς καὶ θείων καρπῶν ἀπογευσάμενοι.

The passage is difficult to understand, and Zacagni, apparently in despair, has inserted de suo the word τροφῆς and translates as if people were 'daily fed upon this blessed meat'! But this will not do : ἡμεροτρωθέντες cannot mean 'supplied from day to day'; if it means anything it means 'gently pierced'; but as a matter of fact, there is no such word. And certainly if τροφῆς were rightly restored, the author could not go on to speak of 'tasting her divine fruits,' i.e. the fruits of the τροφή. But suppose we leave out the word added by Zacagni and read the clause

τῷ τῆς ἀγλαοφεγγοῦς καὶ μακαρίας ταύτης ἱμέρῳ τρωθέντες
'smitten with passion for this resplendent and blessed creature,' we see that all that is necessary to the sense is a satisfactory feminine antecedent to the clause. And this is at once supplied by writing μελέτην for ἐμμελέτημα, which thinly disguises it. The personification of μελέτη is the key to the perplexity of the passage.

We will now pass on to the more difficult question of the genuineness of the Martyrium Pauli which is usually attached to the Euthalian prologue to the Pauline Epistles. As we have pointed out, this question is not really much affected by the

---

[1] The only alternative would be to credit some lost book of Eusebius with the playful preface addressed to Meletius, who would in that case be Meletius of Pontus, who was seven years in hiding in Palestine during the persecution recorded by Eusebius and in constant intercourse with that father. But we do not need to resort to this hypothesis.

solution of the previous one. We might find a Meletius to whom Euthalius could dedicate his work almost anywhere in the fourth century. So that it is not necessary to decide the Meletian question before discussing the *Martyrium*. It must, however, be remembered that the dependence of Euthalius upon Eusebius is a factor in the solution of both questions, and this dependence is a proved and demonstrated fact. Let us see whether it has any bearing upon the discussion by which Prof. Robinson seeks to shew the dependence of the *Martyrium* upon the Pauline prologue, and its non-authenticity as a work of Euthalius. On p. 29 of his *Euthaliana* Mr Robinson prints for the purposes of comparison the passages of the prologue which correspond to the *Martyrium*; as follows :

Prologue to Pauline Epistles.

Z. 522. Αὐτόθι οὖν ὁ μακάριος Παῦλος τὸν καλὸν ἀγῶνα ἀγωνισάμενος, ὥς φησιν αὐτός, τῷ τῶν ἱερονίκων Χριστοῦ μαρτύρων στεφάνῳ κατεκοσμήθη. Ῥωμαῖοι δὲ περικαλλέσιν οἴκοις καὶ βασιλείοις τούτου λείψανα καθείρξαντες ἐπέτειον αὐτῷ μνήμης ἡμέραν πανηγυρίζουσι τῇ πρὸ τριῶν καλανδῶν Ἰουλίων πέμπτῃ Πανέμου μηνὸς τούτου τὸ μαρτύριον ἑορτάζοντες.

Z. 532. Ἔνθα δὴ συνέβη τὸν Παῦλον τριακοστῷ ἕκτῳ ἔτει τοῦ σωτηρίου πάθους τρισκαιδεκάτῳ δὲ Νέρωνος μαρτυρῆσαι, ξίφει τὴν κεφαλὴν ἀποτμηθέντα.

Z. 533. Περὶ δὲ τῆς δευτέρας (ἀπολογίας) ἐν ᾗ καὶ τελειοῦται τῷ κατ᾽ αὐτὸν μαρτυρίῳ, φησὶν κτέ. Ἔστιν οὖν ὁ πᾶς χρόνος τοῦ κηρύγματος Παύλου κτέ.

Z. 529. Ἀναγκαῖον δὲ ἡγησάμην ἐν βραχεῖ καὶ τὸν χρόνον ἐπισημειώσασθαι τοῦ κηρύγματος Παύλου, ἐκ τῶν χρονικῶν κανόνων Εὐσεβίου τοῦ Παμφίλου τὴν ἀνακεφαλαίωσιν ποιούμενος.

Μαρτύριον Παύλου τοῦ Ἀποστόλου. Ἐπὶ Νέρωνος τοῦ Καίσαρος Ῥωμαίων ἐμαρτύρησεν αὐτόθι Παῦλος ὁ ἀπόστολος, ξίφει τὴν κεφαλὴν ἀποτμηθείς, ἐν τῷ τριακοστῷ καὶ ἕκτῳ ἔτει τοῦ σωτηρίου πάθους, τὸν καλὸν ἀγῶνα ἀγωνισάμενος ἐν Ῥώμῃ, πέμπτῃ ἡμέρᾳ Πανέμου μηνὸς ἥτις λέγοιτο ἂν παρὰ Ῥωμαίοις ἡ πρὸ τριῶν καλανδῶν Ἰουλίων, καθ᾽ ἣν ἐτελειώθη ὁ ἅγιος ἀπόστολος τῷ κατ᾽ αὐτὸν μαρτυρίῳ ἑξηκοστῷ καὶ ἐννάτῳ ἔτει τῆς τοῦ σωτῆρος ἡμῶν Ἰησοῦ Χριστοῦ παρουσίας. Ἔστιν οὖν ὁ πᾶς χρόνος ἐξ οὗ ἐμαρτύρησε τριακόσια τριάκοντα ἔτη μέχρι τῆς παρούσης ταύτης ὑπατείας, τετάρτης μὲν Ἀρκαδίου τρίτης δὲ Ὀνωρίου τῶν δύο ἀδελφῶν αὐτοκρατόρων Αὐγούστων, ἐννάτης ἰνδικτιῶνος τῆς πεντεκαιδεκαετηρικῆς περιόδου, μηνὸς Ἰουνίου εἰκοστῇ ἐννάτῃ ἡμέρᾳ. Ἐσημειωσάμην ἀκριβῶς τὸν χρόνον τοῦ μαρτυρίου Παύλου ἀποστόλου.

We have printed this passage with the spaced type by which

Prof. Robinson indicates the coincidence between the two sets of statements. His first remark upon these coincidences is that the comparison 'disposes of Zacagni's view that it is the work of the early Father from whom Euthalius borrowed his chapter-divisions, for it is redolent of Euthalius: the only question is whether it is not too redolent.' It will be recognized at once that this question of redolence has been somewhat complicated by the proved dependence of Euthalius upon Eusebius. The prologue itself has 'an ancient and fish-like smell.' Almost every word of it is from Eusebius, as we will shew in detail. And consequently when Mr Robinson makes his first general criticism of the *Martyrium* by saying that 'it is almost inconceivable that a writer who has so great a wealth of expression as the author of the Prologue should repeat his own language in this slavish manner,' we may very well reply that the objection disappears as soon as it is found that the wealth of language is an illusion, and that the repetition is a repetition of the words of some other person. There is no law of criticism which expresses in the language of minute probability the chance that a person who has made a patchwork out of some other person's writings will repeat the offence or which affirms the extreme unlikeliness that he will put the stolen pieces together a little differently. We come now to three detailed objections which Mr Robinson makes to the authenticity of the *Martyrium*, which would be fatal if they were all correctly taken, without the possibility of reply: we will take them in order: they are intended to demonstrate that the *Martyrium* is a later document, produced by an epitomiser working on the former.

1.   At first the author of the *Martyrium* embodies from the Prologue the Roman date for June 29, viz. ἡ πρὸ τριῶν καλανδῶν Ἰουλίων; but later on he gives the date as μηνὸς Ἰουνίου εἰκοστῇ ἐννάτῃ ἡμέρᾳ.

2.   It is objected that the phrase in the *Martyrium* τῷ κατ' αὐτὸν μαρτυρίῳ is extremely harsh, whether αὐτὸν be referred to Paul or Nero; but in the Prologue it is quite clear that it is referred to Nero. The obscurity in the *Martyrium* is due to the careless work of the epitomiser.

3.   The strongest objection of all lies in the fact that the *Martyrium* places the actual martyrdom on June 29th, which is a deduction from the fact that the Roman Church kept the

festival of SS. Peter and Paul on that day, which we know from
the Liberian catalogue (A.D. 354) to have been simply the day
of the Deposition in A.D. 258. This mistake, according to
Mr Robinson, was not made by the author of the Prologue.
These are formidable objections; it only remains to see
whether they can claim to be insuperable.

Probably the best way to proceed will be to try and get a clear
idea of how much of the matter quoted from the Prologue is
Euthalius and how much Eusebius.

To begin with, the adverb αὐτόθι, which stands at the head of
the first extract, is a Eusebian word, probably the most frequent
adverb which he employs, and quite one of his style-words, as any
one may see by turning the pages of the History. In Eusebius it
never stands, as far as I know, at the beginning of the sentence,
and never is far removed from the preceding note of place.
Euthalius is struck with it and gives it a prominent position, but
at the same time it is thirteen lines of the text since Euthalius
has mentioned Rome[1]. Probably in the passage of Eusebius upon
which Euthalius was working the matter was better arranged.

The words that follow τῷ τῶν ἱερονίκων Χριστοῦ μαρτύρων
στεφάνῳ κατεκοσμήθη we have already shewn to be Eusebian.
We are next told of the Depositio Martyrum, and the curious
words are used περικαλλέσιν οἴκοις καὶ βασιλείοις.

Is it Euthalius or Eusebius that speaks of the churches in
which the martyrs' bones are laid as 'gorgeous and palatial
dwellings'? Let us turn to the oration of Eusebius at the conse-
cration of the Church at Tyre: we find (H. E. x. 4) that he speaks
of Christ as having filled the world with his royal dwellings (βασι-
λικῶν οἴκων αὐτοῦ) which are adorned with περικαλλῆ κοσμήματά
τε καὶ ἀναθήματα. Later on in the same discourse he twice
speaks of the Church at Tyre in the same style, calling it τὸν
βασίλειον οἶκον (pp. 473, 478) and a little later on again it is τὸν
μέγαν καὶ βασιλικὸν ἐξ ἁπάντων οἶκον by which he describes the
Spiritual Church. We may be pretty sure that Euthalius is
working over some Eusebian statement.

The expression τοῦ σωτηρίου πάθους is easily seen to be from

---

[1] The Eusebian usage may be seen from scores of passages; there are three in
the beginning of H. E. iii. 5 πρὸς τῶν αὐτόθι στρατοπέδων ἀναγορευθεὶς...τοῦ τὸν αὐτόθι
τῆς ἐπισκοπῆς θρόνον...τοῖς αὐτόθι δοκίμοις δι' ἀποκαλύψεως ἐκδοθέντα. The commonest
use of the word is in such phrases as ἡ αὐτόθι ἐκκλησία, ἡ αὐτόθι παροικία.

the same source; it is Eusebius' regular term, and occurs not only prominently in the Chronicon, but throughout the History: e.g. *Mart. Pal.* Prol. τῆς τοῦ σωτηρίου πάθους ἑορτῆς, *Mart. Pal.* 11 ταύτὸ τοῦ σωτηρίου μαρτύριον πάθους. Cf. also *H. E.* viii. 2, x. 3. We should not, of course, dwell on comparatively colourless expressions like these, if we had not proved that Eusebius was the principal source for Euthalian language, a fact which entitles us to make identifications of common words and turns of speech as well as rare ones.

The expression τρισκαιδεκάτῳ δὲ Νέρωνος...ἀποτμηθέντα is based partly upon the Chronicon, where the years of Nero are counted separately, but can also be illustrated from *H. E.* ii. 25 ἐπὶ τὰς κατὰ τῶν ἀποστόλων ἐπήρθη σφαγάς· Παῦλος δὴ οὖν ἐπ᾽ αὐτῆς Ῥώμης τὴν κεφαλὴν ἀποτμηθῆναι κτέ., where the only thing we miss is the ξίφει which occurs both in the Prologue and in the *Martyrium*. We have already shewn that Euthalius had pilfered from this passage.

Coming now to the disputed passage ἐν ᾗ καὶ τελειοῦται τῷ κατ᾽ αὐτὸν μαρτυρίῳ we find that this is not Euthalius but Eusebius (*H. E.* ii. 22), δεύτερον δ᾽ ἐπιβάντα τῇ αὐτῇ πόλει, τῷ κατ᾽ αὐτὸν τελειωθῆναι μαρτυρίῳ. And the obscurity which attaches to the phrase κατ᾽ αὐτὸν will be found to be involved in Eusebius himself, so that the *Martyrium* is actually nearer to Eusebius than is the Prologue.

As there seems to be no doubt that Euthalius has transcribed a number of sentences from this chapter of the History it will be convenient to set down the very words of Eusebius, indicating what Euthalius has borrowed in spaced type:

τούτου δὲ Φῆστος ὑπὸ Νέρωνος διάδοχος πέμπεται· καθ᾽ ὃν δικαιολογησάμενος ὁ Παῦλος, δέσμιος ἐπὶ Ῥώμης ἄγεται. Ἀρίσταρχος δ᾽ αὐτῷ συνῆν, ὃν καὶ εἰκότως συναιχμάλωτόν που τῶν ἐπιστολῶν ἀποκαλεῖ. καὶ Λουκᾶς δὲ ὁ τὰς πράξεις τῶν ἀποστόλων γραφῇ παραδούς, ἐν τούτοις κατέλυσε τὴν ἱστορίαν, διετίαν ὅλην ἐπὶ τῆς Ῥώμης τὸν Παῦλον ἄνετον διατρίψαι καὶ τὸν τοῦ Θεοῦ λόγον ἀκωλύτως ·κηρύξαι ἐπισημηνάμενος. τότε μὲν οὖν [Euthal. add. ἐπὶ Νέρωνος] ἀπολογησάμενον [Euthal. add. τὸν Παῦλον] αὖθις ἐπὶ τὴν τοῦ κηρύγματος διακονίαν λόγος ἔχει στείλασθαι τὸν ἀπόστολον, δεύτερον δ᾽ ἐπιβάντα τῇ αὐτῇ πόλει, τῷ κατ᾽ αὐτὸν τελειωθῆναι μαρτυρίῳ.

I suppose we must explain κατ' αὐτὸν here by reference to καθ' ὃν at the beginning of the chapter[1], but the harshness of the construction is as great in Eusebius as in the *Martyrium*, and no argument for a later date of the *Martyrium* can be deduced from the expression in question. Mr Robinson's second objection, therefore, falls to the ground.

The strongest objection is, no doubt, the third, which is based upon an apparent confusion between the Martyrdom and the Depositio of the Apostles which, according to Robinson, exists in the *Martyrium* but not in the Prologue. Did Eusebius say anything about the Depositio, and did he say it clearly? We have by this time little reason to confide in Euthalius as an independent investigator: and the prejudice is in favour of the use of Eusebian matter. It is very unfortunate that just at this point we lack the reference which would decisively clear the matter up, for Eusebius' book of Martyrs to which he several times refers in his history is not extant. No doubt it contained the Martyrdom of the great Apostles as well as of later worthies. We may, however, get some light upon the matter by referring to *H. E.* iii. 31, where Eusebius records the death of John and Philip and says Παύλου μὲν οὖν καὶ Πέτρου τῆς τελευτῆς ὅ τε χρόνος καὶ ὁ τρόπος καὶ προσέτι ὁ τῆς μετὰ τὴν ἀπαλλαγὴν τοῦ βίου τῶν σκηνωμάτων αὐτῶν καταθέσεως χῶρος, ἤδη πρότερον ἡμῖν δεδήλωται. Here κατάθεσις is the equivalent of the Latin *depositio*, and while at first sight it seems that Eusebius is speaking of the later Depositio and carefully distinguishing it from the Martyrdom, the previous passage in the History to which he refers (*H. E.* ii. 25) shews conclusively that this is not his meaning: he is describing the Depositio of SS. Peter and Paul in the Vatican and in the Church on the Ostian Way. Now this very chapter is one of those from which we have already convicted Euthalius of borrowing; and we say therefore that not only is the language of the Prologue at the point in question Eusebian language; but that it certainly does not refer to the Catacombs, for the resting places of the Martyrs are splendid churches, in the plural; this must mean the Vatican and the church on the Ostian Way. It appears therefore that the confusion between the Martyrdom and the Depositio exists equally

---

[1] It is Eusebius' way of describing coincidence in chronological position: *vide* Chronicon *passim*.

in the Prologue and the *Martyrium*. This would seem to meet
Mr Robinson's third objection.

And now as to the method of dating the Martyrdom or
Depositio. In the first place, while we have reason to regard
Eusebius as the proximate source for both the Prologue and the
Martyrium, the actual date given, the 5th of Panemus, is older
than Eusebius. We can see this by comparing Eusebius' method
of dating Martyrdoms in the account of the Palestine Martyrs.
For example, we have Ξανθικὸς μὴν ὃς λέγοιτ᾽ ἂν ᾽Απρίλλιος
παρὰ ῾Ρωμαίοις· Δεσίου μηνὸς ἑβδόμῃ, πρὸ ἑπτὰ εἰδῶν ᾽Ιουνίων
λέγοιτ᾽ ἂν παρὰ ῾Ρωμαίοις [1] and so on, from which it is clear that
the months used by Eusebius, writing at Cesarea, are the Roman
months with Syro-Macedonian names; the Syro-Macedonian
calendar has, therefore, been displaced. It is not unreasonable to
suppose, then, that a reference to Panemus in the account of
Paul's Martyrdom, where Panemus is clearly the Syro-Macedonian
month and not the later Roman substitute, belongs to an earlier
time than Eusebius. If he found it in his sources, he was almost
bound to explain it. The document from which our information
comes must have contained more than the allusion to the fifth
day of Panemus. But even with the attached Roman date there
is still some ambiguity; for Panemus itself has become ambiguous:
and we may regard it as certain that the calendar which in
Eusebius' time had been changed from Syro-Macedonian arrangement to Roman arrangement, while retaining the names, would in
the end take up the Roman names as well as the Roman arrangement of the months : and these names amongst a Greek-speaking
people will appear as Greek names. It is therefore quite natural
that we should find in the *Martyrium* in the passage in which the
writer brings the dates down to his day, the statement that the
Martyrdom is commemorated on the 25th of June.

I do not see, then, that any convincing reason has been brought
forward for making the *Martyrium* later than the Pauline Prologue, or assigning them to different hands. Euthalius is proved
to have been an epitomizer of previous materials; why should we
assume a second epitomizer to go over what Euthalius has collected;
he was quite capable of doing the summarizing himself, either by

---

[1] That is the 7th of Desius is the 7th of June, and so constantly. Notice the
agreement of the Eusebian method of dating with the language of the *Martyrium*:
ἥτις λέγοιτ᾽ ἂν παρὰ ῾Ρωμαίοις.

going over his prologue and picking up the allusions, as Prof. Robinson thinks was done, or by going once more, which is the likelier hypothesis, to the sources from which he had derived his information.

The probability that Euthalius went to his sources for the summary which we find in the *Martyrium* is increased by the appearance in the reckoning of the Eusebian phrase ἥτις λέγοιτ' ἂν in connection with the equivalent date.

There are other reasons for refusing to Euthalius the extreme antiquity with which Mr Robinson wishes to credit him. One of them has been pointed out by Zahn in *Theol. Lit. Blatt* for Dec. 20, 1895; he shews that in Euthalius' list of quotations there is one which is professedly taken from the Apostolic Constitutions (Acts xx. 35), to which pseudapostolic work an extreme antiquity was therefore assigned in Euthalius' mind. But Zahn points out that the quotation in question does not appear in the first form of the Constitutions, the Syriac Didascalia, which belongs to the third century, and that the Constitutions in their later form can hardly have existed as early as 370 and may be later than 400 A.D. Zahn suggests that a later hand should be credited with this quotation; but this is quite unnecessary; the difficulty only arises from a wrong chronological idea about Euthalius.

A further consideration of some weight is to be found in the fact that Euthalius speaks of Eusebius in a way which implies that he had been some time dead and had already acquired a literary canonisation. At the close of the Pauline prologue he imagines an objector who refuses to believe the details of Paul's second captivity on the ground that there is nothing of the kind mentioned in S. Luke. And the reply is that we should, on such a point, receive the testimony of Eusebius the Chronographer, and of his History. For it is those who follow the teaching of the Fathers and accept their traditions who will attain unto eternal life. The idea of replying to such objections comes from Euseb. *H. E.* ii. 22, but the manner of making the reply in which such deference is paid to the opinion of Eusebius, who is styled the Chronographer (which can hardly be a contemporary title), shews that Euthalius is writing after the death of Eusebius, and probably some time after. Now Eusebius died in 340. It would seem, therefore, a very unlikely supposition to assign Euthalius, with Prof. Robinson, to some date between 330—350 A.D.

𝕮𝖆𝖒𝖇𝖗𝖎𝖉𝖌𝖊:

PRINTED BY J. AND C. F. CLAY

AT THE UNIVERSITY PRESS

THE REST OF THE WORDS

OF BARUCH.

London: C. J. CLAY AND SONS,
CAMBRIDGE UNIVERSITY PRESS WAREHOUSE,
AVE MARIA LANE.

Cambridge: DEIGHTON, BELL, AND CO.
Leipzig: F. A. BROCKHAUS.

THE REST OF THE WORDS
OF BARUCH:

A CHRISTIAN APOCALYPSE OF
THE YEAR 136 A.D.

THE TEXT REVISED WITH AN INTRODUCTION

BY

J. RENDEL HARRIS

FORMERLY FELLOW OF CLARE COLLEGE, CAMBRIDGE,
AND NOW PROFESSOR OF BIBLICAL LANGUAGES IN HAVERFORD COLLEGE,
PENNSYLVANIA.

LONDON:
C. J. CLAY AND SONS,
CAMBRIDGE UNIVERSITY PRESS WAREHOUSE
1889

𝕮𝖆𝖒𝖇𝖗𝖎𝖉𝖌𝖊:
PRINTED BY C. J. CLAY, M.A. AND SONS,
AT THE UNIVERSITY PRESS.

THE REST OF THE WORDS OF BARUCH.

THE present work is designed to draw attention to an important but hitherto much-neglected fragment of Apocalyptic literature which seems to me to be valuable, in spite of the contemptuous treatment which it has met with at the hands of the critics, both to the Ecclesiastical Historian and to the Christian Dogmatist; to the former, on account of the light which it throws on one of the most obscure periods in the growth of the Church, that, viz., which includes the revolt of the false Messiah; to the latter, because it helps us to see the manner in which one of the leading doctrines of the Christian Faith polarized the worshippers for and against itself (as almost every point of Christian doctrine does at some time or other in the history of the Church), and setting a man at variance spiritually with his fellow brought it to pass that the sword came down in the house itself to separate the undecided and half-hearted from the convinced and the faithful, that the many who were called might make way for the few who were chosen. And certainly when we say that in this tract the reader will hear the final farewell of the Church to the Synagogue, and that the parting words will be concerned with the doctrine of the Divine Nature of Jesus Christ, we have a right to ask for it a closer and a more careful perusal than it has hitherto met with. Nor is this the only reason why it should be made an object of attentive study. We hear much said now-a-days about the interpolation of Jewish Apocalypses by Christians, and it becomes a very interesting matter for critical study to determine how far such a tendency to the absorption and republication of earlier literary productions prevailed in those centuries which were especially marked by Apocalyptic activity, and in what manner that republication was commonly effected: for it is certain that in the early Christian literature we constantly disinter fragments of earlier workmanship, and equally certain that nothing leads to such reckless criticism as the unskilled or half-skilled attempt to detach the embedded earlier form from its surroundings. The present tract is one in which we are able to point out not only, as I have intimated above, the exact date of its publication, but a great part of the earlier material which the writer appropriated. We can watch the bookmaker at his task, and can, so to speak, mark the places where the scissors and paste have been used; for this Apocalypse is the degenerate offspring of an illustrious line, perhaps the very last scion of a noble house. The Apocalyptic literature connected with Jeremiah and his companions must have been extensive and popular, widely read and full of household words; and a great part of this literature is still extant. We are therefore favourably placed for the study of an interesting problem in early religious teaching.

We may remark further that the Semitic and quasi-Semitic literature is at its best in the region of Apocalypse: the historical situations are better preserved because of the way in which they have been disguised; the cipher in which the story was written has prevented the text from being tampered with. Apocalyptic writers do not deal in the flatteries which so often deface ancient history. Josephus, for example, writing of the expected Messiah and in the hope of pleasing his patrons, will have Vespasian for his Coming One; but this adroit deviation from popular belief would not be worth publication unless it were made known both to the princes whom he designed to propitiate, and to the masses whom he proposed to enlighten. If he had held a contrary opinion or wished to inculcate it (for no one knows what the real opinions of this agreeable diplomatist were) he would have been obliged to write in allegory, cipher, or Apocalypse, and for the few rather than the many. Vespasian would have been an eagle or a dragon, or a dense forest or something of the kind. But we should at least be sure that we had got at his real opinions. Apocalypses, then, are the truer by their very falsity. The opinions which the writer disguises are his genuine opinions.

Further than this, they are his opinions, generally speaking, upon burning questions. Apocalypses concern themselves with the most critical situations in the experiences of men and nations; they touch the deeper exigencies of life; they debate the inconsistencies of man's conceptions of God and the Universe; they discourse on the Providence and Fore-ordination of the Almighty, as it were, to His very face. St Paul is content to state his belief that Adam sinned and, ergo, all men sinned. With the Apocalyptic Baruch or Ezra, the calm theological statement becomes a burning passionate question, "O thou Adam! wherefore hast thou sinned?" In the same way the decline of the Jewish polity is predicted or recorded with much calmness by the Apostles; "the wrath is come upon them to the uttermost" is the sum total of it; .an Apocalyptist, on the contrary, is spurred to write not so much by the fact, as by grief over the fact. His head must needs be waters, and his eyes a fountain of tears. The highest national hopes, too, find their expression in this way: the coming of Messiah, the fall of Rome, the end of a captivity, the imminence of judgments,—all these things require bated breath in the speaker; and we hear him more clearly because he whispers. We know more of the national aspirations of the Jews from their Apocalypses than from all the histories that are extant: which is the same as saying that Apocalypse is one of the highest forms of historical record.

Our document furnishes us, as we shall see, with an illustration of the truth that almost all apocalyptic literature belongs to special historical crises: there are very few books of this kind which do not shew, in addition to disguised facts, disguised figures; the chronology is in cipher as well as the story: the number of years to Messiah's kingdom and to the fall of the great Eagle must be given, but not so that the great Eagle can read it. Time, times and half-a-time, says the Apocalyptist in answer to the passionate 'How long, Lord' which is being repeated inwardly by the people; and then a convenient key is given, and some note which shall epigrammatically attract attention, such as ὁ ἀναγινώσκων νοείτω, or a rude hexameter scrap, like

$$\text{˚Ωδε ὁ νοῦς ὁ ἔχων σοφίαν.}$$

These crises in history and their associated revolutions in thought furnish the Apocalyptic situation: and it is therefore no surprise to us to find a redundance of this kind of literature near the period calculated for the birth of the Messiah, or subsequent to the fall of the city under Titus, or its further desolation under Hadrian. But there is one further point which is not so evident and which does not indeed lie in the nature of the case, but which is very important for the appreciation of Jewish Apocalypses; namely, the tendency which they shew to periodicity. The apocalyptic is not merely a prophet; he has become so by taking a cyclical view of the history of his people: that which furnishes his time-key in determining the duration of a captivity is the duration of a previous captivity. So many flights of the Phœnix, so many Jubilee periods, and then human things will return upon themselves. He expects God to repeat himself in history, and the more so as he sees history repeating itself. It was inevitable that the Jews should indulge Messianic hopes seventy years after the capture of the city by Titus: and they indulged them the more actively as the seventy years ran out.

Nor were they without some encouragement to this belief from actual event. One of the things written across Jewish history was the fatality connected with the 10th of Ab. We may get some idea of the import of this day by recalling the language of Josephus concerning it: "the fated round of times was come, the tenth day of the month Lous, on which aforetime the city had been burnt by the Babylonians" (*Bell. Jud.* VI. 4. 5). He does not hesitate to say that the time had been calculated by God; "one might rightly marvel at the accuracy of the cycle; for it was the very same month and day on which the city was formerly burnt by the Babylonians" (*Bell. Jud.* VI. 4. 8).

So deeply was this day marked with black in their calendar that there is reason to suspect that from that day to this it has been kept as a day of mourning both by Jews and Christians. With the Jews, of course, this is obvious: but the following considerations suggest that the Christian Church also shared this mourning with them. The Greek Church keeps a special memorial of the fall of the city on the 4th of November, and reads on that day, as we shall see, a portion of the very Apocalypse which we are engaged upon. But the question naturally arises as to how a memorial designed for the Fall of the City came to be read on this date. The answer is that Ab, which is the eleventh month of the Hebrew Calendar, has been replaced by November, the eleventh in the Julian year, while some reason not known to us has displaced the day from the tenth to the fourth[1]. We may,

---

[1] We shall see by and bye that our Christian Baruch has the month of Ab in his mind as the commencement of the Exile. According to the Talmud Bether was captured on the 9th of Ab.

therefore, suspect that Christians as well as Jews concerned themselves to note the fatal day[1]. And it was inevitable that the observed periodicity in the dated fortunes of the city should lead to a belief that the period of oppression would also run parallel with the history of the earlier Captivity. At all events this is a sufficient explanation of the excited state of the Jews in the last decade of the seventy years which followed the destruction of the city. Perhaps a similar consideration of other periods mentioned in history or prophecy will furnish us the explanation of the appearance of the other Apocalyptists, Ezras, or Jeremiahs, or Baruchs. This reasoning finds its confirmation when we proceed to the examination of our own especial document. We shall shew presently that it is a disguised history of the 66th year after the fall of the city: and the meaning attached to the number 66 is sufficiently evident from the fact that in many MSS. it has been corrected to 70. The number was seen to belong to the close of a cycle, what we may call the iron number of the captivity of Zion[2]. We will return to this point presently; but before discussing our Christian Baruch more closely, it is as well to say a few words about the earlier Apocalypses from which it is descended.

The Baruch literature begins, of course, with the Apocryphal Baruch of the Old Testament, a work which is still much in dispute, both as to the language in which it was written and the place and period to which it should be assigned. That it is præ-Christian may, however, probably be assumed; so that it differs from the rest of the writings which bear the name of Baruch, all of which belong to the period of the second Captivity (using this term for the result of the Roman War under Vespasian and Titus). At the same time this Apocryphal Baruch, though belonging to an earlier period, furnishes the suggestion for the later writings, and it may be anticipated before comparison that there will be numerous parallelisms in thought and expression between the

---

[1] We observe that the Menaeum heads the service for this day, Διήγησις εἰς τὸν θρῆνον τοῦ προφήτου Ἱερεμίου περὶ τῆς Ἱερουσαλήμ, καὶ εἰς τὴν ἅλωσιν ταύτης καὶ περὶ τῆς ἐκστάσεως Ἀβιμέλεχ. This of itself is strongly suggestive of the commemoration of the fatal day, and the allusion to the lamentation of Jeremiah shews that our tract has replaced an earlier book which was used in the commemoration service.

[2] The chronological parallels have been strained by the Jews to the detriment of the history, so as to make the Hadrian war last three years and a half; the time of the earlier hostilities: Renan rightly remarks (*Origines*, Vol. VI. p. 208, note) "ce dernier chiffre suspect; on a modelé le siége de Béther sur celui de Jérusalem."

early apocryphon, the prototype, and the later brood. But these parallelisms hardly come into account in what we are occupied about, and it is sufficient to refer to any of the good writers upon Apocalyptic literature for the verification of the relations that have been intimated. We call this book, for distinction, the Apocryphal Baruch (or simply Baruch).

With the next book, which we call the Apocalyptic Baruch, we have more to do; for not only is it a very important work, but, as we shall see, the connexion between it and our Christian Baruch is very marked. It was first published by Ceriani in *Monumenta Sacra et Profana*, Tom. I. fasc. i., from a Syriac MS. in the Ambrosian Library[1]; Ceriani at first reserved the Syriac for a future edition of the Old Testament, and gave only a Latin translation; but in response to appeals which were made to him by various scholars, he printed the whole of the Syriac text in the fifth volume of the *Monumenta*. Until Ceriani's publication nothing was known of this apocalyptic Baruch, except the letter of Baruch at the close of the book, which is extant in many MSS. and has often been printed. An examination of this book, in detail, is not within our scope; it will be sufficient to enumerate a few of the more definite results which come to light when the processes of criticism are applied to the book. First of all, then, the writer was a Jew, and a pious Jew, living in troublous times. He laments many who have deserted the Covenant and have cast from them the yoke of the Law, but consoles himself on the other hand that there are many 'who have left their vanities and taken refuge under the shadow of thy wings.' The last expression is the proper one for indicating proselytism. For example, it is the term used by the Jewish Fathers in describing the persuasive powers of the good Hillel; "the gentleness of Hillel brought us near under the wings of the Shekinah;" nor should we be wrong in inferring that those who have deserted the law have done so under the influence of an adverse proselytism which is undermining or replacing Judaism. The Law, too, is his last Jewish citadel. The city was in ruins when he wrote (and we need scarcely say that this desolation was not that of the Babylonian Captivity), and in the face of this disaster, the only religious anchorage was the Law; we know well the zeal with which the Jew turned in his exile from the

---

[1] The MS. is said to be as old as the sixth cent. Its class mark is B. 21 Inf. Ceriani has given a lithographic specimen of it.

Holy City to the pages of his holy book: "Unless thy law," said Zion, "had been my delight, I should then have perished in my affliction." To hold fast by the Law is the main precept; and the more so, because the end must be near: we pass away, but the Law remains. The end of all things is at hand; the pitcher is near the fountain, the ship almost in the harbour, the journey has the city in sight, life speeds to its ending: preaching and penitence, alms and intercession have had their allotted season. Such is the final sentiment of the apocalyptic writer, after he has given his views of the Messianic Kingdom, of the fall of Rome, of the future world and other matters which press upon the mind of the God-fearing people.

And it is not difficult to see the period to which this lamentation belongs. He is a pious Jew of the time of the desertion of Zion; how long after the year A.D. 70 he lived and wrote is more difficult to decide, and indeed no one has handled this point with adequate clearness. We will indicate presently the chief opinions which have been held.

Not only is the writer a Jew, but he is a Palestine Jew,—a Jerusalem Jew, we may say with a good degree of confidence. He is acquainted with the Holy City and its surroundings. The imagined Baruch, for example, receives a word from the Lord (c. 21) 'to go and sit in the valley of the Kedron in a cave of the earth;' how did he know that the Kedron valley was full of caves? In c. 47 he says, "Lo! I am going to Hebron, for thither hath the strong Lord sent me;" he does not say, "I am going from Jerusalem to Hebron;" the city is taken for granted in the story. Add to this, that Hebron would hardly be known out of Palestine. The writer is a Jew, dwelling in the neighbourhood at least of the Holy City; we do not know how far the actual right of dwelling in the city or its environs was restricted at this time; it cannot have been completely forbidden, for that is a regulation which history shews and our later Baruch confirms to have been the result of the revolt of Bar-Cochba. We shall shew presently that the Christian Baruch was also written in the city or near it.

Returning to the question of the time when the Apocalyptic Baruch was written, we observe that those who have written on the subject have dealt with (1) its similarity to another, even more famous Apocalypse, the fourth book of Ezra; (2) the evidences of the influences of Christian Scriptures upon the writer;

(3) the actual notes of time which it contains; (4) the fact that it is quoted in the second century by Papias. For example: the connexion between fourth Ezra and the Apocalypse of Baruch, both in ideas and language, is undoubted. P. Hofstede de Groot in his work on Basilides[1] determines the date of the fourth book of Ezra to be A.D. 97 (reign of Nerva), and he decides, in agreement with Volkmar, that at this time the Gospel of John was either unwritten, or current only in a limited circle. Then in a note he remarks that shortly before 4th Ezra there appeared the Apocalypse of Baruch, a work originally written in Greek, but transmitted to us only in Syriac, which is later than the destruction of the temple, earlier than Papias, and has references to Matthew, Luke and Romans. And this Apocalypse he affirms to be the work of a Jew. De Groot's conclusions may be traversed, perhaps, on some points, and we are not concerned to defend them; the connexion, however, between Ps. Ezra and Apocal. Baruch which he remarks is recognized by other writers; and the only question is whether Apocal. Baruch or Ps. Ezra is the earlier.

Fritzsche on the other hand, in his account of the Apocryphal Books of the Old Testament (Lips. 1871), will have it that the Apocalypse is written not long after the fall of the city. This is a good deal earlier than De Groot's estimate. H. Ewald[2] argues the date something as follows in his review of the earlier numbers of Ceriani's *Monumenta*. He points out that in c. 28 the reckoning from the destruction of the city to the expected Messiah is ' two parts weeks of seven weeks,' which he interprets to mean, in accordance with Hebrew parlance, two-thirds of 49 years: thus bringing us to the year 103 ($70 + \frac{2}{3}49$). But then allowing for twelve periods of final tribulation through which the world must pass from the time when the book is written until the end of the age, he subtracts 12 years and so brings us back to the year 91. It will be evident that this process of calculation and sub-calculation is very uncertain; and the same thing must be said of Ewald's other chronological points.

It is interesting to find, by way of contrast, that Hilgenfeld puts the date as far back as A.D. 72[3]!

---

[1] *Basilides am Ausgange des Apostolischen Zeitalters*, Leipzig, 1868.
[2] *Gottingische gelehrte Anzeigen*, 1867, p. 1705 sqq.
[3] *Messias Judaeorum*, p. lxiii.

It is a difficult thing then to determine the date with precision; and it does not seem that the critics have arrived at any more definite conclusion as to the upper time-limit of the book, than that it was written after the Roman Captivity. For the lower limit the only evidence (apart from that afforded by our Christian Baruch) seems to be that there is good reason to believe that it was from the Apocal. Baruch that Papias derived his Chiliastic story about the rate of produce of corn and wine in the millennium. The passage of Papias is well known by frequent quotation: that of Baruch is sufficiently like to it (x. 29). "In one vine there shall be a thousand shoots, and one shoot shall produce a thousand clusters, and one cluster a thousand berries, and one berry shall give a cor of wine......And they shall eat (of the manna) who come to the end of that time." It must be admitted, however, that there are elements in Papias' story which do not seem to be reproduced here; so that even at the lower time-limit we are a little uncertain. Nor do we arrive at much greater certainty when we try to determine the date of the Apocal. Baruch by the companion volume, the 4th of Ezra. Ewald goes so far as almost to assume that the two books are twin sisters, and if either is earlier than the other it is Apocal. Baruch. But this again is very uncertain. What we do seem to have arrived at is that it is generally admitted that 4th Ezra and Apocal. Baruch are closely related; that Baruch shews some parallels with the Christian Gospels; that its time of production is in the last thirty years of the first century, and that there is some reason to believe it is quoted by Papias. It is unfortunate that we cannot speak with greater confidence, because, since the Christian Baruch as we shall see is exactly dated, we should have been able to get an estimate of the time between the publication of a Jewish Apocalypse and its appropriation by a Christian writer, which estimate might have served us as a rough guide in other and similar cases.

In addition to the three Baruch books to which we have been alluding (Apocryphal Baruch, or simply Baruch, Apocalyptic Baruch, and Christian Baruch) it is very likely that there are other Baruch and Jeremiah books which have perished. The titles Baruch and Jeremiah are interchangeable: our Christian book sometimes bears the name which we have adopted, *Rest of the words of Baruch,* and sometimes it is called the *Paralipomena of Jeremiah.* And it is probable that similar confusion has prevailed with regard to the Baruchs and Jeremiahs which are not now extant, but of which we find traces.

For example, we find that it is to an apocryphal Jeremiah that Euthalius refers the quotation in Ephes. v. 14, "Awake thou that sleepest &c." Others, I believe, suppose it to be taken from an Apocryphal Adam. There is much confusion in these references to Apocryphal authors: but we may well imagine that the sentences come from some unrecovered part of the Baruch-Jeremiah literature, earlier of course than the Apocalypse.

An apocryphal Baruch is alluded to in Hippolytus[1], as being the text-book of a Gnostic named Justin. This Baruch is one of the superior angels, and not a prophet. Hippolytus gives a sketch of the system of Justin, and describes the oath which the initiated take that they will not divulge the mysteries nor relapse from the Good One to the creature: after which the worshipper is introduced to the secrets of the order, and beholds "what eye hath not seen and ear hath not heard, and which have not entered into the heart of man." This is the passage which Euthalius regards St Paul in 1 Cor. ii. as quoting, not from Isaiah, but from Apocryphal Elias. As it is one of the chief Gnostic formulæ in Justin's system, it is at least conceivable that Elias may be a mistake for Baruch.

In the *Altercation of Simon the Jew and Theophilus the Christian*[2], a work of the fifth century, to which Harnack has recently drawn attention[3], there is an allusion to a book of Baruch, from which Theophilus quotes what he considers to be a convincing argument against Simon: "Quomodo ergo prope finem libri sui de nativitate eius et de habitu vestis et de passione eius et de resurrectione eius prophetavit dicens: Hic unctus meus, electus meus, vulvae incontaminatae iaculatus, natus et passus dicitur"? This is in answer to Simon's statement that "Baruch de Christo nihil meminit." The passage is not in any of our known books of Baruch.

In Cyprian's *Testimonia* iii. 29 there has been inserted in some MSS. a quotation from Baruch which has never been identified, as far as I know, in the known Baruch literature. It runs as follows: "Veniet enim tempus et quaeretis me vos et qui post

---

[1] *Philosophumena*, v. 24—27.

[2] *Texte und Untersuchungen*, Bd. i. Heft 3, Leipzig, 1883.

[3] See Schürer, *Neutest. Zeitgeschichte*, iii. 83 (Eng. translation). Schürer's notes on the Baruch literature are very valuable.

vos cupiant audire verbum sapientiae et intellectus et non in-
venient. Nationes autem cupient videre sapientem et non con-
tinget eis; non quia deerit aut deficiet sapientia huius saeculi
terrae sed neque deerit sermo legis saeculo. Erit enim sapientia
in paucis vigilantibus et taciturnis et quietis sibi confabulantibus,
quoniam quidam eos horrebunt et timebunt ut malos. Alii autem
nec credent verbo legis Altissimi. Alii autem ore stupentes non
credent, et credent et contradicentes erunt contrarii et impedientes
spiritum veritatis. Alii autem erunt sapientes ad spiritum erroris,
et pronuntiantes sicut Altissimi et Fortis dicta. Alii autem
personales fidei: alii capaces et fortes in fide Altissimi et odibiles
alieno." The passage is certainly in the Baruch manner, as we
may see by comparing Apocal. Bar. c. 48, "Non enim multi
sapientes reperientur illo tempore, et intelligentes singulares
aliqui erunt: sed etiam qui sciunt, maxime conticescent......et
dicent multi multis illo tempore: Ubinam occultavit se multitudo
intelligentiae?" But we can hardly identify it with any known
passage: so we must still leave a margin for lost literature under
the names of Baruch and Jeremiah.

We come now to our special subject, the Christian Baruch, a
work which, as we said at the commencement, has met with a
somewhat cold reception from the learned. Fritzsche describes it
as much later in date and inferior in character to the Apocalypse
of Baruch[1]. De Groot speaks of it as belonging to the Gnostic
school, whatever that may mean. Kneucker[2] calls it "a tasteless
working over" of the Apocalypse of Baruch. Dillmann refers it to
the third or fourth century, which can hardly be meant as a
commendation. Schürer is more guarded, and simply says that it
is "a Christian book akin to our Apocalypse of Baruch, and has
borrowed largely from it." The question of the literary excellence
of the work is of course quite a subordinate one; it is of more
importance to know that it is admittedly and obviously a
Christian book; and therefore not to be despised even if it
should turn out to be of the third or fourth century. But the
fact is, as we have said, it is much earlier, and its chronology is
susceptible of exact determination.

---

[1] He expressed a hope of editing it, however, at some future time; a promise
which he does not seem to have redeemed; 18 years having elapsed since the
announcement.

[2] *Das Buch Baruch*, Lips. 1879, p. 195.

We will first of all shew that the book was written by a Judæo-Christian living in the city of Jerusalem. The action of the story, being concerned with the exile of the people, is divided between Jerusalem and Babylon; but the writer betrays himself by an excessive knowledge of the topography of the Holy City. Jeremiah wishes to send Abimelech the Ethiopian away from the city in order that he may not see the destruction thereof: and the Lord directs him to send him *to the gardens of Agrippa*, where he shall be hidden in the mountain side until the return of the people from exile. Accordingly Jeremiah directs Abimelech to take a basket and go to the garden of Agrippa *by the mountain road* and bring back figs. Abimelech goes, falls asleep under a tree, wakes after a sufficient sleep of 66 years, and coming back to the ruined city fails to recognize it. "Alas!" says he, "I have lost my way because I took the mountain road."

Now the mention of the garden of Agrippa would of itself be a sufficient betrayal of the locality of the writer, but when it is intimated that there were two roads thither, we are not only convinced that the writer was speaking of a spot well-known to him, but we are even encouraged to attempt an identification of the spot mentioned. It is very likely that the gardens of Herod alluded to are in the fertile valley below Solomon's pools, frequently spoken of by travellers and their guides as Solomon's gardens, and bearing to-day the name of Artas, which is an evident perversion of the Roman *hortus*. I know no more likely place for a royal garden in the vicinity of Jerusalem. And the curious thing is that there are decidedly two roads from Jerusalem to Artas; one the high-road to Bethlehem and Hebron, with a short divergence to the left at Solomon's pools; and the other the track round the hills which follows the line of Solomon's aqueduct from the pools to the city. It certainly looks as if the geography were real geography; and if this be the case the book was written in Jerusalem, as was its prototype the Apocalypse of Baruch. And in any case the allusion to the gardens of Agrippa remains whether we have correctly identified their position or not.

But we may go further than this: not only have we a geographical limit in the gardens of Agrippa, but we have also both superior and inferior chronological limits. Superior, by the fact that the book was written later than Agrippa whichever of the family may be intended; inferior, because it could not be written after the time when his name ceased to be popularly attached to the place described. And it seems to me that this consideration alone would be fatal to Dillmann's hypothesis of the third or fourth century as the time of production of the book. The writer then is a Jerusalem Christian.

The next thing is to give the chronological identification. We have already alluded to this by anticipation. The word of the Lord to Jeremiah concerning Abimelech is that "I will cover him in the mountain *until I cause the people to return to the city.*" Now on the hypothesis, allegorical and cyclical, of a Babylonian captivity, the conventional duration of exile is 70 years. Yet the writer makes Abimelech fall asleep for 66 years. The Greek service-book corrects this to 70, and inserts the 70 again in the passage where Abimelech, meeting the old man outside of the city, obtains from him the information that Jeremiah is with the people in Babylon; where it adds the words 'since 70 years.' The correction was perfectly natural and every way likely: but we must read sixty-six years, and not seventy. The same exchange of numbers will be found in c. vi. where Abimelech shews his basket of figs, and remarks that, though sixty-six years had elapsed since they were gathered, they were not spoiled. And since this is the date of the suggested return from exile, and the book professes to be describing contemporary movements (for it records almost nothing of subsequent date), then the year of the expected return is A.D. 70 (the date of the Captivity) + 66 years = A.D. 136, and the book must have been written very soon after that time.

Very soon after; because, as we shall see, it is an Eirenicon addressed to the people of that time, a time marked perhaps more deeply than any other in the history both of Jews and Christians (unless perhaps it be the capture of the city by Titus), when severe political regulations produced greater changes in six months in the relations of the Church and Synagogue than had taken place in all the preceding years of the century. We know very little, as we would wish to know, of the details of the new settlement of Jewish affairs by Hadrian: but we learn from the history and the coins that Jerusalem was no more, that it was replaced by Aelia Capitolina; that the plough was passed over the sacred soil in token of its renewed subjugation; that Roman statues, the emperor and his gods, were in the holy places; and that an edict

of the emperor prohibited the Jew from approaching the holy
city. Turning to the lists of bishops in Eusebius, we find that
Gentile names appear now for the first time. It is not necessary
to assume the accuracy of Eusebius' list of Jerusalem bishops;
many of these lists, especially the earlier portions of them, are
afterthoughts. But the tradition which makes Marcus bishop of
Jerusalem at the close of the Hadrian War can hardly be incorrect. It means at least that there has been, from political
necessity, a change in the organic life of the Church. The last
have become first, and the first last. The Judæo-Christian party
with its antique traditions and venerable Mosaism is passing away.
The breach with Judaism, which Paul usually effected in a few
months in any city where he laboured, was not really accomplished
in Jerusalem until the false Messiah had run his course. But
then when it came, it came quickly.

Now our document is the Church's Eirenicon to the Synagogue,
at the time of the Hadrian edict. The problem is, how to evade
the edict of banishment from the holy City which is pronounced
on the race. Granted that we are carried away captive, and that
there is a possibility of return from captivity, how is this return
to be brought about? And the answer is contained in the letter
which Baruch is instructed to send from Jerusalem to Jeremiah in
Babylon. So we find in c. vi. as follows: "If ye obey my voice,
saith the Lord, by the mouth of Jeremiah, I will separate you
from Babylon; but he that will not obey, let him be as *a stranger
to Jerusalem* ($\xi \acute{\epsilon} \nu o \varsigma \ \tau \hat{\eta} \varsigma \ \text{'} I \epsilon \rho o \upsilon \sigma a \lambda \acute{\eta} \mu$), and I will test you by the
water of Jordan, and there he that will not obey will be made
manifest." If nothing more had been said, we should have con-
jectured that this meant the rite of baptism; but lest we should
have any doubt on the matter, the writer continues parenthetically,
" this is the sign of the great seal," the conventional Patristic term
for baptism. It is possible that these words may be a later interpolation, but they are not the less striking on that account, for
they would disclose the interpretation that primitively attached
to the passage. The meaning of it all is that the Christians, who
are evidently not affected by the imperial edict, for they took no
part in the rebellion, have suggested to Jews that by becoming
Christians by the way of baptism they can evade the force of the
edict, and no longer be *strangers to Jerusalem.* The people are
to be brought down to Jordan's side from Babylon, and there the

precious and the vile are as far as possible to be separated one
from another. Those that will make the necessary renunciation
are received, the rest rejected. The story runs that Jeremiah
sorted them out by families, and when a whole family was clear
in renouncing Babylon and its customs they were accepted, and if
not they were rejected. It is not easy to imagine the manner of
the selection. The writer does not mean Rome when he speaks of
the people renouncing Babylon and passing over Jordan, and talks
of mixed families where men had married Babylonish women. I
think he here means the old school of Jews (those who are Babylonians by choice and who make no move towards Jordan), between
whom and the Gentile Church lies the conflict for the possession of
the intermediate party, the Judæo-Christians of various types.
The selection being made by families is thoroughly in the Eastern
manner, where religion is always bounded by social and racial
limits, just as population is to this day reckoned by households.
"Himself believed and his house" is the conventional formula for
a change of religion: "as for me and my house" is a similar term.
What makes one a little more confident in this interpretation that
it was an appeal on the part of the Gentile Christians or at least
of the Gentilising Christians to the more conservative, half convinced among their Jewish brethren, is that we find from the
account that some undecided people in the middle ground came
part way to Jerusalem and then returned; and that on their returning to Babylon, they were received with an intimation that
as they had secretly departed from them, they would not be
received again: Babylon would have none of them. This according to the story leads to the formation of a new colony which
is derisively called Samaria. Now this is not difficult of interpretation, if we imagine that there were those who had gone so
far from Judaism as to provoke an edict against their being received again into ecclesiastical fellowship, and yet had not come
so near to Christianity as to be able to pass the baptismal stand-
ards. In this case, then, one result of the Hadrian edict is the
formation of a new Ebionite movement in Palestine. This exactly agrees with the statements of Epiphanius and Jerome as to
the origin of Ebionism: they attempted to be both Jews and
Christians, and ended by being neither.

It is just possible that this accepting and rejecting of families
of Jews by unauthorized or half-authorized persons may be the

origin of a story in the Talmud which seems to cover some irritation of national feeling[1] on the subject of proselytism.

The story is apparently referred to the time of Rabbi Joshua who is talmudically the second generation from Hillel the Great. "R. Joshua said, I received from R. Johanan ben Zakkai, who received it from his teacher as a tradition in a direct line from Moses on Mount Sinai, that Elias would not come to pronounce clean or unclean, *to reject or admit families* in general, but only to reject those that had entered by violence, and to admit those who had been rejected by violence. There was, beyond Jordan[2], a family of the name of Beth Zerefa, which a certain Ben Zion *had excluded by violence.* There was there another family (of impure blood) whom this Ben Zion had *admitted by violence.* He comes to pronounce such clean or unclean, to reject or to admit them." It is quite possible that this story refers to the admission of proselytes by Jewish Christians of the city of Jerusalem (note the Ben Zion) who rank practically in the city as Jews, at all events up to the time of the final rupture, although in foreign cities they had long been known as a ' third race.'

In Jerusalem itself the line of demarcation between Jews and Christians was for a long time very faintly marked. The ecclesia was *intra synagogam.* Witness the account of the relations between the Pharisees and S. James the Just which Hegesippus furnishes; no difference of opinion seems to exist, except on the one point of the person of Jesus Christ, whom St James affirms to be coming in the clouds of heaven. Something of the same sort is implied in the story of Stephen. We shall see by and bye that this is the very point which provokes the people in the story to stone Jeremiah, just as in the history they had done to St James.

We have shewn, then, that the date suggested by the Baruch-story is exactly the right date for the interpretation of the events that are there adumbrated. It is very interesting to see that baptism, which at first served to initiate proselytes into Judaism,

---

[1] Mishna *Edujoth,* viii. 7, quoted in Schürer *Neutest. Zeitgesch.* ii. 156, Eng. trans.

[2] We must not strain allegory in order to see here a reference to baptism. I use the passage to shew that the Jews in the first century quarrelled over and discussed their family membership and its purity or impurity just as our Apocalypse shews them to be doing in the early part of the second century.

but which does not seem to have been applied to Jews of good standing, has now become one of the means for distinguishing the Jews from the proselytes, and that the baptized are baptizing the baptizers.

Before leaving the question of chronology, we must say a word or two about another time-note in the book. The people stone Jeremiah, and when dying he predicts the coming of Jesus Christ, the Son of God, after a lapse of four hundred and seventy-seven years[1]. It is a little difficult to see what he means by these figures and how he arrives at them. It must be either that the Apocalyptist is giving 'the actual period from the first return from Exile to the Messiah, or he is fabricating a similar period for the second advent, the numbers being assumed to repeat as in the case of the duration of the Exile. That the former is the right interpretation may be gathered from the prediction which Jeremiah makes that the Messiah will choose to himself 12 apostles in order that they may preach the gospel amongst the Gentiles. (c. ix. 18.) But how does he calculate the period? For we have no possibility of deducing 477 years from the interval between Jeremiah's death and the birth of Christ. The building of the walls under Ezra and Nehemiah is, however, not very far from the time intimated; if we assume this to have taken place in 458 B.C. or thereabout we should not be 20 years out in the reckoning. But it would be idle to assume a great acquaintance with chronology on the part of our simple-minded Apocalyptist; and we might perhaps leave this part of the question unsettled without feeling that the interpretation would suffer. We will, however, venture one suggestion for clearing the matter up. At the close of the sixth book of Josephus' Jewish Wars will be found a table of the leading periods in the history of Jerusalem from conquest to conquest and captivity to captivity. Now in this list the time from David to the Babylonian exile is given as 477 years: so that it is just possible that the Apocalyptist made an error in taking a number from Josephus' tables.

We will now pass on to consider the literary debts of the Christian Baruch to his predecessors, beginning with some passages which are founded on the Apocalypse of Baruch.

Apocal. ii. Haec autem dixi tibi, ut dicas Jeremiae, et omnibus qui similes sunt vobis, ut recedatis ab urbe ista, quia opera vestra

---

[1] The MSS. are very confused over this number; the Ethiopic in particular fluctuating between 303, 330, and 333 *weeks*.

sunt urbi huic tanquam columna firma et preces vestrae tanquam murus validus.

This passage is imitated in the later Baruch as follows: c. i. 1, ἔξελθε ἐκ τῆς πόλεως ταύτης σὺ καὶ ὁ Βαρούχ......αἱ γὰρ προσευχαὶ ὑμῶν ὡς στῦλος ἑδραῖός ἐστιν ἐν μέσῳ αὐτῆς καὶ ὡς τεῖχος ἀδαμάντινον περικυκλοῦν αὐτόν. (We are thus able to restore some parts of the original Greek of the Apocalypse of Baruch.)

The remote source of either sentence is to be sought in Jer. i. 18.

Apocal. vi. Et factum est crastino die, et ecce exercitus Chaldaeorum circumdedit urbem, et tempore vesperae reliqui populum ego Baruch et exivi et steti apud quercum : et contristabar super Sion et ingemiscebam super captivitatem quae supervenerat populo : et ecce subito spiritus fortitudinis sustulit me et extulit me supra Jerusalem in altum. et vidi et ecce quatuor angeli stantes super quatuor angulos urbis, tenentes unusquisque ex eis lampada ignis in manibus suis.

Compare with this the account by the later Baruch of the capture of the city, especially

iii. 2. Καὶ ἐγένετο φωνὴ σάλπιγγος, καὶ ἐξῆλθον ἄγγελοι ἐκ τοῦ οὐρανοῦ, κατέχοντες λαμπάδας ἐν ταῖς χερσὶν αὐτῶν, καὶ ἔστησαν ἐπὶ τὰ τείχη τῆς πόλεως.

The angels then in Bar. Apocal. wait until one of their number takes the holy vessels and delivers them to the earth, which opens her mouth and swallows them up. The Christian Baruch makes this hiding of the vessels to be done by Jeremiah and Baruch.

x. Dic Jeremiae ut vadat et confirmet captivitatem populi usque ad Babylonem ; tu autem mane hic in vastitate Sion et ego ostendam tibi post hos dies quod futurum est ut contingat in fine dierum. et dixi Jeremiae sicut praecepit mihi Dominus. et ipse quidem ivit cum populo ; ego autem Baruch reversus sum et sedi ante portas templi et lamentatus sum lamentationem istam super Sion et dixi.

The whole of these details are absorbed by the later Baruch, with the single exception of the mention of the 'gates of the temple.' Each writer makes Baruch the one that laments over the city.

A more striking case of absorption of the earlier story is the account of the priests throwing the keys of the Sanctuary up to heaven.

Apocal. x. Vos autem sacerdotes sumite claves sanctuarii et proiicite in altitudinem coeli et date eas Domino et dicite; Custodi domum tuam tu: nos enim ecce inventi sumus oeconomi mendaces.

Bar. Christ. iv. 3. Ἱερεμίας δὲ ἄρας τὰς κλεῖδας τοῦ ναοῦ, ἐξῆλθεν ἔξω τῆς πόλεως καὶ ἔρριψεν αὐτὰς ἐνώπιον τοῦ ἡλίου, λέγων· Σοὶ λέγω, ἥλιε, λάβε τὰς κλεῖδας τοῦ ναοῦ τοῦ Θεοῦ, καὶ φύλαξον αὐτὰς ἕως ἡμέρας ἐν ᾗ ἐξετάσει σε Κύριος περὶ αὐτῶν. Διότι ἡμεῖς οὐχ εὑρέθημεν ἄξιοι τοῦ φυλάξαι αὐτὰς, ὅτι ἐπίτροποι ψεύδους ἐγενήθημεν.

The passage in *Apocal.* xi. Dicite mortuis: Beati vos magis quam nosmetipsi, qui vivi sumus, becomes in *Bar. Christ.* iv. 9 Μακάριοί εἰσιν Ἀβραὰμ Ἰσαὰκ καὶ Ἰακὼβ, ὅτι ἐξῆλθον ἐκ τοῦ κόσμου τούτου.

It will be seen that the coincidences in the opening chapters of the two Apocalypses are very marked. The same coincidence is to be traced on referring to the closing chapters of the Apocalyptic Baruch. Baruch writes a letter to the nine and a half tribes who are in Babylon and sends it by means of an eagle.

Apocal. lxxvi. Accersivi aquilam et locutus sum ei verba ista: Te fecit Altissimus ut sis excelsior prae omnibus avibus: et nunc vade, neque commoreris in loco, neque ingrediaris nidum, neque consistas super quamvis arborem, donec transieris latitudinem aquarum multarum fluminis Euphratis, et ieris ad populum illum qui habitat ibi et proice ad eos epistolam hanc: recordare autem quod tempore diluvii a columba accepit Noe fructum olivae cum eam emisisset de arca; sed et corvi ministrarunt Eliae deferentes ei cibum, sicut praeceptum erat eis; etiam Salomon tempore regni sui quocumque volebat mittere, aut quaerere aliquid, avi praecipiebat, et obediebat ei sicut praecipiebat ei: et nunc ne taedeat te, neque declines ad dexteram aut ad sinistram, sed vola et vade via recta ut custodias mandatum Fortis sicut dixi tibi. (lxxvii.) Et fuit cum consummassem omnia verba epistolae huius et scripsissem eam cum cura usque ad finem eius et plicuissem eam et obsignassem eam diligenter et ligassem eam ad collum aquilae et dimisi et misi eam.

This is imitated in c. vii. of the Christian Baruch with no loss of force in the transcription:

Bar. Christ. vii. Σοὶ λέγω, βασιλεῦ τῶν πετεινῶν, ἄπελθε ἐν εἰρήνῃ μεθ᾽ ὑγείας καὶ τὴν φάσιν ἔνεγκέ μοι. Μὴ ὁμοιωθῆς τῷ κόρακι ὃν ἐξαπέστειλε Νῶε, καὶ οὐκ ἀπεστράφη εἰς τὴν κιβωτόν·

ἀλλὰ ὁμοιώθητι τῇ περιστερᾷ ἥτις ἐκ τρίτου φάσιν ἤνεγκε τῷ
δικαίῳ· οὕτω καὶ σύ, ἆρον τὴν καλὴν φάσιν ταύτην τῷ Ἰερεμίᾳ,
καὶ τοῖς σὺν αὐτῷ, ἵνα εὖ σοι γένηται, ἆρον τὴν χάρτην ταύτην
τῷ λαῷ τῷ ἐκλεκτῷ τοῦ Θεοῦ. Ἐὰν κυκλώσωσί σε πάντα τὰ
πετεινὰ τοῦ οὐρανοῦ, καὶ πάντες οἱ ἐχθροὶ τῆς ἀληθείας βουλόμενοι πολεμῆσαι μετὰ σοῦ, ἀγώνισαι· ὁ Κύριος δώῃ σοι δύναμιν.
Καὶ μὴ ἐκκλίνῃς εἰς τὰ δεξιὰ ἢ ἀριστερά, ἀλλ᾽ ὡς βέλος ὕπαγον
ὀρθῶς οὕτως ἄπελθε κτέ.

These instances will be sufficient to shew the kind of use which
the later Apocalyptist made of the earlier. And that the earlier
form had attached to it the epistle of Baruch appears not only
from the legend of the carrier-eagle but from the admission[1] at
the close of the Christian Baruch that "the rest of the words of
Jeremiah and all his might are written, not here, but in the
epistle of Baruch."

The traces of the use of the beautiful Apocalypse, known as
the fourth book of Ezra, are less marked, but they are decided.
The famous passage in c. v. foretelling that "blood shall drop
from wood *and the stone shall utter its voice*" was known to our
Apocalyptist: it furnished him with the idea of the closing situation
in his book; that in which Jeremiah sets up a stone, which takes
his likeness, and deceives thereby the people who wish to kill him,
until he has finished communicating the mysteries which he has
seen to the crowd and his companions Baruch and Abimelech.
The riotous folk stone the stone, thinking it to be Jeremiah.
But at last the stone cries out with a human voice, "O foolish
children of Israel, wherefore do ye stone me, thinking that I am
Jeremiah?" The motive for this story is evidently the single
sentence quoted above from Ezra[2]. Another clause in the same
connexion, where Ezra foretells amongst the signs of the end
that "salt water shall be found in sweet water and friends be at
war with one another," is copied by the Christian writer (c. ix.
16), "Snow shall become black and sweet waters salt."

The writer was also acquainted with the Apocryphal Isaiah.
In c. ix. 18, 19 the text of our author runs as follows: "He shall
come, and he shall come forth and he shall choose him twelve

---

[1] This may however be a later appendix.

[2] IV. Esd. v. 5. It is quite possible that the whole sentence is a confused allusion to the sawing asunder of Isaiah and the stoning of Jeremiah, and that Ezra
himself may be drawing on legendary sources: but compare what is said on this
point on pp. 43, 44.

apostles that they may preach the Gospel amongst the Gentiles: whom I beheld adorned by his Father and coming into the world on the mount of Olives; and he shall fill the hungry souls. While Jeremiah was saying these things concerning the Son of God, that he is coming into the world, the people was enraged, and said; These are the same words as were spoken by Isaiah the son of Amos, when he said, I beheld God and the son of God. Come then and let us kill him with a different death to that wherewith we killed Isaiah." The people are not alluding here immediately to the famous sixth chapter of Isaiah in which the prophet sees the Lord on his throne, or as the Targumists prefer to render it, so as to avoid the anthropomorphic conception, the glory of the Lord on his throne[1]; but they are speaking of a prophecy or pseudo-prophecy in which the manner of his death seems also to have been recorded as well as his ecstasy. And this can hardly be anything else than the Ascension of Isaiah, in which Justin Martyr is supposed to have found his information about the sawing in twain of Isaiah with a wooden saw, and to which Origen definitely appealed as an authority for the manner of the prophet's martyrdom. We will not saw him asunder, they say, as Isaiah was martyred, but, for the sake of variety, we will stone him. It is, of course, possible that the writer might have based his fiction on mere traditions, but the reference to Jeremiah as seeing the coming of the Son of God and his sending forth of the twelve apostles to preach is conclusive in favour of the Ascension of Isaiah as the origin from which he drew. The reason why Isaiah is arrested is because "Berial was in great wrath against Isaiah on account of the vision and the revelation which Sammael had unveiled and because by him was seen the coming of the Beloved from the seventh heaven, and his transformation,...and the tortures wherewith the children of Israel would torture him, and the coming and the teaching of the twelve apostles..."[2] And that the writer had the actual book to refer to will appear from the use he has made of another detail of the Martyrdom of Isaiah. When the writer describes the tortures of the prophet and his final ascent in rapture through the seven heavens before his death, he makes the prophet fall into a death-like trance in which speech and breathing cease. And

---

[1] A conception which lies underneath the passage in the Gospel: "He saw his glory and spake of him," John xii. 41.

[2] *Ascensio Isaiae*, ed. Dillmann, c. iii.

what Isaiah sees in that vision he tells afterwards to the king and the circle of the prophets. "While he was speaking by the Holy Ghost, in the hearing of all, he held his peace and his mind was rapt away and taken upward so that he saw not those that stood around ; his eyes were open but his mouth was still and the mind of his body was rapt away upward, but his breath was in him, for he saw a vision." (I think that we should read here 'his breath was *not* in him.') The writer explains further that the "vision which he saw was not of this world, but of the world which is hidden from mortal eyes. And after Isaiah saw this vision, he narrated it to Hezekiah and Josab his son and the rest of the assembled prophets." All of this is imitated in our Christian Baruch: Jeremiah falls into a death-like trance, but after three days he revives, his soul revisits her tenement, and he tells the Glory of the Father and the Son. This use of Apocryphal Isaiah begins in the earlier part of the prophet's ecstasy (c. ix. 3) where he cries out "Holy, holy, holy...beyond the sweet voice of the two seraphim :" here the direct reference is to Isaiah vi., as is seen from the trisagion and the mention of two seraphim ("one cried unto another"), but that Ps. Isaiah is in mind with its full Christology appears from the insertion of the words "the true light that lighteneth me."

We need not hesitate to say then that the writer has used the Ascension of Isaiah, and used it too, for it is an interpolated Apocalypse, augmented and expanded by Christian hands, in its later and Christian form. The date of this work is discussed by Dillmann in his preface, and we need not dispute his conclusion in referring the book to the beginning of the second century[1].

We have thus determined three earlier Judæo-Christian works which have been used and imitated in the process of manufacture of the Christian Baruch. We will pass on to examine the possible use which the writer may have made of other traditions concerning Jeremiah, or, which is for our purpose the same thing, of lost books incorporating traditions.

That traditions concerning Jeremiah were widely circulated in early times appears from many considerations : the second book of the Maccabees, for instance, has the whole story of the hiding of the sacred vessels, in a form which does not agree with the Apo-

---

[1] *Ascensio*, p. xvi. Quibus omnibus perpensis Ascensionem iam primis secundi saeculi decenniis exstitisse censeo.

calyptic Baruch, and which is not in perfect harmony with the Christian Baruch. And its version professes to be that of official documents. " It is also found in the records that Jeremiah the prophet commanded them that were carried away to take some of the fire, as it hath been signified: and that the prophet on giving them the law charged them that were carried away not to forget the commandments of the Lord, and that they should not be led astray in their minds on seeing images of silver and gold with their ornaments. And with other such admonitions exhorted he them that the law should not depart from their heart. It is also contained in the writing that the prophet being warned of God commanded that the tabernacle and the ark should be brought along after him: and that he went forth into the mountain where Moses climbed up and saw the heritage of God. And Jeremiah on coming thither found a kind of ·cave-dwelling, and he carried in there the tabernacle and the ark and the altar of incense and closed up the door. And certain of those that followed him came up to mark the way and they could not find it. But when Jeremiah learned of it, he blamed them and said, The place shall be unknown until God gather his people again together, and become propitious. And then shall the Lord shew these things[1]."

There is one point in which the later Baruch agrees better with this than the Apocalypse: it makes Jeremiah hide the vessels and not the angels. Possibly, therefore, the writer was under the influence of the Maccabean tradition, which need not be very early. The date of the second of Maccabees is, however, one of the unsolved problems.

Another very important tradition concerning Jeremiah is that he was stoned. This is not an original idea of the Christian Baruch. We find it in the Epistle to the Hebrews. The famous passage "they were stoned, they were sawn asunder, &c." is a summary of the sufferings of the worthies of Faith, and each statement is based on the history of some real person : it has always been known that "they were sawn asunder" referred to Isaiah, just as "stopped the mouths of lions" referred to Daniel, and "quenched the violence of fire" to the three Hebrew children; but it is not so generally felt that "they were stoned" belongs to Jeremiah.

[1] 2 Macc. ii.

Yet such is the case, as the Baruch-Jeremiah legends shew :
and the Epistle to the Hebrews is therefore one of the early wit-
nesses to the tradition.   But whence was it derived ?   We may
not easily reply, but it was from the same source in written or
unwritten tradition that Christian Baruch derived his information.

There is other important evidence of the diffusion of the
tradition.   The place of burial of Jeremiah is still shewn in Jerusalem in a cave which passes by the name of Jeremiah's grotto.
This grotto lies in the southern side of the conspicuous hill to the
north of the city which is supposed by many persons to be the
place called Calvary.   On the north-west side of the same hill are
the ruins of the early Church which commemorated the martyrdom of St Stephen who was said to have been stoned here.   And
it is said that this hill is the Tarpeian rock of ancient Jerusalem,
the Beth-hassaqelah or 'Place of Stoning' of the Talmud.   It
seems then that there is some connexion between the death
which Jeremiah met, according to tradition, and the place where
he is said to be buried.   And the tradition concerning his stoning
in Jerusalem must be early : for the uniform church tradition of
later days, as we find it in the life of Jeremiah attributed falsely
to Epiphanius, or the life that is given on his commemoration
day in the Greek Church (see Menaeum for May 1), is that he was
stoned indeed, but at Tahpanhes in Egypt, and not, as the Jerusalem tradition and the Christian Baruch say, in Jerusalem.   Can
we be wrong in affirming the antiquity of the tradition which we
find in our authority ?   The opinion of the first and second centuries seems to be that Jeremiah was stoned in Jerusalem[1].

But did the traditions of our document centre round any
actual person ?   Are Jeremiah and Baruch the background of the
picture or the foreground ?   Do the historical features of the
romance limit themselves to the City and the time of the Jewish
expulsion and the baptismal suggestion of the Christians to the
Jews : or may we go further ?   The writer has, according to some

---

[1] I do not forget that an attempt might have been made to bring the legends
into harmony with our Lord's words "O Jerusalem which killest the prophets and
stonest them that are sent unto thee;" but such a tendency would not have
produced an earlier tradition but a later one.   It is more reasonable, though the
hypothesis is not necessary, and might even be fanciful, to understand our Lord as
saying this in allusion to the legends.   When he said it he was in view of the place
of supposed martyrdom of Isaiah on the south of the city and of Jeremiah on the
north.

MSS., changed 'Baruch the scribe' of the old Testament into 'Baruch the reader.'· Does he mean a real official of the Church? It would be hard to say: but with Jeremiah the case is easier: for there is reason to believe that Judah, the last bishop of Jerusalem before the definitely Christian régime, died at the hands of the party of Barcochba. The Chronicon of Eusebius declares that many of the Christians suffered for not taking arms against Rome; and marks the close of the war by the arrival of the first Gentile Bishop. Now if Judah the supposed fifteenth bishop had outlived the war, he would certainly not have been exiled by the Romans: so he must have vacated his office by death.

A further interesting question arises with regard to the relations of our writer to the Christian records. We see him quoting freely and incorporating adroitly from many of the Judæo-Christian books which were current at that time in Palestine; Isaiah, Ezra, and Baruch—he knows them all. Baruch the Apocalyptist, whom he quotes most freely, though hardly to be called a Christian, has been affirmed by careful critics to be under the influence of the sentiments and to shew traces of the language of our Gospels. What of the Christian Baruch? Had he any acquaintance with the New Testament Scriptures? *There is some ground for believing that he was acquainted with the Gospel of John.* This will no doubt sound somewhat strange, but we will not prejudge the question by choosing for the time of production of the fourth gospel a period as *late* as is consistent with what has been hitherto known of the literature of the second century: there has been too much *à priori* reasoning in the dating of the fourth Gospel. Nor is the Nemesis which attaches to this arbitrary and *ex silentio* criticism exhausted. Neither will we on the other hand over-emphasise coincidences of thought and expression between our writer and the Gospel; although it might be possible to argue that when a writer (ix. 13) calls Jesus Christ the light of all the ages, the unquenchable lamp, the life of the faith, it is natural to refer to the Light of the World, the Light of Men and the Light of Life, and to the contrast which Christ makes between himself and John the Baptist, when he calls him the lamp *which has been kindled* and shines. We might point out also that the conjunction of φῶς and ζωή is frequently recognized as not merely Christian, but Johannine. M. Clermont-Ganneau has established a number of cases of the occurrence of φῶς + ζωή as a

Christian formula in Syria. The two words are often arranged crosswise, thus φ ω c ; and M. Ganneau says we must seek the
origin of the formula in the Gospel of John[1]. And with less judgment it would be possible to quote the words (ix. 18) ἐρχόμενον εἰς τὸν κόσμον as a reminiscence of John i. 9, the interpretation of which is however doubtful. As none of these coincidences would definitely convince me of a quotation from John, so neither do I unduly desire to convince any one by them; but I would draw attention to one clause in the adoration of Jeremiah (ix. 3) where he addresses the Lord as τὸ φῶς τὸ ἀληθινὸν τὸ φωτίζον με, the true Light that lighteneth me: where the collocation of words is so peculiar, that it is almost impossible to refer the language to any other than St John, and in view of this fact the previous coincidences acquire new force. Further the passage is found, not only in the Greek, which exhibits at many points a text that has undergone some correction, but in the Ethiopic version, which often approaches very nearly, as we shall see, to the original form of the Apocalypse. Unless then it can be shewn that these words are a later addition, in the Ethiopic as well as in the Greek, we must admit a quotation from the fourth Gospel, which quotation happily allows of being dated in or about the year 136 A.D.

Authorities for the Text.

In the year 1866 Dillmann published the Ethiopic version of the Christian Baruch from several MSS.; and in the preface to the Ethiopic Chrestomathy[2], in which the text appeared, he pointed out that it was a regular part of the Ethiopic Bible, where it appears along with the Book of Baruch, the Lamentations of Jeremiah, and the Epistle of Jeremiah[3]. The Ethiopic version is translated from the Greek, and becomes a very important witness for the text. I follow, in my ignorance of Ethiopic, the best translations I can get of Dillmann's text; good ones fortunately are not lacking. There is a German translation by Prätorius in Hilgenfeld's *Zeitschrift für wissenschaftliche Theologie* 1872, p. 230—247 : and a later revised translation with notes by König in *Theologische*

---

[1] *Archéologie Orientale*, p. 171.   [2] Lips. 1866.
[3] Cf. Wright, *Cat. of Ethiopic MSS. in the British Museum;* Codd. 7, 8, 14, 16, 20.

Studien und Kritiken for 1877, pp. 318—338. I cite the evidence of this version as *aeth.*

The Menaea for Nov. 4th are a direct authority for the Greek text, which they contain in a somewhat abbreviated form, and in a less pure text. For example the Menaeum printed at Venice in 1843 gives the first five chapters only of the text. The whole of the text, according to Ceriani, is found in the Menaeum printed at Venice in 1609. Ceriani quotes occasionally a MS. Menaeum of the Ambrosian Library; and no doubt the evidence of this class of documents might be multiplied a hundredfold. Their combined evidence is given as *men.*

To this Ceriani added a MS. (marked AF. IX. 31) of the fifteenth century, which he describes as belonging to the Bibliotheca Regia Braidensis; which I take to represent the convent library of the Italian town of Bra in Piedmont. From this MS., with the aid of the Menaeum, Ceriani published the text which appears in the fifth volume of his *Monumenta Sacra* pp. 11—18. This MS. I call *a.*

To these authorities we may add the following from the library of the Patriarchate of Jerusalem.

Cod. *b* = Cod. 34, of the S. Sepulchre portion of the Library, of the eleventh century, containing the Ἐρωτήσεις καὶ Ἀποκρίσεις of Anastasius the Sinaite. At the end there are a number of questions concerning the dissonances of the Evangelists *de resurrectione Christi*: a fragment from Irenæus, the same as is printed in Tischendorf's *Anecdota Sacra et Profana* p. 120 from Cod. Coislin. 120; and on f. 251, at the end of the life of Jeremiah the prophet, comes the title τὰ παραλειπόμενα Ἰερεμίου τοῦ προφητοῦ.

Cod. *c* = Cod. 6 S. Sepulcri of the tenth century has been collated with the foregoing. It contains a valuable text which often deviates widely from that of the foregoing MS. The text begins on f. 242 of the MS.

The next two manuscripts belong to a totally different recension; but they are related *inter se*: the text which they give is an epitome of the Paralipomena, probably taken from the Menaea with appendices from collateral sources: they are as follows:

Cod. *d* = Cod. 66 S. Sep. a late MS. (15th cent. ?) containing a collection of apocryphal matters of all kinds: a brief summary may be useful. It begins with an extract from Chrysostom, followed by

f. 6 b. Τοῦ ἁγίου ἀποστόλου καὶ εὐαγγελιστοῦ Ἰωάννου τοῦ

θεολόγου λόγος περὶ τῆς κοιμήσεως τῆς ὑπερευλογημένης καὶ ἐνδόξου δεσποίνης ἡμῶν θεοτόκου καὶ ἀειπαρθένου Μαρίας.

f. 14. Τῆς σεβασμίας μεταστάσεως τῆς ὑπερενδόξου δεσποίνης ἡμῶν καὶ ἀειπαρθένου.

f. 23. Περίοδοι τοῦ ἁγίου καὶ ἐνδόξου ἀποστόλου καὶ εὐαγγελιστοῦ παρθένου ἐπιστηθίου φίλου Ἰωάννου τοῦ θεολόγου.

f. 93 b. Πράξεις τοῦ ἁγίου καὶ ἐνδόξου καὶ πανευφήμου ἀποστόλου Θωμᾶ.

f. 109 b. Ἐκ τῶν περιόδων τοῦ ἁγίου καὶ ἐνδόξου ἀποστόλου Φιλίππου. ὑπὸ (l. ἀπὸ) πράξεως πέντε καὶ δεκάτου μέχρι τέλους τοῦ μαρτυρίου αὐτοῦ.

f. 124. Πράξεις Ματθία καὶ Ἀνδρέα ἐν τῇ χώρᾳ τῶν ἀνθρωποφάγων.

f. 146 b. Πράξεις τῶν ἀποστόλων Πέτρου καὶ Παύλου καὶ πῶς ἐν Ῥώμῃ ἐμαρτύρησαν ἐπὶ Νέρωνος.

f. 165. Μαρτύριον τοῦ ἁγίου ἀποστόλου καὶ εὐαγγελιστοῦ Μάρκου.

f. 169 b. Τοῦ ἁγίου ἀποστόλου καὶ εὐαγγελιστοῦ Λουκᾶ.

f. 177. Ὑπόμνησις εἰς τὸν ἅγιον ἀπόστολον καὶ εὐαγγελιστὴν Ματθαῖον.

f. 181 b. Τοῦ ἁγίου ἐνδόξου ἀποστόλου Ἰακώβου ἀδελφοῦ τοῦ ἁγίου Ἰωάννου τοῦ θεολόγου.

f. 182. Διήγησις περὶ τῆς ἀντιλογίας τοῦ διαβόλου μετὰ τοῦ κυρίου ἡμῶν Ἰησοῦ Χριστοῦ.

f. 186. Βίος σύντομος καὶ πολιτεία τοῦ ὁσίου πατρὸς ἡμῶν Ἰωάννου τοῦ ἐν τῷ φρέατι.

f. 188 b. Βίος τοῦ ἁγίου Γερασίμου.

f. 190 b. Διήγησις Μάλχου μοναχοῦ.

f. 194. Διήγησις περὶ…Νικολάου.

f. 196. Μαρτύριού Μενίγνου (sic).

f. 199. Ἄθλησις…Θεοδώρου.

f. 202 b. Μαρτύριον Φωτείνου.

f. 209 b. Διήγησις…ἐν τῷ βίῳ…Παχωμίου.

f. 212 b. Διήγησις περὶ τοῦ θρήνου τοῦ προφήτου Ἱερεμία περὶ τῆς Ἱερουσαλήμ. καὶ περὶ τῆς ἁλώσεως ταύτης καὶ περὶ τῆς ἐκστάσεως Ἀβιμέλεχ. εὐλόγησον δέσποτα.

A life of Jeremiah is prefixed to the text of the Paralipomena.

f. 215. περὶ τῆς ἁλώσεως Ἱερουσαλήμ· τὰ λαληθέντα ὑπὸ κυρίου πρὸς Ἱερεμίαν· καὶ ὅπως ἡ αἰχμαλωσία γέγονεν ἔχει οὕτως.

f. 222 b. Ὀπτασία Κοσμᾶ μοναχοῦ.
f. 229. Διήγησις ἑτέρας ὀπτασίας.
f. 231 b. Διήγησις περὶ τοῦ γενομένου θαύματος ἐν Ἀφρίκῃ
[ἐν] τῇ πόλει Καρταγένῃ.
f. 233. Ἐφραίμ· εἰς τὸν πάγκαλον Ἰωσήφ.
f. 252. Χρυσοστόμου· εἰς τὸν μάταιον βίον.
f. 260. Διήγησις καὶ διαθήκη τοῦ δικαίου καὶ πατριάρχου
Ἀβραάμ· δηλοῖ δὲ καὶ τὴν πεῖραν τοῦ θανάτου αὐτοῦ. εὐλόγησον
δέσποτα.

It will be seen that the MS. though late contains a great deal of valuable apocryphal matter: for example, I found it worth while when working at Jerusalem to copy the whole of the Ἀντιλογία τοῦ διαβόλου and the Διαθήκη Ἀβραάμ, as well as the Baruch matter.

The title attached to the Baruch extracts seems to imply that they were taken from a Menaeum.

Cod. *e* = Cod. 35 S. Crucis (the library of the Convent of the Holy Cross now removed to the Patriarchal Library at Jerusalem). This is also a late paper MS. (xvth cent.) and contains a similar text of the Paralipomena to the preceding. It contains also the prefixed life of Jeremiah. The MS. opens with a διήγησις Ἰακώβου εἰς τὸ γενέσιον τῆς θεοτόκου. We have collated the Baruch text with Cod. *d*.

We have thus the following authorities for the text:

> *aeth* = Ethiopic version as edited by Dillmann.
> *men* = The Menaea.
> *a* = Cod. Braidensis.
> *b* = Cod. 34 S. Sepulcri.
> *c* = Cod. 6 S. Sepulcri.
> *d* = Cod. 66 S. Sepulcri.
> *e* = Cod. 35 S. Crucis.

In using these authorities, we find that *d* and *e* are only transcripts, with occasional modifications, from the Menaeum; and a very little examination will shew that the text of the Menaeum is only a secondary authority. Of the remaining MSS., *a* and *b* present an almost identical text, and constitute together a single authority. The text is thus reduced to three principal authorities, which vary widely *inter se* from time to time; viz aeth, *a* + *b*, and *c*. In comparing the readings we shall find that the Ethiopic text

is on the whole much superior to the text of *a, b*; and that where
it diverges from this, it almost always has *c* associated with it [1].

We should thus be led to take generally the consensus of
aeth and *c* as furnishing the earliest reading; but this would
require, first, that there should be a margin left for occasional
cases in which *a, b* may have preserved the right reading: and
second, that the consensus of *a, b* with either of the pair *aeth* and
c against the other should be regarded as, almost to a certainty,
the primitive reading. The MSS. would thus be represented by

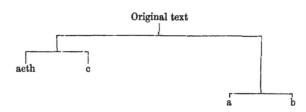

Original text

aeth   c

a   b

The scheme will test itself readily as we edit the text; but a
few instances may perhaps be taken to shew the relation of the
authorities and the generally corrupt state of transcription.

v. 23.   *a.* εἰ μὴ ἧς πρεσβύτης, καὶ ὅτι οὐκ ἐξὸν ἀνθρώπῳ Θεοῦ
ὑβρίσαι τὸν μείζονα αὐτοῦ· ἐπεὶ κατεγέλων ὅτι μαίνῃ.

b. εἰ μὴ εἷς πρεσβύτης· καὶ ὅτι οὐκ ἐξὼν ἀνθρώπῳ Θεοῦ
ὑβρίσαι τὸν μείζονα αὐτοῦ· ἐπεὶ καταγέλων σου καὶ ἔλεγον ὅτι
μένει.

c. εἰ μὴ εἷς πρεσβύτης· καὶ οὐκ ἐξὼν ἀνθρώπων ὑβρίσαι τὸν
μείζονα αὐτοῦ· ἐπικατεγέλουν σοι καὶ ἔλεγον ὅτι μὲν [ἠχμαλώ-
τευσον κτέ].

aeth. Wenn du nicht ein bejahrter Mann wärest, so würde ich
dich schmähen und über dich lachen, doch nicht soll es geschehen,
dass man einen Menschen verachtet, und zwar einen bejahrten
Mann; und wenn du nicht ein solcher wärest, so würde ich sagen,
dass du ausser dir bist.

Comparing these readings we see that the Θεοῦ is to be
rejected in *a, b*: while the consensus of *b, c* and the Ethiopic makes
it certain that the word ἐπικατεγέλων was followed more or less

---

[1] The superiority of the Ethiopic text is affirmed also by König (*Stud. u. Krit.*
1877, p. 319) : "In der That hat mir eine durchgängige Vergleichung beider Texte
gezeigt, dass beide weit von einander abweichen, ja dass der äthiopische dem
Originale der Schrift näher als der bis jetzt veröffentlichte griechische Text steht."

closely by καὶ ἔλεγον; while the similarity of the endings ἐγέλων and ἔλεγον is sufficient reason for the omission of a clause.

Nor can we be far wrong if, restoring the particle ἂν from the Menaea, we read ἐπικατεγέλων ἄν σοι καὶ ἔλεγον ὅτι μαίνῃ.

vi. 22. *a.* ὁ ἀκούων, ἀφορίσω αὐτὸν ἐκ τῆς Βαβυλῶνος, ὁ δὲ μὴ ἀκούων, ξένος γένηται τῆς Ἱερουσαλήμ.

b. ὁ ἀκούων, κτέ..
...................γενήσεται κτέ...................

c. ὁ ἀκούων ἀναφέρω αὐτὸν ἐκ τοῦ λάκκου τῆς Βαβυλῶνος· ὁ δὲ μὴ ἀκούων ξένος γίνεται τῆς Ἱερουσαλὴμ καὶ τῆς Βαβυλῶνος.

aeth. Diejenigen, welche (auf sie) gehört haben, werde ich aus Babylon ausführen und sie werden nicht verbannt von Jerusalem in Babylon sein.

The chief point here is the addition of the words 'and from Babylon' by Cod. *c*: they evidently stood in the Ethiopic archetype but being unintelligible they were corrected to 'in Babylon.'

Thus we have the consensus of *c* and *aeth* for an apparently unintelligible reading: but the story explains it, as we proceed, for those who will not obey Jeremiah are not only refused admission to Jerusalem, but they are rejected also on their attempt to return to Babylon. So that the clause is a genuine one.

vii. 12. *a, b.* ἐὰν κυκλώσουσί σε πάντα τὰ πετεινὰ τοῦ οὐρανοῦ καὶ βούλωνται πολεμῆσαι μετὰ σοῦ, ἀγώνισαι· (*b* ἀγώνησαι).

c. ἐὰν κυκλώσωσίν σε πάντα τὰ πετεινὰ τοῦ οὐρανοῦ, καὶ πάντες οἱ ἐχθροὶ τῆς ἀληθείας βουλόμενοι πολεμῖσαι μετὰ σοῦ, ἀγώνισαι.

The missing clause being found also in the Ethiopic, we are entitled to restore it to the text.

There are some places, however, in which the text is extremely obscure in all authorities: and we may even be obliged to resort to conjecture for a reading. For example:

iv. 10. *a, b.* ταῦτα εἰπὼν Βαροὺχ, ἐξῆλθεν ἔξω τῆς πόλεως, κλαίων καὶ λέγων, Ὅτι διὰ σὲ, Ἱερουσαλήμ, ἐξῆλθον ἀπὸ σοῦ.

c. ταῦτα εἰπὼν, ἐξῆλθεν κλαίων καὶ λέγων, Ὅτι λοιποῦ διὰ σὲ, Ἱερουσαλήμ· καὶ ἐξῆλθεν ἐκ τῆς πόλεως.

aeth. Und nachdem er dieses geredet hat, ging er weinend hinaus.

Here the Ethiopic has cut the knot of a difficult passage by the simple process of omission of a clause and *a, b* by the omission of a word: we may suggest the reading "Ὅτι λυπούμενος διὰ σὲ, Ἱερουσαλήμ, ἐξῆλθον ἀπὸ σοῦ. This furnishes the necessary material for the explanation of the variants.

vi. 16. *a, b.* Ἀποστείλας δὲ εἰς τὴν διασπορὰν τῶν ἐθνῶν, ἤνεγκεν χάρτην καὶ μέλανα καὶ ἔγραψεν ἐπιστολήν.

c. ὁ δὲ Βαροὺχ ἀπέστειλεν εἰς τὴν ἀγωρὰν (sic!) τῶν ἐθνῶν καὶ ἤνεγκεν χάρτην καὶ μέλαν καὶ ἔγραψεν ἐπιστολήν.

aeth. Und Baruch geleitete ihn bis zur Strasse und holte Papier und Tinte und schrieb.

The Ethiopic text shews that διασπορὰ is a corruption: for it gives *Strasse* which is equivalent in Eastern language to ἀγορά: (e.g. Sûk in Arabic is either *street* or *market;* and this interchangeability of the two words has given rise to variant and conflate readings in the New Testament in Mark vi. 56 ἐν ταῖς ἀγοραῖς καὶ ἐν ταῖς πλατείαις :) so that we may safely read ἀγορά: but ἀγορὰ τῶν ἐθνῶν is more difficult: yet the τῶν ἐθνῶν cannot be omitted since it is found in *c* as well as in *a, b.* Let us see, then, whether there are any considerations that will throw light on this difficult reading. Is there any market that might be called the Gentiles' market; or any street that might bear the name of the Gentiles' street? This question brings before us some very interesting matter. We may establish the following points: (*a*) that there was a famous fair held annually at Abraham's oak near Hebron; (β) that this was especially a fair of the Gentiles; (γ) that this fair is closely connected in history with the Jewish war under Hadrian; and (δ) that the introduction of the city Hebron, and the terebinth of Abraham, into the story was suggested to the writer by the earlier Baruch whom he so largely draws upon in other details. And first, with regard to the fair: Sozomen in his Ecclesiastical History devotes a chapter to the account of the religious disorders that prevailed at this fair, and to the suppression by Constantine of the forms of idolatry that had associated themselves with it. At this Terebinth, says he, there assemble annually the inhabitants of the country and the remoter parts of Palestine, and the Phœnicians and the Arabians, during the summer season to keep a feast, and very many resort thither for the sake of trade, both buyers and sellers. The feast is diligently frequented by all nations, by the Jews because they boast of their descent from Abraham; by the Greeks because angels there appeared to men, and by

Christians. On this famous spot Constantine ordered the erection of a Christian Church[1].

This concourse of the Gentiles at the Terebinth-fair appears also from the *Onomasticon* of Eusebius, who says that the oak and sepulchre of Abraham are an object of religious veneration πρὸς τῶν ἐχθρῶν, where Reland long ago[2] saw that we must correct ἐχθρῶν into ἐθνῶν, as Lagarde has done in his edition of the *Onomasticon*[3].

Sozomen, indeed, speaks of the Jews as frequenting the fair, but there is evidence to set against this statement, according to Jerome[4], who says that "exsecrabile fuisse Judaeis mercatum celeberrimum visere." We may, therefore, call this annual gathering a market of the Gentiles, in agreement with our text of Baruch.

The reason of the detestation which the Jews felt for this fair will be found according to Jerome in the consideration of the connexion between the fair and the Hadrian War. Many thousands of men had been sold at this market, after the capture of Bether, the last stronghold of the Jews, some of them at miserable rates, such as the price of a horse's feed of corn. Thus Jerome says, "quod ultima captivitate sub Hadriano, quando et urbs Jerusalem subversa est, innumerabilis populus diversae aetatis et utriusque sexus in mercato Terebinthi venumdatus sit. Et idcirco exsecrabile etc.," and again in his Commentary on Zechariah[5], "legamus veteres historias et traditiones plangentium Judaeorum, quod in tabernaculo Abrahae, ubi nunc per annos singulos mercatus celeberrimus exercetur, post ultimam eversionem quem sustinuerant ab Hadriano multa hominum millia venumdata sint et quae vendi non potuerint translata in Aegyptum." It is clear, therefore, that the market, however famous, and widely attended, could never have been popular with the Jews. It has even been questioned whether in the time subsequent to the war, they were not disqualified by edict from

[1] Sozomen *H. E.* ii. 4, ἐνταῦθα δὲ λαμπρὰν εἰσέτι νῦν ἐτήσιον πανήγυριν ἄγουσιν ὥρᾳ θέρους οἱ ἐπιχώριοι, καὶ οἱ προσωτέρω Παλαιστινοί, καὶ Φοίνικες καὶ Ἀρράβιοι. Συνίασι δὲ πλεῖστοι καὶ ἐμπορείας ἕνεκα, πωλήσοντες καὶ ἀγοράσοντες.

[2] Reland, *Palestina* pp. 711 sqq. *sub voce* Chebron.

[3] Ἡ δρῦς Ἀβραὰμ καὶ τὸ μνῆμα αὐτοθὶ θεωρεῖται καὶ θρησκεύεται ἐπιφανῶς πρὸς τῶν ἐχθρῶν. Cf. Jerome, *De situ et nominibus*, *sub voce* Arboc, A cunctis in circuitu gentibus terebinthi locus superstitiose colitur.

[4] Jerome, *Comm. in Jer.* xxxi. 15.

[5] Jerome, *Comm. in Zach.* xi. 4, 5.

coming as near to Jerusalem as Hebron; some persons maintain that they were absolutely exiled from the soil of Palestine; but in any case we can see clearly that the market was a foreigners' market, and that it was closely connected historically with Hadrian's victories. Indeed it is quite possible that Hadrian established the fair. Something of the kind seems to be implied in the statement of the Paschal Chronicle, which under the date 119 A.D. (!) reports as follows: Ἦλθεν Ἀδριανὸς εἰς Ἱεροσόλυμα καὶ ἔλαβεν τοὺς Ἰουδαίους αἰχμαλώτους, καὶ ἀπελθὼν εἰς τὴν λεγομένην Τερέβινθον προέστησεν πανήγυριν καὶ πέπρακεν αὐτοὺς εἰς ταγὴν ἵππου ἕκαστον, καὶ τοὺς ὑπολειφθέντας ἔλαβεν εἰς Γάζαν καὶ ἐκεῖ ἔστησεν πανήγυριν καὶ ἐπώλησεν αὐτούς. καὶ ἕως τοῦ νῦν ἡ πανήγυρις ἐκείνη λέγεται Ἀδριανή.

There is here some confusion of dates, and it is also a question whether Hadrian visited Palestine himself or whether he merely established the fairs at the Terebinth and at Gaza by military authority; there is, however, reason for believing that the time of Hadrian is the time to which we must refer the establishment of these annual gatherings.

It appears then that we may put in a good claim for the identification of the Gentiles' market, and for the justification of the difficult reading of our best manuscript.

Nor need we be at all surprised at the allusion to Hebron in the story: for in the Apocalypse of Baruch, which our writer follows, we find the very same thing. Baruch goes to Hebron in search of a theophany or at least of an angelophany. It is the proper place to look for heavenly visitants[1]. Our Ethiopic Version, if we could accept its reading, would make the Christian Baruch

---

[1] The parallelism between the two writers may be seen by placing the passages side by side:

Apocal. Bar.

xxi. 1. Et abii inde et sedi in Valle Cedron in caverna terrae.

xlvii. Et cum exissem ac dimisissem eos, abii inde et dixi eis; Ecce ego vado usque ad Hebron: illuc enim misit me Fortis.

lxxvii. 18. Et fuit prima et vigesima mense octavo veni ego Baruch et sedi subtus quercum in umbra ramorum (? is this the Terebinth)...et scripsi has duas epistolas.

Bar. Christ.

iv. 11. καὶ ἔμεινεν ἐν μνημείῳ καθεζόμενος.

vi. 16. ὁ δὲ Βαροὺχ ἀποστείλας εἰς τὴν ἀγορὰν τῶν ἐθνῶν ἤνεγκε χάρτην καὶ μέλανα καὶ ἔγραψεν ἐπιστολήν.

also go to Hebron, as the proper place to finish the interview with the angel. This would bring the two Apocalypses into even closer relation: but we need not assume this. If our supposition be correct that the book belongs to the close of the Hadrian War, it is certain that the thoughts of the writer must have turned to the market where the Jews were sold into slavery; and conversely, if we have properly identified the Gentiles' market, the argument is in favour of referring the book to the time of Hadrian as the most likely period for an allusion to the Terebinth.

These instances, then, will perhaps suffice to shew the nature of the text with which we are dealing. It need scarcely be remarked that a host of insignificant itacisms and cases of corrupt transcription have been neglected. The chapters and verses are taken from the text of Ceriani.

Note on the Geography of Ezra and Baruch.

As we study the parallels between this pair of Apocalypses, or between any pair of the triad, 4 Ezra, Apocal. Baruch, Bar. Christ., we derive great advantage for the interpretation of the three texts. It is a great gain, for instance, to see how much, in each case, depends on a proper knowledge of the suburbs of Jerusalem and the country between that city and Hebron. We will take the matter a little further and try to apply our results to a problem that has been hitherto unsolved. Let us ask ourselves the question whether it is possible to identify the field of Arphad or Ardath mentioned in the 4th book of Ezra as the locality of one of the visions of that Apocalypse. The passage runs "ibis in campum florum ubi domus non est aedificata, et manduces solummodo de floribus campi......et profectus sum, sicut dixit mihi, in campum qui vocatur Arphad et sedi ibi in floribus" (iv. Esd. ix. 24—26). The MSS. are, as might be expected, in the greatest confusion over this Ardath: the Latin texts reading Ardath, Ardat, Ardoch, or Ardach, which are evidently modifications of a primitive Ardat, or Ardath; the Arabic reads Araat, the Armenian Ardab; while the Syriac and Ethiopic agree in reading Arphad, and the weight of their combined testimony is so great that it is the accepted reading in Fritzsche's text. On the other hand the Arabic reading is very close, when written in uncial Greek, to the Latin reading; nor is the Armenian very far from it. The question being insoluble from the MSS. alone, we turn to the known relations between the group of Apocalypses mentioned above: the first thought that suggests itself is that perhaps the field in question may be the field of Agrippa mentioned in Christian Baruch. The two names are not so remote as to render identification impossible, and if we imagine the γ to drop out we can come very near to the Arphad of the Syriac version. But perhaps this assumption is a little too difficult, and so we will try another and easier one.

Observing the fact that Hebron is mentioned in Apocal. Baruch as one of the seats of prophetic inspiration, and that Hebron is also implied in the Christian Baruch, we ask ourselves whether it is mentioned in 4 Ezra. Now if we turn to the Apocalypse of Baruch, we find that the vision at Hebron is preceded by a seven days' fast, and that before the prophet begins his fast or sets out for Hebron he bids farewell to the people and their elders who are extremely unwilling that he should depart from amongst them. The parallel to this passage in 4 Ezra is in c. xii. v. 40—51 ; as we may see from the following :

Apocal. Bar.	4 Esdras.
c. xlvi. Et responderunt filius meus et seniores populi et dixerunt mihi : Usque ad istiusmodi humiliavit nos Fortis, ut recipiat te a nobis cito et vere erimus in tenebris, &c. &c.	c. xii. 40. Et factum est cum audisset omnis populus quoniam pertransierunt septem dies et ego non fuissem reversus in civitatem et congregant se omnis a minimo usque ad maximum et venit ad me et dixerunt mihi dicentes,
	41. Quid peccavimus tibi et quid iniuste egimus in te...tu enim nobis superasti... sicut lucerna in loco obscuro.
c. xlvii. Et cum exissem ac dimisissem eos abii inde et dixi eis; Ecce ego vado usque ad Hebron...et veni ad eum locum ubi sermo factus fuerat ad me et sedi ibi et ieiunavi septem diebus, et factum est post dies septem....	50. Et profectus est populus sicut dixi ei in civitatem: ego autem sedi in campo septem diebus sicut mihi mandavit et manducavi de floribus, &c. Et factum est post dies septem....

We suspect, then, that the place of the fifth vision of Ezra (the vision of the great Eagle) may be taken to be Hebron ; but a glance at the text will shew that the scene is the same as in the fourth vision (the vision of the Sorrowing Woman): and this scene is the field of Arphad, or Ardath, or whatever may be its right name. It seems, therefore, that Hebron as a place for visions turns up in all three Apocalypses, and that Ardath is in its neighbourhood. With some likelihood we may say further that the oak of Abraham as a place for celestial communications turns up in all three writings: in the Christian Baruch by implication in the allusion to the Gentiles' market or fair at the Terebinth; and in the Apocalypse of Baruch the oak is suggested in the parallel passage to this, quoted in a previous note (Apocal. Bar. c. lxxvii. 18)[1]. But it is also in Ezra, for we find in c. xiii. 57, " Et profectus sum et transii in campum (sc. Ardath)...et sedi ibi tribus diebus. (c. xiv.) Et factum est tertio die, et ego sedebam sub quercu (sc. Terebintho)."

Now observe further that the place of vision is described in Ezra as "campum...ubi domus non est aedificata," and compare the description which Sozomen gives of the sacred oak and its surroundings. "The place is open and cultivated ground, nor are there any buildings except the well and the ancient Abrahamic buildings around the oak" (αἴθριος γὰρ καὶ ἀρόσιμός ἐστιν ὁ χῶρος καὶ οὐκ ἔχων οἰκήματα ἢ μόνα τὰ περὶ τὴν δρῦν πάλαι τοῦ Ἀβραὰμ γενόμενα καὶ τὸ φρέαρ τὸ παρ᾽ αὐτοῦ κατασκευασθέν). At first sight the parallelism of these two passages seems a little artificial; but this objection disappears as soon as we observe that in either case the absence of buildings is a corollary from the sanctity of the place. It had been rendered holy by the Theophany which had occurred there. Each of our three Apocalyptists is occupied with the subject of the Upper Jerusalem, and examination shews that *it was believed that Abraham had seen this Heavenly City at Mamre.* Let us then compare what Ezra and Apocalyptic Baruch say on this point:

Bar. Apocal.	4 Esdras.
iv. 3. " Ostendi eam (sc. Jerusalem) Adamo priusquam peccaret; cum vero abjecit mandatum, sublata est ab eo, ut etiam paradisus. Et postea ostendi eam servo meo Abrahamo noctu inter divisiones victimarum."	x. 50. Ostendit tibi Altissimus claritatem gloriae eius (sc. Jerusalem) et pulchritudinem decoris eius. Propterea enim dixi tibi ut venires in agrum ubi non est fundamentum aedificii; nec enim poterat opus aedificii hominis sustinere in loco ubi incipiebat Altissimi civitas ostendi.

The place of Ezra's vision is the same as that of Abraham.

We have thus proved that the scene of the 14th chapter of Ezra is geographically identified with the neighbourhood of Abraham's oak; if any doubt remained on our mind as to the correctness of

[1] p. 34.

the investigation, it might be dispelled by the following further
consideration : when Ezra is sitting under the oak, a voice comes
to him out of the bush saying, Ezra, Ezra ; and the speaker goes
on to say that it was in the burning bush that he appeared to
Moses when the people was in bondage in Egypt. Now we may
very well ask, What is the reason for this abrupt allusion to the
burning bush ; how came the author's mind to travel that way ?
The answer is that the Terebinth of Mamre was supposed to have
the same virtue of non-inflammability as the bush in Mount Sinai.
The evidence for this will be found in Reland, *Palestina*, under
the heading Chebron, and is as follows :

Ps. Eustathius, writing a commentary on the *Hexaemeron*,
says (Migne, *Patr. Gr.* xviii. 778) that Joseph was buried in the
same place as his ancestor Abraham, and that in this place is
the Terebinth where Jacob hid the idols of Laban, and which is
still reverenced by the people of the neighbouring countries....
And if this Terebinth be set on fire it is swallowed in flame and
one would think it to have been consumed ; but as soon as the
fire is extinguished the Terebinth is seen to be unharmed. The
same account is given by Georgius Syncellus in his *Chronographia*
(ed. Niebuhr, Vol. I. 202): and it appears that Syncellus and
Eustathius are drawing from a common authority, since their
language is similar, and they both make the mistake of confound-
ing the oak at Shechem with the tree at Mamre. This common
authority is named by Syncellus ; it is the chronographer Julius
Africanus, who must therefore be also responsible for the blunder[1].

---

[1] We give the passages side by side :

Ps. Eustathius.

Ἐπὶ τέλει δὲ καὶ τὸν Ἰωσήφ, τῆς Αἰγύπτου ἀποχωρήσαντες, κηδεύουσιν ἔνθα ὁ προ-
πάτωρ αὐτῶν Ἀβραὰμ προκεκήδευτο· ἐν ᾧ
τόπῳ ὑπῆρχε καὶ ἡ τερέβινθος, ὑφ' ᾗ
ἔκρυψεν Ἰακὼβ τῆς (sic) Λάβαν τὰ εἴδωλα,
ἥτις ἔτι καὶ νῦν εἰς τιμὴν τῶν προγόνων ὑπὸ
τῶν πλησιοχώρων θρησκεύεται· ἔστι γὰρ
ἄχρι τοῦ δεῦρο παρὰ τὸν πρέμνον αὐτῆς
βωμός, ἐφ' ὃν τά τε ὁλοκαυτώματα καὶ τὰς
ἑκατόμβας ἀνέφερον· εἶναί τε φασὶ ῥάβδον
αὐτὴν ἑνὸς τῶν ἐπιξενωθέντων ἀγγέλων
τῷ Ἀβραάμ, ἥνπερ τῷ τόπῳ τότε παρὼν
ἐνεφύτευσε καὶ ἐξ αὐτῆς ἡ ἀξιάγαστος ἀνε-
φύη τερέβινθος. Ὑφαφθεῖσα γὰρ ὅλη πῦρ

Georgius Syncellus.

Ἡ ποιμενικὴ σκήνη τοῦ Ἰακὼβ ἐν Ἐδέσῃ
σωζομένη κατὰ τοὺς χρόνους Ἀντονίνου
Ῥωμαίων βασιλέως διεφθάρη κεραυνῷ ὥς
φησιν ὁ Ἀφρικανός, ἕως τῶν χρόνων αὐτοῦ
Ἀντωνίνου ἱστόρησας. Ἰακὼβ ἀπαρεσθεὶς
τοῖς ὑπὸ Συμεὼν καὶ Λευὶ πραχθεῖσιν ἐν
Σικίμοις διὰ τὴν τῆς ἀδελφῆς φθορὰν εἰς
τοὺς ἐπιχωρίους, θάψας ἐν Σικίμοις οὓς
ἐφέρετο θεοὺς παρὰ τὴν πέτραν ὑπὸ τὴν
θαυμάσιαν τερέβινθον ἥτις μέχρι νῦν εἰς
τιμὴν πατριαρχῶν ὑπὸ τῶν πλησιοχώρων
τιμᾶται, μετῆρεν εἰς Βαιθήλ· ταύτης παρὰ
πρέμνον βωμὸς ἦν, ὥς φασιν ὁ Ἀφρικανός,
τῆς τερεβίνθου, ἐφ' ὃν τὰς ἐκτενὰς ἀνέφερον

We have thus a perfect explanation of the allusion made by Ezra to the burning bush. There was a tradition that the Terebinth was incombustible. It appears, therefore, that we ought to identify the field of Esdras' vision with the neighbourhood of Hebron and the sacred oak. This suggests that we should read *Arbaa*[1] as the name of the field (the ancient name of Hebron being Kiriath-Arba). Writing this in uncial characters, the word easily becomes ΑΡΒΑΔ, from which the *Ardab* of the Armenian is a mere transposition, and Arphad of the Syriac a slight change of two closely related letters. The other variants readily explain themselves in a similar manner.

The Ezra-Baruch legends in the Koran.

We have in the preceding section traced the process of corruption by which the manuscripts of the fourth book of Ezra have disguised the writer's geography almost beyond identification. We will now add something further to the subject, though only in a tentative manner, by trying to demonstrate that traces of our group of Apocalypses or at least of some of them are to be found in the Koran and in Commentaries on the Koran.

The second chapter of the Koran entitled 'the Cow' contains near the close a curious passage which Sale renders as follows: "Hast thou not considered how he behaved himself who passed by a city which had been destroyed even to her foundations? He said, How shall God quicken this city after she hath been dead? And God caused him to die for an hundred years and afterwards raised him to life. And God said, How long hast thou tarried here? He answered, A day or a part of a day. God said, Nay thou hast tarried here an hundred years. Now look on thy food and drink, they are not yet corrupted ; and look on thine ass: and this have we done that we might make thee a sign unto them." And Sale remarks that it is the opinion of the Arabic commentators

γίνεται καὶ νομίζεται τοῖς πᾶσιν εἰς κόνιν ἐκ τῆς φλογὸς ἀναλύεσθαι, καίτοι σβεσθεῖσα μέντοι ἀσινὴς ὅλη καὶ ἀκέραιος δείκνυται.

ἐν ταῖς πανηγύρεσι τῆς χώρας ἔνοικοι, ἡ δ' οὐ κατεκαίετο δοκοῦσα πίπρασθαι. παρὰ ταύτην ὁ τάφος Ἀβραὰμ καὶ Ἰσαάκ. φασὶ δέ τινες ῥάβδον εἶναί τινος τῶν ἐπιξενωθέντων ἀγγέλων τῷ Ἀβραὰμ φυτευθεῖσαν αὐτόθι.

[1] The LXX give uniformly Arboc, which Jerome corrects to *Arbee*: "corrupte in nostris codicibus Arboc scribitur cum in Hebraeis legatur Arbee"

that the person spoken of here is Ozair or Ezra. He gives some
further expansion of the legends, which it is quite likely that he
took from Maracci. At all events there is in this author's *Pro-
dromus ad Refutationem Alcorani* Pt. iv. 85 a good note on the
subject, as follows: "Conveniunt omnes, quos videre potui, Alco-
ranum hic loqui de Ozair, id est Ezra, qui transiens iuxta civitatem
Jerusalem iam a Chaldaeis destructam, insidens asino cum canistro
ficorum et cyatho pleno musto, coepit ambigere, quomodo posset
Deus illam urbem restituere, et habitatores eius in ea exstinctos
suscitare. Deus autem mori fecit eum, mansitque mortuus per
centum annos; post quos suscitatus a Deo, vidit ficus et musti
cyathum adhuc integros et incorruptos; asinum vero extinctum
et in ossa redactum : ad quae respiciens Ezra iussu Dei vidit illa
elevari, atque inter se compacta carne vestiri, et fieri asinum, in
quem cum Deus spiritum immisisset statim coepit rudere." D'Herbelot in his *Bibliothèque Orientale*, under the heading *Ozair*, gives
the same traditions more at length : "Les interprètes de l'Alcoran
disent sur ce passage que l'homme dont il est parlé ici est Ozair
ou Esdras lequel ayant été mené in captivité par Bakht-al-Nassar
ou Nabuchodonosor à Babylone, et delivré ensuite miraculeuse-
ment de sa prison, se transporte à Jerusalem, qui étoit pour lors
ruinée, et s'arrêta à un village, fort proche de cette ville, nommé
Sair abad, maison de promenade, et *Deir anab*, lieu de vignoble,
une vigne dans la signification que les Italiens donnent à ce mot.
Ce lieu qui n'étoit couvert que de mazures, avoit cependant dans
son terroir des Figuiers et des Vignes chargez de fruits. Esdras
en prit pour sa provision et alla se loger auprès de quelque pan de
muraille qui restoit encore sur pied. Ce fut là qu'il établit un
hermitage où il vivoit des fruits qu'il avoit cueillis et tenoit un
asne que luy avait servi de monture pendant son voyage, attaché
auprès de luy. Ce saint homme en considerant de ce lieu là les
ruines de la ville Sainte pleuroit amèrement devant le Seigneur et
disoit souvent en luy même, plûtost en admirant la puissance de
Dieu, qu'en murmurant contre elle : 'Comment les ruines de
Jerusalem, pourroient-elles jamais se relever.' Mais il n'eût pas
plûtost concu cette pensée que Dieu le fit mourir sur le champ et
le tint caché aux yeux de hommes avec tout ce qu'il avoit autour
de lui, l'espace d'un siècle entier, au même état qu'il se trouvoit
pour lors. Cependant, soixante et dix ans après la mort de
Nabuchodonosor, Dieu suscita Noschek Roy de Perse, qui ordonna

le rétablissement de la Ville et du Temple de Jerusalem, et trente ans après les ordres de ce Roy ayant été executez Dieu resuscita Esdras en un tel état qu'il luy parut n'avoir dormi que pendant un jour, mais ayant ouvert les yeux, il connut bientôt, que Dieu avoit operé un grand miracle en sa personne, et s'écria aussitôt, Dieu certainement est tout puissant; car, il peut faire tout ce qu'il luy plait."

Upon the passage which we have quoted from the Koran, Maracci endeavours to shew that the legend, though it contains more figments than words, agrees better with the history of Nehemiah than Ezra; the cup of wine being a reminiscence of the office which Nehemiah held at the Persian court, and the ass a reflection of the beast on which he made the circuit of the ruined city. But he asks in despair "Whence the death of Nehemiah and his ass: and their resurrection after the lapse of a century; and whence this story of the marvellous conservation of wine and figs? Some persons say that it is not Ezra, nor Nehemiah, but a certain *Alchedrum.*" The story certainly is a queer confusion of legends; it must be evident that we have many single gentlemen rolled into one, and that the principal one amongst them is our friend Abimelech the Ethiopian, whose basket of figs furnishes the explanation which Maracci searched the Scriptures for in vain.

The mythical Alchedrum is therefore Abimelech: and the sentence in which God directs the supposed Ezra to look on his marvellously conserved food and drink has its origin in the passage where the old man tells Abimelech to look into the basket and see that the figs have no evil smell though they were gathered 66 years ago. We may, if we please, refer the story of the ass and the wine-cup to Nehemiah, but as we have here a practically certain origin for the Mohammedan legends, it is best to exhaust this source before seeking a second, and we find that the story of the sleep of Abimelech is the origin of the one hundred years' death-sleep of the Ezra of the Koran. And indeed although the Koran gives the time as 100 years, the legends quoted by D'Herbelot shew traces of a knowledge of the number 70 as given in corrected copies of the Christian Baruch. Why else should it have been said that the 100 years was made up of 70 years from the death of Nebuchadnezzar together with 30 years to the time of Noschek, king of Persia?

Further, the passage in the Koran is used to prove the resurrection of the dead by the resurrection of the city. And it is to be noticed that Abimelech when he sees that the figs exude still their milky juice, breaks into an exultant apostrophe to his flesh which God is able to revive.

The writer, too, who made his Ezra sleep 100 years and think it to be a day or part of a day, is in exact consonance with Abimelech who thinks he has slept a very little and would in fact like to sleep a little more.

But, as we have said, the legends collected in D'Herbelot are not totally explained by the introduction of our Abimelech. It looks as if the fourth book of Ezra were here, if not some biblical allusion also to Nehemiah. The account which he gives of Ezra finding a hermitage in a desolate spot not far from the city, is marvellously like the story of the sojourn in the Field of Arphad; his diet of figs may be only a correction for the flowers which Ezra is directed to live on. And even the allusion to the ruins which covered the ground may be an adaptation of Ezra's note that the spot was clear of buildings. We will even go so far as to suspect that the field of Arbaa (Arbad) underlies the perplexing names which D'Herbelot quotes for the place of Ezra's hermitage.

It seems, therefore, to sum up, that there is good reason to believe that Mohammed was acquainted with the Christian Baruch, and that the Commentators who explained his allusion were acquainted also with the fourth book of Ezra. In view of the uncertainty which prevails with regard to the literary sources of Mohammedanism especially on the Christian side, it may be not wholly useless to have given some confirmation of the theory of Ceriani, that the second chapter of the Koran draws on the story contained in the last words of Baruch.

The Christian Baruch, 4 Ezra, and Barnabas.

An interesting question arises in one passage of our author as to the possibility of a reference to the epistle of Barnabas, and the subject is important enough in view of the uncertainty of the date of that epistle; so that it seems hardly fair to dismiss the matter in the compass of a foot-note. In c. ix. 15, we find a prediction that the tree of life which is planted in the midst of Paradise will come into the world, and that this tree will cause the fruitless trees to become fruitful, and the boastful trees to wither; and the tree which is established will make them to bend. So at least we have edited, deserting the reading of our MSS.: which give the sense 'will make them to be judged.' The difference between the two readings is only a single letter. Our best MS. has failed here, and the text of the Ethiopic version is so confused, that it is almost unintelligible. That our emendation, however, is substantially correct may be seen from the following passage quoted in Gregory of Nyssa amongst a number of Testimonies against the Jews[1]:

Καὶ τότε ταῦτα συντελεσθήσεται, λέγει Κύριος, ὅταν ξύλον ξύλων (l. ξύλῳ) κλιθῇ καὶ ἀναστῇ καὶ ὅταν ἐκ ξύλου αἷμα στάξει (l. στάξῃ). The two corrections which we have given in brackets, obvious enough of themselves, are given by Ceriani from an Ambrosian MS.[2]

Now this bending of tree to tree is exactly what is spoken of in our author, when he intimates that the tree of life will make all the other trees to bow before it. So that our correction of the text is justified, as we shall see more clearly as we proceed.

Two questions then arise, first as to the origin of the quotation which Nyssen makes: second as to the meaning of the similar matter in the text of our author. We will take these points in order. The passage is very like one in the twelfth chapter of Barnabas, which runs as follows: Ὁμοίως πάλιν περὶ τοῦ σταυροῦ ὁρίζει ἐν ἄλλῳ προφήτῃ λέγοντι· Καὶ πότε ταῦτα συντελεσθήσεται; λέγει Κύριος· ὅταν ξύλον κλιθῇ καὶ ἀναστῇ καὶ ὅταν ἐκ ξύλου αἷμα στάξῃ.

We may regard it as almost certain that Gregory Nyssen is quoting from Barnabas; the differences being so slight that we can at once allow for them by the ordinary processes of transcription. We have only to imagine the text of Barnabas to have dropped ξύλῳ after ξύλον and all is clear. But this brings

---

[1] Zacagni, *Collectanea Monumenta*, p. 309; Ceriani, *Mon. Sac.* v. i. 108.
[2] Cod. C. 135, Inf.

Barnabas into very close relation with the language of the Christian Baruch.

We must not, however, assume any direct quotation between them, inasmuch as the passage in Barnabas is distinctly given as a quotation from one of the prophets. Nor should we have much difficulty in identifying this prophet with the Apocalyptic Ezra, because a great part of the quotation can at once be found in his text, and because the Christian Baruch, who exhibits parallel language to that part of Barnabas' quotation which cannot be found in the text of Ezra as edited, has been shewn to have internal relations with the fourth book of Ezra. We will place the passages side by side for the sake of comparison:

Gregory Nyss., and Barnabas (xii. 1).	Christian Baruch (ix. 15, 16).	4 Ezra iv. 33, v. 5, 9.
Καὶ πότε ταῦτα συντελεσθήσεται; λέγει Κύριος· Ὅταν ξύλον κλιθῇ καὶ ἀναστῇ καὶ ὅταν ἐκ ξύλου αἷμα στάξῃ.	Γίνεται δὲ μετὰ τοὺς καιροὺς τούτους, καὶ ἔρχεται εἰς τὴν γῆν τὸ δένδρον τῆς ζωῆς τὸ ἐν μέσῳ τοῦ παραδείσου φυτευθέν, ... καὶ τὰ βεβλαστηκότα καὶ μεγαλαυχοῦντα................... ποιήσει κλιθῆναι τὸ δένδρον τὸ στηριχθέν....................... .... τὰ γλυκέα ὕδατα ἁλμυρὰ γενήσονται.	Et respondi et dixi, Quomodo et quando haec?...... .... et de ligno sanguis stillabit, et lapis dabit vocem suam .... et in dulcibus aquis salsae invenientur.

We must then, I think, conclude that the Recension of 4 Ezra which Barnabas and the Christian Baruch used contained a clause answering to ὅταν ξύλον ξύλῳ κλιθῇ. This is, I think, the very conclusion arrived at by Le Hir in his discussion of the fourth book of Ezra[1]. Le Hir, however, goes further and very ingeniously seeks the origin of the whole Ezra passage in the prophet Habakkuk, where the stone cries from the wall that is builded by deceit and the cross-beam answers back to it, and where woe is denounced on those who build houses by blood. The conjunction of stone, tree and blood is suggestive even in a translation, especially when it is a talking stone, too, as in 4 Ezra and in the later Baruch. But M. Le Hir goes so far as to restore the whole passage of Habakkuk into close textual agreement with Barnabas and Ezra, as the following will shew:

---

[1] Études Bibliques, p. 198.

Habakkuk ii. 11.

כפים מעץ יעננה: הוי בנה עיר בדמים וכונן...

Suggested corruption of Le Hir,

כפים מעץ יענה ויעיר: בדם ימוך

Now without endorsing the whole of the suggestions of this
reading, we may say that the first one, which turns on the equiva-
lence of the two Hebrew roots which mean respectively *to answer*
and *to bend*, is so striking that we may be pretty sure we have
tracked the quotations to their source; and we may add to this,
what I do not think Le Hir noted, that the words which precede in
Habakkuk "the stone shall cry out of the wall," answer exactly to
"the stone shall give its voice" of Ezra, and, in fact, furnish the
momentum for the misunderstandings which culminate in the
personification of the dying Jeremiah by a stone. We may therefore follow with confidence the greater part of Le Hir's reasoning.

And, bearing in mind that the Hebrew text of the passage in
Habakkuk is perfectly satisfactory, and needs neither textual correction nor any subtleties of interpretation, we may say that in
a certain circle, probably Jerusalem, there prevailed a flagrant
corruption or mistranslation of the passage: that this corruption
became the basis of exegetical subtleties on the part of Apocryphal
writers, both Jews and Christians: the former, probably, explained
the 'blood that drops from wood' of the martyrdom of Isaiah:
while the latter, who never missed the chance of seeing the 'cross'
in any reference to 'beams,' 'trees,' 'rods' or 'timber,' were able
to find a prophetic testimony to the central object of their faith in
the fact that 'wood should bend to wood,' or that 'blood should
trickle' therefrom.

And this brings us to the second point; viz. the meaning which
our Christian Baruch attached to the words which he has absorbed.
He is preaching the triumph of the Cross; this may be regarded to
be as certain as if he had followed Barnabas' example and prefixed a
paragraph saying that the prophet is here speaking of the Cross.
But it is not quite so clear whether he is speaking of the assumption of the Cross, which is of course the Tree of Life, into Paradise
and its adoration by the rest of the trees of the garden, or of the
descent of the Tree from Paradise and its adoration by the rest of
the trees of the world. The former opinion derives some weight
from the fact that some of the early Christians believed the Cross

had been caught up into Paradise, a natural belief when we consider that they had so persistently taught that it was the Tree which had been planted in the midst of the garden.

But the latter opinion agrees better with the statement of the writer that the tree is coming to the earth and that the fruitless trees (i.e. the Gentiles) will under its influence bear fruit, while those that have sprouted and are high-minded (i.e. the extreme section of the Jews) will have to bow before it.

ΤΑ ΠΑΡΑΛΕΙΠΟΜΕΝΑ ΙΕΡΕΜΙΟΥ ΤΟΥ ΠΡΟΦΗΤΟΥ.

I. Ἐγένετο, ἡνίκα ᾐχμαλωτεύθησαν οἱ υἱοὶ Ἰσραὴλ ἀπὸ 1
τοῦ βασιλέως τῶν Χαλδαίων, ἐλάλησεν ὁ Θεὸς πρὸς Ἱερεμίαν·
Ἱερεμία, ὁ ἐκλεκτός μου, ἀνάστα, ἔξελθε ἐκ τῆς πόλεως
ταύτης, σὺ καὶ Βαρούχ· ἐπειδὴ ἀπολῶ αὐτὴν διὰ τὸ πλῆθος
τῶν ἁμαρτιῶν τῶν κατοικούντων ἐν αὐτῇ. Αἱ γὰρ προσευχαὶ 2
ὑμῶν ὡς στῦλος ἑδραῖός ἐστιν ἐν μέσῳ αὐτῆς, καὶ ὡς τεῖχος
ἀδαμάντινον περικυκλοῦν αὐτήν. Νῦν ἀναστάντες ἐξέλθατε 3
πρὸ τοῦ τὴν δύναμιν τῶν Χαλδαίων κυκλῶσαι αὐτήν. Καὶ 4
ἀπεκρίθη Ἱερεμίας, λέγων· Παρακαλῶ σε, Κύριε, ἐπίτρεψόν
μοι τῷ δούλῳ σου λαλῆσαι ἐνώπιόν σου. Εἶπεν δὲ αὐτῷ
ὁ Κύριος· Λάλει, ὁ ἐκλεκτός μου Ἱερεμίας. Καὶ ἐλάλησεν 5
Ἱερεμίας, λέγων· Κύριε παντοκράτωρ, παραδίδως τὴν πόλιν
τὴν ἐκλεκτὴν εἰς χεῖρας τῶν Χαλδαίων, ἵνα καυχήσηται ὁ
βασιλεὺς μετὰ τοῦ πλήθους τοῦ λαοῦ αὐτοῦ, καὶ εἴπῃ ὅτι,
Ἴσχυσα ἐπὶ τὴν ἱερὰν πόλιν τοῦ Θεοῦ; Μὴ, Κύριέ μου· ἀλλ᾽ 6
εἰ θέλημά σού ἐστιν, ἐκ τῶν χειρῶν σου ἀφανισθήτω. Καὶ 7
εἶπε Κύριος τῷ Ἱερεμίᾳ· Ἐπειδὴ σὺ ἐκλεκτός μου εἶ, ἀνάστα
καὶ ἔξελθε ἐκ τῆς πόλεως ταύτης, σὺ καὶ Βαρούχ· ἐπειδὴ
ἀπολῶ αὐτὴν διὰ τὸ πλῆθος τῶν ἁμαρτιῶν τῶν κατοικούντων

Title, with abc; aeth, The rest of the words of Baruch.

I. 1 ηνικα ab; οτε c | οι; c om | απο ab; υπο c | Ιερεμιαν cum c aeth; ab add
τον προφητην λεγων | Ιερ...Βαρουχ ab, aeth; αναστηθη και συ και Βαρουχ c | απολω
c; απολλω ab | αυτην ab aeth; τὴν πολιν ταυτην c | κατοικουντων ab; ενοικουντων c |
v. 2 εστιν; c om | περικυκλουν a; περικυκλων b; περι τα τειχη αυτης c (not aeth) | v. 3 νυν
αναστ. εξελθατε ab (a εξελθετε); νυν ουν c, inserting ανασταντες εξελθατε at the end of
the verse | προ του κτέ following the Menaea and de; but abc προ του ἡ δυναμις των
χαλδαιων κυκλωσει (κυκλωση a) αυτην | v. 4 απεκριθη ab; ελαλησεν c | επιτρεψον μοι ab ;
κελευσον με c | τω δουλω σου ab aeth; c om | ενωπιον σου ab; λογον εναντιον σου c | αυτω
c aeth; ab om | v. 5 ελαλησεν ab; ειπεν c | λεγων ab; om c | παραδιδως a; παραδιδης b;
παραδιδοις c | πολιν; aeth add ταυτην | μετα...αυτου ab aeth; c om | v. 6 σου (1°); b
σον | σου (2°); c om | v. 7 Ks; ab o ks | τω Ιερ. ab; προς Ιερεμιαν c | αναστα ab; αναστηθι
c | εκ...ταυτης aeth om | απολω bc; a om | κατοικ. ab; ενοικ. c | end of verse a adds
απολλω.

8 ἐν αὐτῇ. Οὔτε γὰρ ὁ βασιλεύς, οὔτε ἡ δύναμις αὐτοῦ, δυνήσεται εἰσελθεῖν εἰς αὐτήν, εἰ μὴ ἐγὼ πρῶτος ἀνοίξω τὰς πύλας
9 αὐτῆς. Ἀνάστηθι οὖν, καὶ ἄπελθε πρὸς Βαρούχ, καὶ ἀπάγγειλον
10 αὐτῷ τὰ ῥήματα ταῦτα. Καὶ ἀναστάντες ἕκτην ὥραν τῆς νυκτός, ἔλθετε ἐπὶ τὰ τείχη τῆς πόλεως, καὶ δείξω ὑμῖν, ὅτι, ἐὰν μὴ ἐγὼ πρῶτος ἀφανίσω τὴν πόλιν, οὐ δύνανται εἰσελθεῖν
11 εἰς αὐτήν. Ταῦτα εἰπὼν ὁ Κύριος, ἀπῆλθεν ἀπὸ τοῦ Ἱερεμίου.
1 II. Ἱερεμίας δὲ διέρρηξεν τὰ ἱμάτια αὐτοῦ καὶ ἐπέθηκεν χοῦν ἐπὶ τὴν κεφαλὴν αὐτοῦ· καὶ εἰσῆλθεν εἰς τὸ ἁγιαστήριον
2 τοῦ Θεοῦ· καὶ ἰδὼν αὐτὸν ὁ Βαρούχ χοῦν πεπασμένον ἐπὶ τὴν κεφαλὴν αὐτοῦ, καὶ τὰ ἱμάτια αὐτοῦ διερρωγότα, ἔκραξε φωνῇ μεγάλη, λέγων· Πάτερ Ἱερεμία, τί ἔστι σοι, ἢ ποῖον ἁμάρτημα
3 ἐποίησεν ὁ λαός; Ἐπειδὴ ὅταν ἡμαρτάνεν ὁ λαός, χοῦν ἔπασσεν ἐπὶ τὴν κεφαλὴν αὐτοῦ ὁ Ἱερεμίας, καὶ ηὔχετο ὑπὲρ τοῦ λαοῦ,
4 ἕως ἂν ἀφεθῇ αὐτῷ ἡ ἁμαρτία. Ἠρώτησε δὲ αὐτὸν ὁ Βαρούχ,
5 λέγων· Πάτερ, τί ἔστι σοι; Εἶπε δὲ αὐτῷ Ἱερεμίας· Φύλαξαι τοῦ σχίσαι τὰ ἱμάτιά σου, ἀλλὰ σχίσωμεν τὰς καρδίας ἡμῶν· καὶ μὴ ἀντλήσωμεν ὕδωρ ἐπὶ τὰς ποτίστρας, ἀλλὰ κλαύσωμεν καὶ γεμίσωμεν αὐτὰς δακρύων· ὅτι οὐ μὴ ἐλεήσῃ
6 τὸν λαὸν τοῦτον ὁ Κύριος. Καὶ εἶπε Βαρούχ· Πάτερ Ἱερεμία, τί
7 γέγονε; Καὶ εἶπεν Ἱερεμίας ὅτι, Ὁ Θεὸς παραδίδωσι τὴν πόλιν εἰς χεῖρας τοῦ βασιλέως τῶν Χαλδαίων, τοῦ αἰχμαλωτεῦσαι
8 τὸν λαὸν εἰς Βαβυλῶνα. Ἀκούσας δὲ ταῦτα Βαρούχ, διέρρηξε καὶ αὐτὸς τὰ ἱμάτια αὐτοῦ, καὶ εἶπε· Πάτερ Ἱερεμία, τίς σοι
9 ἐδήλωσε τοῦτο; Καὶ εἶπεν αὐτῷ Ἱερεμίας· Ἔκδεξαι μικρὸν

v. 8 εις ab; προς c | τας π. αυτης ab; αυτοις τας πυλας c | v. 10 δειξω ab; δικνυω | εαν μη c; εαν μητι ab | αφαν. την πολιν ab aeth; απολεσω αυτην c | πολιν; ab add και ανοιξω, not c, aeth | δυνανται ab; δυνησονται c | εις αυτην ab; εν αυτη c | v. 11 απηλθεν ab; ανεχωρησεν c | Ιερ.; c adds εις τον ουνον; not ab aeth.
II. 1 Ιερ...θεου (b)c aeth; ab δραμων δε Ιερεμιας ανηγγειλε τω Βαρουχ ταυτα (b ταυτα τω B.) και ελθοντες εις τον ναον του θεου; b adds διερρηξεν τα ιματια αυτου Ιερεμιας και επεθηκεν χουν επι την κεφαλην αυτου· και ηρξαντο αμφοτεροι κλεειν εν τω αγιαστηριω του θεου | v. 2 και ιδων ab; ειδων δε c | χουν; c om | αυτου (1°); c add χουν | φωνη μεγαλη λεγων a; φωνην μεγαλην λεγ. b; c om | πατερ ab aeth; c om | τι εστιν ab aeth; απεστην c | εποιησεν ab aeth; ημαρτεν c | v. 3 ημαρτανεν ab aeth; ημαρτεν c | εως αν ab; οπως c | αυτω ab aeth; αυτοις c | αμαρτια; c add αυτη | v. 4 ερωτησεν ab; επερωτησεν c | αυτον ab; αυτω c | o; c om | πατερ τι εστι σοι c aeth; τι εστιν τουτο ab | v. 5 τα ιματια σου; c om | αλλα (1°); ab add μαλλον (not c aeth) | και (1°); c om | ποτιστρας; b ποτιστριας | αλλα(2°); c add μαλλον | τον λαον τ. ο κ. ab; κυρ. τ. λ. τ. c | v. 6 πατερ Ιερ. ab aeth; προς Ιερεμιαν c | v. 7 Ιερεμιας ab aeth; c om | παραδιδωσει a; παραδιδει b; παραδω c | την πολιν ab aeth; c add την εκλεκτην | του βασιλεως ab aeth; c om | του αιχ.; και αρουσι c | v. 8 ταυτα ab aeth; c om | και αυτος ab (aeth); c om | και ειπεν ab aeth; λεγων c | εδηλωσε ab; απηγγειλεν c.

μετ' ἐμοῦ ἕως ὥρας ἕκτης τῆς νυκτός, ἵνα γνῷς, ὅτι ἀληθές ἐστι
τὸ ῥῆμα. Ἔμειναν οὖν ἐν τῷ θυσιαστηρίῳ κλαίοντες. 10
III. Ὡς δὲ ἐγένετο ἡ ὥρα τῆς νυκτός, καθὼς εἶπεν ὁ Κύριος 1
τῷ Ἱερεμίᾳ, ἦλθον ὁμοῦ ἐπὶ τὰ τείχη τῆς πόλεως Ἱερεμίας καὶ
Βαρούχ. Καὶ ἐγένετο φωνὴ σάλπιγγος, καὶ ἐξῆλθον ἄγγελοι 2
ἐκ τοῦ οὐρανοῦ, κατέχοντες λαμπάδας ἐν ταῖς χερσὶν αὐτῶν,
καὶ ἔστησαν ἐπὶ τὰ τείχη τῆς πόλεως. Ἰδόντες δὲ αὐτοὺς 3
Ἱερεμίας καὶ Βαρούχ, ἔκλαυσαν, λέγοντες· Νῦν ἐγνώκαμεν ὅτι
ἀληθές ἐστι τὸ ῥῆμα. Παρεκάλεσε δὲ Ἱερεμίας τοὺς ἀγγέλους, 4
λέγων· Παρακαλῶ ὑμᾶς μὴ ἀπολέσθαι τὴν πόλιν ἄρτι, ἕως
ἂν λαλήσω πρὸς Κύριον ῥῆμα. Καὶ εἶπεν Κύριος τοῖς ἀγγέλοις·
Μὴ ἀπολέσητε τὴν πόλιν ἕως ἂν λαλήσω πρὸς τὸν ἐκλεκτόν
μου Ἱερεμίαν. Καὶ εἶπε· Δέομαι, Κύριε, κέλευσόν με λαλῆσαι
ἐνώπιόν σου. Καὶ εἶπε Κύριος· Λάλει, ὁ ἐκλεκτός μου Ἱερεμίας. 5
Καὶ εἶπεν Ἱερεμίας· Ἰδοὺ νῦν, Κύριε, ἐγνώκαμεν ὅτι παραδίδως 6
τὴν πόλιν σου εἰς χεῖρας τῶν ἐχθρῶν αὐτῆς, καὶ ἀπαροῦσι τὸν
λαὸν εἰς Βαβυλῶνα. Τί ποιήσωμεν τὰ ἅγιά σου ἢ τὰ σκεύη τῆς 7
λειτουργίας σου, τί θέλεις αὐτὰ ποιήσωμεν; Καὶ εἶπεν αὐτῷ ὁ 8
Κύριος· Ἆρον αὐτά, καὶ παράδος αὐτὰ τῇ γῇ καὶ τῷ θυσιαστηρίῳ
λέγων, Ἄκουε, γῆ, τῆς φωνῆς τοῦ κτίσαντός σε ἐν τῇ περιουσίᾳ
τῶν ὑδάτων, ὁ σφραγίσας σε ἐν ἑπτὰ σφραγίσιν, ἐν ἑπτὰ και-
ροῖς, καὶ μετὰ ταῦτα λήψῃ τὴν ὡραιότητά σου· φύλαξον τὰ
σκεύη τῆς λειτουργίας ἕως τῆς συνελεύσεως τοῦ ἠγαπημένου.

v. 9 το ρημα bc aeth; ab add τουτο | ουν c aeth; ab add αμφοτεροι | at the end
ab add και ησαν διερρωγοτα τα ιματια αυτων και η γη επι τας κεφαλας αυτων.
III. 1 ως ab; οτε c | της νυκτος ab aeth; c om | Ιερ. και Βαρ. ab ; c aeth om | at
end aeth adds und setzen sich nieder indem sie warteten | v. 2 και ιδου a; και aeth; c
om | εγενετο; c om | σαλπιγγος c aeth; σαλπιγγων ab | και (2°); c om | αγγ.; c οι
αγγ. | κατεχοντες; c εχοντες | εν τ. χ. αυτων ab aeth; c om | επι ab; εις c | της
πολεως ab aeth; c om | v. 3 λεγοντες c aeth; και ειπαν ab | εγνωκαμεν ab; εγνωμεν c |
v. 4 πολιν ; c adds ταυτην (not ab aeth) | προς κ. ρ. c aeth; μετα του θυ του υψιστου
ab | και ειπ...Ιερεμιαν c aeth; ab om | και ειπε (2°); ab add κλαιων; c om | δεομαι...Ιερ.
(v. 5) ab aeth; c om | v. 6 Κυριε; c om | εγνωκαμεν ab; εγνωμεν c | παραδιδως a; παρα-
διδῃς b; παραδιδοις c | σου; c om | των εχθρων αυτης ab aeth; των Χαλδαιων c | απαρουσι;
c αρουσιν | v. 7 text as in c (aeth); ab τι θελεις ποιησω τα αγια σκευη της λειτουργιας |
v. 8 αυτω o; c om | αρον ab aeth; αρατε c | παραδος ab aeth; παραδοτε | και τω θυσ.
c aeth (dem Erdboden und dem Hause des Heiligtums); ab om | λεγων ab aeth; c
om | ακ. γη; οτι γη ακ. c | της φωνης ab (aeth); c om | εν τη π. τ. υδ. ab (aeth durch
die Kraft der Gewässer); c ο πλασας σε εν ουσια των κτισματων | ο σφρ. σε; e men
του σφραγισαντος σε | εν επ. σφρ. ab aeth; c om | εν επ. κ. ab (c καιδροις); aeth
om | και; c om | ληψη τ. ωρ. σου ab (aeth); λημψη την οδον τη ωραιοτητι σου c |
φυλαξον; c και φυλαξης | de men aeth εως της συνελευσεως τ. η; εως της συντελειας τ.
η. ab; c εως ερωτησιν ποιηση κς περι αυτων· οτι ημεις ουκ ευρεθημεν αξιοι φυλαξαι

9 Καὶ ἐλάλησε Ἱερεμίας· Παρακαλῶ σε, Κύριε· δεῖξόν μοι, τί ποιήσω Ἀβιμέλεχ τῷ Αἰθίοπι· ὅτι πολλὰς εὐεργεσίας ἐποίησε τῷ λαῷ καὶ τῷ δούλῳ σου Ἱερεμίᾳ· ὅτι αὐτὸς ἀνέσπασέ με ἐκ τοῦ λάκκου τοῦ βορβόρου· καὶ οὐ θέλω αὐτὸν, ἵνα ἴδῃ τὸν ἀφανισμὸν τῆς πόλεως καὶ τὴν ἐρήμωσιν· ἀλλ᾽ ἵνα 10 μὴ λυπηθῇ. Καὶ εἶπε Κύριος τῷ Ἱερεμίᾳ· Ἀπόστειλον αὐτὸν εἰς τὸν ἀμπελῶνα τοῦ Ἀγρίππα διὰ τοῦ ὄρους· καὶ ἐγὼ σκεπάσω αὐτὸν, ἕως οὗ ἐπιστρέψω τὸν λαὸν εἰς τὴν πόλιν. 11 Εἶπε δὲ Κύριος τῷ Ἱερεμίᾳ· Ἄπελθε μετὰ τοῦ λαοῦ σου εἰς Βαβυλῶνα, καὶ μεῖνον μετ᾽ αὐτῶν εὐαγγελιζόμενος αὐτοῖς, 12 ἕως οὗ ἐπιστρέψω αὐτοὺς εἰς τὴν πόλιν. Κατάλειψον δὲ 13 τὸν Βαροὺχ ὧδε, ἕως οὗ λαλήσω αὐτῷ. Ταῦτα εἰπὼν ὁ 14 Κύριος, ἀνέβη ἀπὸ Ἱερεμίου εἰς τὸν οὐρανόν. Ἱερεμίας δὲ καὶ Βαροὺχ εἰσῆλθον εἰς τὸ ἁγιαστήριον, καὶ τὰ σκεύη τῆς λειτουργίας παρέδωκαν τῇ γῇ, καθὼς ἐλάλησεν αὐτοῖς ὁ Κύριος· καὶ αὔθωρον κατέπιεν αὐτὰ ἡ γῆ· ἐκάθισαν δὲ οἱ δύο, 15 καὶ ἔκλαυσαν. Πρωίας δὲ γενομένης, ἀπέστειλεν Ἱερεμίας τὸν Ἀβιμέλεχ, λέγων· Ἆρον τὸν κόφινον, καὶ ἄπελθε εἰς τὸ χωρίον τοῦ Ἀγρίππα διὰ τῆς ὁδοῦ τοῦ ὄρους, καὶ ἐνεγκὼν ὀλίγα σῦκα, δίδου τοῖς νοσοῦσι τοῦ λαοῦ· ὅτι ἐπὶ σὲ ἡ εὐφρασία 16 τοῦ Κυρίου, καὶ ἐπὶ τὴν κεφαλήν σου ἡ δόξα. Αὐτὸς δὲ ἀπελήλυθεν καθὼς εἶπεν αὐτῷ.

1 IV. Πρωίας δὲ γενομένης, ἰδοὺ ἡ δύναμις τῶν Χαλδαίων ἐκύκλωσε τὴν πόλιν· ἐσάλπισεν δὲ ὁ μέγας ἄγγελος, λέγων·

αυτας (sic! shewing that the scribe has wandered to c. IV. v. 4) οτι επιτροποι του ψευδους ευρεθημεν.

v. 9 και ελαλ. ab; ελ. δε c; ab add κλαιων (not c aeth) | Ιερεμιας; c add προς κ͞υ λεγων | παρακαλω; ab add και δυσωπω | τω λαω και τω δ. σου c aeth; ab om | Ιερεμια: aeth adds weit mehr als alle Leute der Stadt | οτι αυτος ανεσπασεν ab; c αυτος γαρ ανεστησεν | του βορβορου c aeth; ab om | αυτον ινα ιδη ab aeth; ινα αφης αυτον ιδειν c | τον αφαν. ab aeth; την ερημωσιν c | πολεως; ab add ταυτης | και τ. ερ.; c η τον αφανισμον η την ερημωσιν | αλλ ινα μη λυπηθη aeth; ab αλλ ινα ελεησης αυτον και μη λυπ.: c ηδη (sic) και λυπηθη | v. 10 τω Ιερ.; c om | αμπελωνα; c αγρον | δια του ορους και εγω c aeth; ab και εν τη σκια του ορους | εως ου επι. ab; c εως αποστρεψω | εις την πολιν ab aeth; c εις Βαβυλωνα | v. 11; c om | v. 12; c om; aeth om εως ου λαλ. αυτω | v. 13; c λαλησας δε αυτω ο κ͞ς ανεχωρησεν εις τον ο͞υν͞ον απο του Ιερεμιου | v. 14 αγιαστηριον; c adds του θεου | και (2°); ab add επαραντες | τα σκευη; ab add τα αγια | παρεδωκαν; ab add αυτα | γη ab aeth; c adds και του θυσιαστηριω | καθως ελαλησεν αυτ. ο κ͞ς b aeth de men; c καθως ειπεν κ͞ς; α om | αυθωρον c; ab ευθεως | οι δυο c aeth; ab om | εκλαυσαν; ab add αμα | v. 15 αρον...απελθον ab aeth; c απελθε | και...λαου; c om | οτι...δοξα ab (aeth); c οτι ευφρασια κ͞υ εις την κεφαλην σου ηξει | v. 16 c aeth; ab και ταυτα ειπων Ιερεμιας απελυσεν αυτον· Αβιμελεχ δε επορευθη καθα ειπεν αυτω.

IV. 1 την πολιν c aeth; a την πολιν Ιερουσαλημ; b πασαν τ. π. Ιερ.

Εἰσέλθατε εἰς τὴν πόλιν ἡ δύναμις τῶν Χαλδαίων· ἰδοὺ γὰρ ἠνεῴχθη ὑμῖν ἡ πύλη. Εἰσῆλθεν οὖν ὁ βασιλεὺς μετὰ τοῦ 2 πλήθους αὐτοῦ, καὶ ἠχμαλώτευσαν πάντα τὸν λαόν. Ἱερεμίας 3 δὲ ἄρας τὰς κλεῖδας τοῦ ναοῦ, ἐξῆλθεν ἔξω τῆς πόλεως, καὶ ἔρριψεν αὐτὰς ἐνώπιον τοῦ ἡλίου, λέγων· Σοὶ λέγω, ἥλιε, λάβε τὰς κλεῖδας τοῦ ναοῦ τοῦ Θεοῦ, καὶ φύλαξον αὐτὰς ἕως ἡμέρας, ἐν ᾗ ἐξετάσει σε Κύριος περὶ αὐτῶν. Διότι ἡμεῖς οὐχ εὑρέθημεν 4 ἄξιοι τοῦ φυλάξαι αὐτάς, ὅτι ἐπίτροποι ψεύδους ἐγενήθημεν. Ἔτι κλαίοντος Ἱερεμίου τὸν λαόν, εἵλκοντο εἰς Βαβυλῶνα. 5 Ὁ δὲ Βαροὺχ ἐπέθηκε χοῦν ἐπὶ τὴν κεφαλὴν αὐτοῦ, καὶ ἐκάθισε, 6 καὶ ἔκλαυσε τὸν θρῆνον τοῦτον, λέγων· Διὰ τί ἠρημώθη Ἱερουσαλήμ; Διὰ τὰς ἁμαρτίας τοῦ ἠγαπημένου λαοῦ παρεδόθη εἰς χεῖρας ἐχθρῶν, διὰ τὰς ἁμαρτίας ἡμῶν καὶ τοῦ λαοῦ. Ἀλλὰ 7 μὴ καυχάσθωσαν οἱ παράνομοι, καὶ εἴπωσιν ὅτι, Ἰσχύσαμεν λαβεῖν τὴν πόλιν τοῦ Θεοῦ ἐν τῇ δυνάμει ἡμῶν. Ἠδυνήθητε ἐπ' αὐτῇ· ἀλλὰ διὰ τὰς ἁμαρτίας ἡμῶν παρεδόθημεν. Ὁ δὲ Θεὸς 8 ἡμῶν οἰκτειρήσει ἡμᾶς, καὶ ἐπιστρέψει ἡμᾶς εἰς τὴν πόλιν ἡμῶν· ὑμεῖς δὲ ζωὴν οὐχ ἕξετε. Μακάριοί εἰσιν οἱ πατέρες ἡμῶν, 9 Ἀβραάμ, Ἰσαὰκ καὶ Ἰακώβ, ὅτι ἐξῆλθον ἐκ τοῦ κόσμου τούτου, καὶ οὐκ εἶδον τὸν ἀφανισμὸν τῆς πόλεως ταύτης. Ταῦτα εἰπών, 10 ἐξῆλθεν, κλαίων καὶ λέγων ὅτι, Λυπούμενος* διὰ σέ, Ἱερουσαλήμ, ἐξῆλθον ἀπὸ σοῦ. Καὶ ἔμεινεν ἐν μνημείῳ καθεζόμενος, 11 τῶν ἀγγέλων ἐρχομένων, καὶ ἐκδιηγουμένων αὐτῷ περὶ πάντων.

V. Ὁ δὲ Ἀβιμέλεχ ἤνεγκε τὰ σῦκα τῷ καύματι, καὶ 1 καταλαβὼν δένδρον, ἐκάθισεν ὑπὸ τὴν σκιὰν αὐτοῦ τοῦ ἀνα-

---

v. 1 η δυναμις; ab πασα η δυν. | πυλη ab; c θυρα | v. 2 εισηλθεν; ab εισελθετω | του πλ. αυ. ab; c του ιδιου πλ. | ηχμαλωτευσαν; ab αιχμαλωτευσατω | παντα; c om | λαον; c adds εις Βαβυλωνα | v. 3 κλειδας; c κλεις | εξω...λεγων ab aeth; και ειπεν c | σοι a aeth; συ bc | λαβε ab; c δεξαι | κλειδας; c κλεις | του θεου; c om (not ab aeth) | εως (v. 3)... εγενηθημεν (v. 4) with ab aeth; c εως ερωτησιν ποιησει ͞κ͞ς περι αυτων εως της συνελευσεως του ηγαπημενου | end c adds εξενεγκαι ουν αυτον | v. 5 Ιερεμιου; c αυτου | τον λαον; c om | ειλκοντο; c ειλκοντες | Βαβυλωνα; ab add υπο του βασιλεως των χαλδαιων | v. 6 ὁ δε Βαρ.; c Ιερεμιας δε διερρηξεν τα ιματια αυτου και | και του λαου ab aeth; c om | v. 7; c ισχυσαμεν; ηδυνηθημεν ab aeth (?) | τη; c om | ηδυνηθητε επ' αυτη c (aeth); ab om | παρεδοθημεν ab (?aeth παρεδοθη μεν); c om | v. 8 ημων (1°) ab aeth; c om | οικτειρησει; c. οικτιρησεν | και επιστρ. ημ. ab aeth; c. om | v. 9 της π. τ. ab aeth; c. ͞ι͞λ͞η͞μ | v. 10 ειπων; ab add Βαρουχ | εξηλθεν; ab add εξω της πολεως | λυπουμενος; c λοιπου; ab aeth om | Ιερουσαλημ; c adds και | εξηλθον; c εξηλθεν | απο σου; c εκ της πολεως | και λεγ.... σου; aeth om | v. 11 καθεξομενος; c om; aeth? | ερχομενων; ab add προς αυτον, not c aeth | παντων; ab add ων ο ͞κ͞ς εμηνυεν αυτω δι' αυτων.

V. 1 καυματι; aeth adds von dort wohin ihn Jeremias gesandt hatte | καταλαβων; c κατελαβεν | δενδρον; c adds και | υπο την σκιαν αυτου; c om (not ab aeth) | του ανα-παηναι bc (b om του); του αναπαυσαι a.

παῆναι ὀλίγον, καὶ κλίνας τὴν κεφαλὴν αὐτοῦ ἐπὶ τὸν κόφινον
τῶν σύκων ὕπνωσεν, κοιμώμενος ἔτη ἑξηκονταέξ· καὶ οὐκ
2 ἐξυπνίσθη ἐκ τοῦ ὕπνου αὐτοῦ. Καὶ μετὰ ταῦτα ἐγερθεὶς
ἀπὸ τοῦ ὕπνου αὐτοῦ, εἶπεν ὅτι, Ἡδέως ἐκοιμήθην ἂν ἄλλο
ὀλίγον, καὶ βεβαρημένη ἐστὶν ἡ κεφαλή μου, ὅτι οὐκ ἐκορέσθην
3 τοῦ ὕπνου μου. Καὶ ἀνακαλύψας τὸν κόφινον τῶν σύκων,
4 εὗρεν αὐτὰ στάζοντα γάλα. Καὶ εἶπεν· Ἤθελον κοιμηθῆναι
5 ὀλίγον, ὅτι βεβαρημένη ἐστὶν ἡ κεφαλή μου· ἀλλὰ φοβοῦμαι,
μήπως κοιμηθῶ καὶ βραδυνῶ τοῦ ἐξυπνισθῆναι, καὶ ὀλιγωρήσῃ
Ἱερεμίας ὁ πατήρ μου· εἰ μὴ γὰρ ἐσπούδαζεν, οὐκ ἂν ἀπέστειλέ
6 με ὄρθρου σήμερον. Ἀναστὰς οὖν πορεύσομαι τῷ καύματι, καὶ
7 *ἀπέλθω ὅπου οὐ καῦμα, οὐ κόπος ἔστιν καθ' ἡμέραν*. Ἐγερθεὶς
οὖν ἦρε τὸν κόφινον τῶν σύκων, καὶ ἐπέθηκεν ἐπὶ τῶν ὤμων
ἑαυτοῦ· καὶ εἰσῆλθεν εἰς Ἱερουσαλήμ, καὶ οὐκ ἐπέγνω αὐτήν,
οὔτε τὴν οἰκίαν, οὔτε τὸν τόπον, οὔτε τὸ γένος ἑαυτοῦ, καὶ εἶπεν·
8 Εὐλογητὸς Κύριος, ὅτι μεγάλη ἔκστασις ἐπέπεσεν ἐπ' ἐμέ· οὐκ
9 ἔστιν αὕτη ἡ πόλις· πεπλάνημαι, ὅτι διὰ τῆς ὁδοῦ τοῦ ὄρους
10 ἦλθον, ἐγερθεὶς ἀπὸ τοῦ ὕπνου μου· καὶ βαρείας οὔσης τῆς
κεφαλῆς μου διὰ τὸ μὴ κορεσθῆναί με τοῦ ὕπνου μου, πεπλά-
11 νημαι τὴν ὁδόν. Θαυμαστὸν εἰπεῖν τοῦτο ἐναντίον Ἱερεμίου,
12 ὅτι πεπλάνημαι. Ἐξῆλθε δὲ ἀπὸ τῆς πόλεως· καὶ κατανοήσας
εἶδε τὰ σημεῖα τῆς πόλεως, καὶ εἶπεν· Αὕτη μὲν ἔστιν ἡ πόλις,
13 πεπλάνημαι δέ. Καὶ πάλιν ὑπέστρεψεν εἰς τὴν πόλιν, καὶ
14 ἐζήτησε, καὶ οὐδένα εὗρε τῶν ἰδίων. Καὶ εἶπεν· Εὐλογητὸς
15 Κύριος, ὅτι μεγάλη ἔκστασις ἐπέπεσεν ἐπ' ἐμέ. Καὶ πάλιν

---

v. 1 κλιναs ab; εκλινεν...και c | επιc aeth; υπο ab | των συκων c om (not aeth?) | κοι-
μωμενος ετη εξ. εξ; aeth om; c και εποιησεν εξηκοντα και εξ ετη εκκοιμωμενος | εκ; απο
c | αυτου; ab add κατα προσταξιν θεου δια τον λογον ον ειπεν τω Ιερεμια οτι εγω αυτον
σκεπασω | v. 2 και (1°); c om | εγερθεις; c εξυπνησθεις | ηδεως; b ιδεως | αν αλλο
ολιγον; ab αλλ' ολιγον; c ολιγον; aeth wenn ich doch noch ein wenig schliefe | και
βεβ.; c αλλα βαρια | μου (2°); c aeth om | v. 4 ολιγον; de men αλλο ολιγον | βεβαρη-
μενη; c βαρια | v. 5 ορθρου σημερον c; σημερον ab; beim Lichtwerden aeth | v. 6 text
corrupt; ab· ου γαρ καυμα ου κοπος εστιν καθημεραν; c om; aeth denn die Hitze ist ja
heiss und niemals lässt sie ganz und gar nach | v. 7 εγερθεις; αναστας c | των ωμων
ab; την κεφαλην c; aeth om και επεθηκεν...εαυτου· αυτην...εαυτου ab (adding εαυτου
after τοπον); aeth weder die Stadt noch sein Haus | c om ουτε τον τοπον | και ειπεν;
ab ουτε τινα ευρεν κ. ειπ. | v. 8 επ' εμε c adds σημερον (not ab aeth) | ουκ; c και ουκ;
aeth και ελεγεν· ουκ | v. 9 πεπλανημαι; c adds γαρ την οδον | ηλθον; c om | v. 10 πεπλα-
νημαι; ab add δε | v. 11 ειπειν; c εστιν | Ιερεμιου; c του Ι. | οτι πεπλανημαι; c adds
την οδον; aeth wie sich mir die Stadt verandert hat | v. 12 εξηλ. δε; c και εξηλ | κατα-
νοησας ειδε ab; ευρεν c | της πολεως ab; αυτης c | c adds at end την οδον | v. 13 πολιν;
c οδον | και εξητησε; c om | v. 14 και ειπεν; c om | κυριος; ab ο κυριος; ει κυριε c | εμε;
c adds και ουκ εστιν αυτη η πολις | v. 15 παλιν; c om (not ab aeth).

ἐξῆλθεν ἔξω τῆς πόλεως. Καὶ ἔμεινε λυπούμενος, μὴ εἰδὼς
ποῦ ἀπέλθῃ. Καὶ ἀπέθηκε τὸν κόφινον, λέγων· Καθέζομαι 16
ὧδε, ἕως ὁ Κύριος ἄρῃ τὴν ἔκστασιν ταύτην ἀπ᾽ ἐμοῦ.
Καθη- 17
μένου δὲ αὐτοῦ, εἶδέ τινα γηραιὸν ἐρχόμενον ἐξ ἀγροῦ, καὶ λέγει
αὐτῷ Ἀβιμέλεχ· Σοὶ λέγω, πρεσβῦτα, ποία ἐστὶν ἡ πόλις
αὕτη; Καὶ εἶπεν αὐτῷ· Ἱερουσαλήμ ἐστι. Καὶ λέγει αὐτῷ 18
Ἀβιμέλεχ· Ποῦ ἔστιν ὁ Ἱερεμίας ὁ ἱερεύς, καὶ Βαρούχ ὁ
ἀναγνώστης, καὶ πᾶς ὁ λαὸς τῆς πόλεως ταύτης, ὅτι οὐχ
εὗρον αὐτούς; Καὶ εἶπεν αὐτῷ ὁ πρεσβύτης· Οὐκ εἶ σὺ 19
ἐκ τῆς πόλεως ταύτης, σήμερον μνησθεὶς τοῦ Ἱερεμίου, ὅτι 20
ἐπερωτᾷς περὶ αὐτοῦ μετὰ τοσοῦτον χρόνον; Ἱερεμίας γὰρ 21
ἐν Βαβυλῶνί ἐστι μετὰ τοῦ λαοῦ· ᾐχμαλωτεύθησαν γὰρ ὑπὸ
Ναβουχοδονόσορ τοῦ βασιλέως, καὶ μετ᾽ αὐτῶν ἐστιν Ἱερεμίας
εὐαγγελίσασθαι αὐτοῖς καὶ κατηχῆσαι αὐτοὺς τὸν λόγον. Εὐθὺς 22
δὲ ἀκούσας Ἀβιμέλεχ παρὰ τοῦ γηραιοῦ ἀνθρώπου, εἶπεν· Εἰ 23
μὴ ᾖς πρεσβύτης, καὶ ὅτι οὐκ ἐξὸν ἀνθρώπῳ ὑβρίσαι τὸν
μείζονα αὐτοῦ, ἐπικατεγέλων ἄν σοι καὶ ἔλεγον, ὅτι μαίνῃ·
ὅτι εἶπας, Ἠχμαλωτεύθη ὁ λαὸς εἰς Βαβυλῶνα. Εἰ ἦσαν 24
οἱ καταρράκται τοῦ οὐρανοῦ κατελθόντες ἐπ᾽ αὐτούς; οὔπω
ἐστὶ καιρὸς ἀπελθεῖν εἰς Βαβυλῶνα. Πόση γὰρ ὥρα ἐστίν, 25
ἀφ᾽ οὗ ἀπέστειλέ με ὁ πατήρ μου Ἱερεμίας εἰς τὸ χωρίον τοῦ
Ἀγρίππα ἐπὶ ὀλίγα σῦκα, ἵνα δίδωμεν τοῖς νοσοῦσι τοῦ
λαοῦ, καὶ ἀπελθὼν ἤνεγκον αὐτά, καὶ ἐλθὼν ἐπί τι δένδρον 26
τῷ καύματι, ἐκάθισα τοῦ ἀναπαῆναι ὀλίγον, καὶ ἔκλινα τὴν
κεφαλήν μου ἐπὶ τὸν κόφινον, καὶ ἐκοιμήθην, καὶ ἐξυπνισθεὶς

v. 15 πολεως; ab add και ελεγεν· τα μεν σημεια της πολεως εισιν (sic) | ειδως; c ιδων |
απελθη c; απελθειν ab | και απεθηκεν ab aeth; αφηκεν δε c | κοφινον; c adds των συκων;
aeth? | v. 16 εως; c adds αν | v. 17 καθημενου; καθεζομενου c | γηραιον; c γηραον ανου |
ερχ.; c om | λεγει; c ειπεν | Αβιμελεχ ab aeth; c om | σοι; b συ | πρεσβυτα; abc men
πρεσβύτα | αυτω; c om | Ιερουσαλημ; aeth das alte Jerusalem | v. 18 λεγει; c ειπεν |
που; ab και που | εστιν; ab εισιν | ιερευς aeth; ab ιερευς του θεου; c αρχιερευς | ο ανα-
γνωστης; c om; aeth der Levit | v. 19 αυτω ο πρ. c aeth; ο πρ. τω Αβιμελεχ ab | v. 20
μνησθεις; c εμνησθης | μετα τοσ. χρ.; aeth. obgleich du diese ganze Zeit da sassest |
v. 21 υπο; c υπο του | βασιλεως; c adds Βαβυλωνος; aeth von Persien | εστιν Ιερ.; c
απηλθεν | και κατ. αυτους ab (αυτοις b); c aeth om | τον λογον abc; aeth om | v. 23 οτι;
c om | ανθρωπω (aeth); ab ανθρωπω θεου; c ανθρωπων | επικατεγελων αν; κατ. αν de
men; επει καταγελων ab; επικατεγελουν c | σοι c; σου bde men; a om | και ελεγον; a
om | μαινη a aeth; μενει b; μεν c | οτι ειπας; c om | ηχμαλ.; c ηχμαλωτευσον | v. 24
ουπω; c ουπω ουκ | καιρος; c om | απελθειν; c πορευθηναι | v. 25 αφ᾽ ου; c εξοτου | εις
...Αγριππα; c om (not aeth ab) | επι; c ενεγκαι | συκα; ab add ενεγκαι; c aeth om |
ινα διδ...λαου; c τοις νοσουσιν | v. 26 απελθων; c om | ηνεγκον αυτα και ελθων; ab om;
aeth ich bin gegangen und dorthin gelangt und habe genommen was er mir befehlen
hat und habe mich umgewandt, und indem ich ging | τι; c om | εκαθισα...κοφινον (1°);
c om | εκοιμηθην; ab add ολιγον | εξυπνισθεις; c αναστας.

ἀπεκάλυψα τὸν κόφινον τῶν σύκων, νομίζων ὅτι ἐβράδυνα, καὶ
εὗρον τὰ σῦκα στάζοντα γάλα, καθὼς συνέλεξα αὐτά. Σὺ δὲ
27 λέγεις, ὅτι ἠχμαλωτεύθη ὁ λαὸς εἰς Βαβυλῶνα ; "Ινα δὲ γνῷς,
28 λάβε, ἴδε τὰ σῦκα. Καὶ ἀνεκάλυψε τὸν κόφινον τῶν σύκων
29 τῷ γέροντι. Καὶ εἶδεν αὐτὰ στάζοντα γάλα. Ἰδὼν δὲ αὐτὰ
30 ὁ γηραιὸς ἄνθρωπος, εἶπεν· Ὦ υἱέ μου, δίκαιος ἄνθρωπος εἶ σύ,
καὶ οὐκ ἠθέλησεν ὁ Θεὸς δεῖξαί σοι τὴν ἐρήμωσιν τῆς πόλεως.
Ἤνεγκε γὰρ ταύτην τὴν ἔκστασιν ἐπὶ σὲ ὁ Θεός. Ἰδοὺ γὰρ
ἑξήκοντα καὶ ἐξ ἔτη σήμερόν εἰσιν ἀφ' οὗ ἠχμαλωτεύθη ὁ λαὸς
31 εἰς Βαβυλῶνα. Καὶ ἵνα μάθῃς, τέκνον, ὅτι ἀληθές ἐστιν, ἀνά-
βλεψον εἰς τὸν ἀγρὸν καὶ ἴδε, ὅτι ἐφάνη ἡ αὔξησις τῶν γενημά-
των· ἴδε καὶ τὰ σῦκα, ὅτι καιρὸς αὐτῶν οὐκ ἔστι, καὶ γνῶθι.
32 Τότε ἔκραξε μεγάλῃ φωνῇ Ἀβιμέλεχ, λέγων· Εὐλογήσω σε,
Κύριε ὁ Θεὸς τοῦ οὐρανοῦ καὶ τῆς γῆς, ἡ ἀνάπαυσις τῶν ψυχῶν
33 τῶν δικαίων ἐν παντὶ τόπῳ. Καὶ λέγει τῷ γηραιῷ ἀνθρώπῳ·
Ποῖός ἐστιν ὁ μὴν οὗτος ; Ὁ δὲ εἶπε· Νισσάν· *καὶ ἔστιν ἡ
34 δωδεκάτη*. Καὶ ἐπάρας ἐκ τῶν σύκων, ἔδωκε τῷ γηραιῷ ἀνθρώπῳ, καὶ λέγει αὐτῷ· Ὁ Θεὸς φωταγωγήσει σε εἰς τὴν ἄνω
πόλιν Ἰερουσαλήμ.

1 VI. Μετὰ ταῦτα ἐξῆλθεν Ἀβιμέλεχ ἔξω τῆς πόλεως, καὶ
προσηύξατο πρὸς Κύριον. Καὶ ἰδοὺ ἄγγελος Κυρίου ἦλθε,
καὶ ἀπεκατέστησεν αὐτόν, ὅπου ἦν Βαρούχ· εὗρε δὲ αὐτὸν ἐν
2 μνημείῳ καθεζόμενον. Καὶ ἐν τῷ θεωρῆσαι ἀλλήλους, ἔκλαυσαν

v. 26 απεκαλυψα; c ανεκαλυψα | εβραδυνα; c εχρονησα | τα συκα; c αυτα; (aeth?) |
συνελεξα; c ανελεξαμην | ηχμ. ὁ λαος; c ηχμαλωτευθησαν | v. 30 δικαιος...συ c (aeth); ab
δικαιου αυοῦ υιος ει συ | δειξαι σοι c aeth; ab ιδειν σε | πολεως; ab add ταυτης; not c aeth |
γαρ (1°); c om | ὁ θεος; c om | σημερον εισιν c (aeth); ab om | ηχμ. ὁ λαος; c αιχμα-
λωτευθησαν | v. 31 τεκνον; c om | αληθες εστιν; ab αληθη εισιν απερ λεγω σοι | οτι...
γνωθι aeth, ab (οτι ουκ) (a γεννηματων); c οτι ουκ εστι καιρος των συκων | fin aeth adds
und er erkannte dass die Zeit von alle diesen nicht war | v. 32 τοτε; c και | Αβιμελεχ;
c om | ευλογησω; c ευλογω | κυριε ὁ θεος; ab ὁ θεος; c κυριε; aeth O Herr mein Gott,
Gott | των ψυχων; c om | τοπω ab aeth; c καιρω | v. 33 και λεγει τω γηραιω αυῶ; c το
φως το αληθινον· ἡ αληθινη ανταποδοσις, ὁ ων μεγας, θαυμαστος εις τους αιωνας αμην.
τοτε λεγει τω γη. αν. | Νισσαν και ε. δωδ.; ab Νισσαν· ὁ εστι δωδεκατος; c Ισαακ εστιν
ὁ μην ουτος; aeth der zwölfte des Monats Nisan welcher Mijazja ist. The Ethiopic
text must be right: for Nisan is not the twelfth month, either in civil or ecclesiastical reckoning. A reference to Ezra viii. 15 will shew the passage on which
our writer works: "we departed from the river of Ahava on the twelfth day of
the first month to go unto Jerusalem": the 12th of Nisan is here meant, the return
commencing in Nisan, in order that Jerusalem may be reached in Ab: cf. Ezra pas-
sim. Or can it be Νισσαν ὁ εστιν Αβιβ? v. 34 και επαρας; c ουτος αρας ουν | και
λεγει; c ειπων | εις; ab επι.

VI. 1 προσηυξατο; c ηυξατο | ηλθε και; ab add κρατησας αυτου της δεξιας χειρος |
αυτον; ab add εις τον τοπον | Βαρουχ; ab add καθεζομενος | ευρε δε; c και ευρε | καθε-
ζομενον; ab om | v. 2 εκλ. αμφ. b (aeth); a om; c εκλαυσαν.

ἀμφότεροι καὶ κατεφίλησαν ἀλλήλους. Ἀναβλέψας δὲ Βαρούχ, εἶδε τὰ σῦκα ἐσκεπασμένα ἐν τῷ κοφίνῳ· καὶ ἄρας τοὺς ὀφθαλμοὺς αὐτοῦ εἰς τὸν οὐρανὸν, προσηύξατο λέγων· Ἔστι Θεὸς ὁ παρέχων μισθαποδοσίαν τοῖς ἁγίοις αὐτοῦ. Ἑτοίμασον 3 σεαυτὴν, ἡ καρδία μου, καὶ εὐφραίνου, καὶ ἀγάλλου ἐν τῷ

r. v. 1. σκηνώματί σου, λέγω τῷ σαρκικῷ οἴκῳ σου· τὸ πένθος σου γὰρ μετεστράφη εἰς χαράν. Ἔρχεται γὰρ ὁ ἱκανὸς, καὶ ἀρεῖ σε ἐκ τοῦ σκηνώματός σου. Οὐ γὰρ γέγονέ σοι ἁμαρτία. Ἀνάψυξον ἡ παρθενική μου πίστις, καὶ πίστευσον ὅτι ζήσεις. 4 Ἐπίβλεψον ἐπὶ τὸν κόφινον τοῦτον τῶν σύκων· ἰδοὺ γὰρ ἐξη- 5 κονταὲξ ἔτη ἐποίησαν, καὶ οὐκ ἐμαράνθησαν, οὐδὲ ὤζεσαν, ἀλλὰ στάζουσι τοῦ γάλακτος. Οὕτως γίνεταί σοι ἡ σάρξ μου, ἐὰν 6 ποιήσῃς τὰ προσταχθέντα σου ὑπὸ τοῦ ἀγγέλου τῆς δικαιο- σύνης. Ὁ φυλάξας τὸν κόφινον τῶν σύκων, αὐτὸς πάλιν 7 φυλάξει σε ἐν τῇ δυνάμει αὐτοῦ. Ταῦτα εἰπὼν ὁ Βαρούχ, 8 λέγει τῷ Ἀβιμέλεχ· Ἀνάστηθι, καὶ εὐξώμεθα, ἵνα γνωρίσῃ ἡμῖν ὁ Κύριος τὸ, πῶς δυνησώμεθα ἀποστεῖλαι τὴν φάσιν τῷ Ἱερεμίᾳ εἰς Βαβυλῶνα διὰ τὴν γενομένην σοι σκέπην. Καὶ 9 ηὔξατο Βαρούχ, λέγων· Ἡ δύναμις ἡμῶν, ὁ Θεὸς ἡμῶν Κύριε, τὸ ἐκλεκτὸν φῶς, τὸ ἐξελθὸν ἐκ στόματος αὐτοῦ, παρακαλῶ καὶ δέομαί σου τῆς ἀγαθότητος· τὸ μέγα ὄνομα, ὃ οὐδεὶς δύναται γνῶναι· ἄκουσον τῆς φωνῆς τοῦ δούλου σου, καὶ γενοῦ γνῶσις 10 ἐν τῇ καρδίᾳ μου. Τί θέλεις ποιήσωμεν; πῶς ἀποστείλω πρὸς

v. 2 αλληλους (2°); b repeats εν τω θεωρ. αλλ. | αναβλεψας; aeth om | δε; ab om | Βαρουχ; ab add τοις οφθαλμοις αυτου (b τους οφθ. α.) | κοφινω; ab add του Αβιμελεχ (not c aeth) | αρας ab; c (aeth) επηρεν | προσηυξατο λεγων ab (aeth); c ειπεν | εστιν ab; εις εστιν o c; gross ist Gott aeth | αγιοις αυτου c (aeth seinen Gerechten); ab τοις αγαπωσι σε | v. 3 η; c om | αγαλλου ab; c αγαλλιασον | εν; c aeth λεγων | λεγω; c aeth om | οικω σου; c τω οικω σου αγιω | μετεστραφη; c μεταστραφητω; aeth μεταστραφησεται | γαρ (2°); c om | αρει; c ερει | εκ τ. σκη; c. εν τω σκηνωματι; aeth und wird dich in deinen Körper zurückkehren lassen | γεγονε; c εγενετο εν; aeth omits clause | v. 4 ab αναψυξον εν τω σκηνωματι σου, εν τη παρθενικη σου ποιμνη; c αναστηθι αναστρεψον εις το ιδιον σου η παρθενικη μου πιστις; aeth schaue auf deine Jungfräulichkeit des Glaubens | οτι; c και | v. 5 τουτον ab (aeth); c om | v. 6 προσταχθεντα σου ab (aeth deinen Befehl); c προστεταχθεντα (!) σοι | v. 8 λεγει τω Αβ.; c ειπεν ο Αβ.; cf aeth, antwortete Abimelech und sagte zu ihm | το; c om | δυνησωμεθα ab; c δυναμεθα | φασιν; c adds ταυτην (not aeth) | δια...σκεπην; ab δια την σκεπην την γενομενην σοι εν τη οδω; c δια την σκεπην σου; aeth die Beschützung mit der du mich bedeckt hast | v. 9 Βαρουχ; ab add και Αβιμελεχ | λεγων; ab λεγοντες | η δυναμις ημων ο θς ημων κε ab; ο θς κς η δυναμις μου c aeth (meine Kraft ist Gott, der Herr) | εκλεκτον; aeth om | εκ; c εκ του | παρακαλω και δεομαι c aeth; ab παρακαλουμεν και δεομεθα | της αγ.; c την αγαθοτητα | ονομα; ab add σου | γνωναι; c add αυτω | v. 10 του δουλου c aeth; ab των δουλων | μου c aeth; ab ημων | τι θε. ποιησ.; ab τι ποιησωμεν; c εως αν το (sic) θελω ποιησω; aeth (?) | πως αποστ.; ab πως αποστειλωμεν; c εως αν αποστειλω; aeth und ich schicke.

11 Ἰερεμίαν εἰς Βαβυλῶνα; Ἔτι δὲ προσευχομένου τοῦ Βαρούχ,
12 ἰδοὺ ἄγγελος Κυρίου ἦλθε, καὶ λέγει τῷ Βαρούχ· Βαρούχ, ὁ
σύμβουλος τοῦ φωτός, Μὴ μεριμνήσῃς τὸ, πῶς ἀποστείλῃς πρὸς Ἰερεμίαν· ἔρχεται γὰρ πρός σε ὥρᾳ τοῦ φωτὸς
13 αὔριον ἀετὸς, καὶ σὺ ἐπισκέψῃ πρὸς Ἰερεμίαν. Γράψον οὖν
ἐν τῇ ἐπιστολῇ ὅτι, Λάλησον τοῖς υἱοῖς· Ἰσραήλ· Ὁ γενόμενος
ἐν ὑμῖν ξένος, ἀφορισθήτω, καὶ ποιήσωσι ιε΄ ἡμέρας· καὶ μετὰ
14 ταῦτα εἰσάξω ὑμᾶς εἰς τὴν πόλιν ὑμῶν, λέγει Κύριος. Ὁ μὴ
ἀφοριζόμενος ἐκ τῆς Βαβυλῶνος, ᾦ Ἰερεμία, οὐ μὴ εἰσέλθῃ εἰς τὴν
πόλιν· καὶ ἐπιτιμῶ αὐτοῖς, τοῦ μὴ ἀποδεχθῆναι αὐτοὺς αὖθις ὑπὸ
15 τῶν Βαβυλωνιτῶν, λέγει Κύριος. Καὶ ταῦτα εἰπὼν ὁ ἄγγελος,
16 ἀπῆλθεν ἀπὸ τοῦ Βαρούχ. Ὁ δὲ Βαροὺχ ἀποστείλας εἰς τὴν
ἀγορὰν τῶν ἐθνῶν, ἤνεγκε χάρτην καὶ μέλανα, καὶ ἔγραψεν
17 ἐπιστολὴν περιέχουσαν οὕτως· Βαροὺχ ὁ δοῦλος τοῦ Θεοῦ γράφει
τῷ Ἰερεμίᾳ· Ὁ ἐν τῇ αἰχμαλωσίᾳ τῆς Βαβυλῶνος, χαῖρε καὶ
ἀγαλλιῶ, ὅτι ὁ Θεὸς οὐκ ἀφῆκεν ἡμᾶς ἐξελθεῖν ἐκ τοῦ σώματος
τούτου λυπουμένους διὰ τὴν πόλιν τὴν ἐρημωθεῖσαν καὶ ὑβρι-
18 σθεῖσαν. Διὰ τοῦτο ἐσπλαγχνίσθη ὁ Κύριος ἐπὶ τῶν δακρύων
ἡμῶν, καὶ ἐμνήσθη τῆς διαθήκης, ἧς ἔστησε μετὰ τῶν πατέρων
19 ἡμῶν Ἀβραὰμ, καὶ Ἰσαὰκ, καὶ Ἰακώβ. Ἀπέστειλε γὰρ πρός
με τὸν ἄγγελον αὐτοῦ, καὶ εἶπέ μοι τοὺς λόγους τούτους, οὓς
20 ἀπέστειλα πρός σε. Οὗτοι οὖν εἰσὶν οἱ λόγοι, οὓς εἶπε Κύριος
ὁ Θεὸς Ἰσραὴλ, ὁ ἐξαγαγὼν ἡμᾶς ἐκ γῆς Αἰγύπτου, ἐκ τῆς
21 μεγάλης καμίνου· Ὅτι οὐκ ἐφυλάξατε τὰ δικαιώματά μου,
ἀλλὰ ὑψώθη ἡ καρδία ὑμῶν, καὶ ἐτραχηλιάσατε ἐνώπιόν μου,
ἐθυμώθην καὶ ἐν ὀργῇ παρέδωκα ὑμᾶς τῇ καμίνῳ εἰς Βαβυλῶνα.
22 Ἐὰν οὖν ἀκούσητε τῆς φωνῆς μου, λέγει Κύριος, ἐκ στόματος
Ἰερεμίου τοῦ παιδός μου, ὁ ἀκούων, ἀναφέρω αὐτὸν ἐκ τῆς Βαβυλῶνος, ὁ δὲ μὴ ἀκούων, ξένος γενήσεται τῆς Ἰερουσαλὴμ καὶ

---

v. 10 Βαβυλωνα; *ab* add την φασιν ταυτην | *v.* 11 Βαρουχ (1°); *ab* add και του Αβι-
μελεχ | ηλθε; *c* om | λεγει; *c* ειπεν | Βαρουχ; *ab* add απαντας τους λογους τουτους |
v. 12 Βαρουχ *c aeth*; *ab* om | φωτος; *ab* add λεγει | μεριμνησης *c aeth*; *ab* μεριμνη-
σητε | αποστειλης *c aeth*; *ab* αποστειλητε | γαρ; *c* om | προς; *c* τον | *v.* 13 λαλησον; *c*
ειπατε | ο; *c* οτι | ξενος; *c* εξ ενος | *v.* 14 ω Ιερ.; *ab* om | επιτιμω *a*; *bc* επετιμων | αυ-
τους *c*; *ab* om | υπο; *ab* om | *v.* 15 και; *c* om | απηλθεν; *c* ανεχωρησεν | *v.* 16 *ab*
αποστειλας δε εις την διασποραν των εθνων ηνεγκεν χαρτην και μελανα και εγραψεν
επιστολην περιεχουσαν ουτως; *c* ο δε Βαρουχ απεστειλεν εις την αγωραν των εθνων και
ηνεγκεν χαρτην και μελαν και εγρ. επ. λεγων οτι; *aeth und Baruch geleitete ihn bis zur
Strasse und holte Papier und Tinte und schrieb folgendermassen* | *v.* 17 ο (2°); *c* om;
aeth τω | αγαλλιω *a*; αγαλλιου *b*; αγαλλιασον *c* | *v.* 19 απεστειλα *ab aeth*; αποστειλω
c | *v.* 20 εκ (2°); *c* om | *v.* 21 εθυμωθην *c*; om *ab aeth* | εν οργη και θυμω *ab*; *c aeth*
om | *v.* 22 ουν; *c* om | αναφερω *c* (*aeth*); αφορισω *ab* | της Βαβ.; του λακκου της Βαβ.
c | γενησεται; *a* γενηται; *c* γινεται | και της Βαβ.; *ab* om; *aeth und sie werden nicht*

τῆς Βαβυλῶνος. Δοκιμάσεις δὲ αὐτοὺς ἐκ τοῦ ὕδατος τοῦ 23
Ἰορδάνου· ὁ μὴ ἀκούων φανερὸς γενήσεται· τοῦτο τὸ σημεῖόν
ἐστι τῆς μεγάλης σφραγῖδος. •VII. Καὶ ἀνέστη Βαρούχ, καὶ ἐξῆλθεν ἐκ τοῦ μνημείου. 1
Καὶ ἀποκριθεὶς ἀνθρωπίνῃ φωνῇ ὁ ἀετὸς, εἶπε· Χαῖρε, Βαρούχ, 2
ὁ οἰκονόμος τῆς πίστεως. Καὶ εἶπεν αὐτῷ Βαρούχ ὅτι, Ἐκλεκ- 3
τός εἰ σὺ ὁ λαλῶν, ἐκ πάντων τῶν πετεινῶν τοῦ οὐρανοῦ· ἐκ
τῆς γὰρ αὐγῆς τῶν ὀφθαλμῶν δῆλόν ἐστι. Δεῖξόν μοι οὖν, τί 4
ποιεῖς ἐνταῦθα; Καὶ εἶπεν αὐτῷ ὁ ἀετός· Ἀπεστάλην ὧδε, ὅπως 5
πᾶσαν φάσιν ἣν θέλεις, ἀποστείλῃς δι' ἐμοῦ. Καὶ εἶπεν αὐτῷ 6
Βαρούχ· Εἰ δύνασαι σὺ ἐπᾶραι τὴν φάσιν ταύτην τῷ Ἰερεμίᾳ
εἰς Βαβυλῶνα; Καὶ εἶπεν αὐτῷ ὁ ἀετός· Εἰς τοῦτο γὰρ καὶ 7
ἀπεστάλην. Καὶ ἄρας Βαρούχ τὴν ἐπιστολὴν, καὶ δεκαπέντε 8
σῦκα ἐκ τοῦ κοφίνου τοῦ Ἀβιμέλεχ, ἔδησεν εἰς τὸν τράχηλον
τοῦ ἀετοῦ, καὶ εἶπεν αὐτῷ· Σοὶ λέγω, βασιλεῦ τῶν πετεινῶν, 9
ἄπελθε ἐν εἰρήνῃ μεθ' ὑγείας, καὶ τὴν φάσιν ἔνεγκόν μοι. Μὴ 10
ὁμοιωθῇς τῷ κόρακι, ὃν ἐξαπέστειλε Νῶε, καὶ οὐκ ἀπεστράφη
ἔτι πρὸς αὐτὸν εἰς τὴν κιβωτόν· ἀλλὰ ὁμοιώθητι τῇ περιστερᾷ,
ἥτις ἐκ τρίτου φάσιν ἤνεγκε τῷ δικαίῳ· οὕτω καὶ σὺ, ἆρον τὴν 11
καλὴν φάσιν ταύτην τῷ Ἰερεμίᾳ καὶ τοῖς σὺν αὐτῷ, ἵνα εὖ σοι
γένηται, ἆρον τὸν χάρτην τοῦτον τῷ λαῷ τῷ ἐκλεκτῷ τοῦ Θεοῦ.
Ἐὰν κυκλώσωσί σε πάντα τὰ πετεινὰ τοῦ οὐρανοῦ, καὶ πάντες 12
οἱ ἐχθροὶ τῆς ἀληθείας βουλόμενοι πολεμῆσαι μετὰ σοῦ, ἀγώνι-
σαι· ὁ Κύριος δώῃ σοι δύναμιν. Καὶ μὴ ἐκκλίνῃς εἰς τὰ δεξιὰ,
μήτε εἰς τὰ ἀριστερὰ, ἀλλ' ὡς βέλος ὕπαγον ὀρθῶς, οὕτως ἄπελθε
ἐν τῇ δυνάμει τοῦ Θεοῦ. Τότε ὁ ἀετὸς ἐπετάσθη, ἔχων τὴν 13

v. 23 δοκιμασω a; δοκιμασει b; δοκιμασης c (aeth) | γενησεται; c γινεται | το; ab om.

VII. 2 Text with ab aeth; c και ευρεν τον αετον καθεζομενον εκτος του μνημιου
και ειπεν αυτω ο αετος | πιστεως ab aeth; πολεως c | v. 3 αυτω; c om | συ ο; c
om | v. 4 ουν; c om | ειπεν αυτω; ab om αυτω | v. 5 απ. ab aeth; c ο θ͞ς απεστειλεν
με | ωδε; ab add προς σε | πα. φα.; c προς πα. φα. | δι' εμου; c με | v. 6 ειπεν;
c λεγει | δυνασαι συ a | δυνη συ b; δυνηση c | επαραι; c αραι | ειπεν; c λεγει | v. 7 εις;
εγω εις ab | γαρ και; ab om | v. 8 αυτω; c om | v. 9 βασιλευ; c ο βασιλευς | πετεινων;
c ορνεων | ενεγκον c; ενεγκαι ab | v. 10 ετι προς αυτον; ab om (not c aeth) | v. 11 τοις συν
αυτω; c τοις δεσμιοις αυτου; aeth. die welcher von Israel bei ihm sind | τον χαρτην
τουτον; sic ab; c aeth ταυτην την χαραν (aeth diese Freudenbotschaft | εκλεκτω;
c και τω εκλεκτω | v. 12 κυκλωσωσι; ab κυκλωσουσι | παντες...αληθειας c aeth; ab
om | βουλομενοι; ab βουλωνται | δωη ab aeth; δωση c | εις τα δεξια ac; δεξια b | μητε εις
τα; ab η | υπαγον ορθως; a υπαγων ορ.; c υπαγων | ουτως; c aeth om | απελθε; c
υπαγε | end of verse; ab add και εσται η δοξα κ͞υ εν παση τη οδω η πορευση (not
c aeth).

ἐπιστολήν, καὶ ἀπῆλθεν εἰς Βαβυλῶνα, καὶ ἀνεπαύσατο ἐπί τι
ξύλον ἔξω τῆς πόλεως εἰς τόπον ἔρημον· ἐσιώπησε δὲ ἕως οὗ
14 διῆλθεν Ἱερεμίας, αὐτὸς καὶ ἄλλοι τινὲς τοῦ λαοῦ· ἐξήρχοντο
γὰρ θάψαι νεκρόν· καὶ γὰρ ᾐτήσατο Ἱερεμίας παρὰ τοῦ Ναβουχοδονόσορ, λέγων· Δός μοι τόπον, ποῦ θάψω τοὺς νεκροὺς τοῦ
15 λαοῦ μου. Καὶ ἔδωκεν αὐτῷ. Ἀπερχομένων δὲ αὐτῶν καὶ
κλαιόντων μετὰ τοῦ νεκροῦ, ἦλθον κατέναντι τοῦ ἀετοῦ· καὶ
ἔκραξεν ὁ ἀετός, λέγων· Σοὶ λέγω, Ἱερεμία ὁ ἐκλεκτὸς τοῦ Θεοῦ,
ἄπελθε, σύναξον τὸν λαὸν ἅπαντα, καὶ ἔλθωσιν ὧδε, ἵνα ἀκού-
σωσι τοῦ καλοῦ κηρύγματος, ὃ ἤνεγκά σοι ἀπὸ τοῦ Βαρούχ καὶ
16 τοῦ Ἀβιμέλεχ. Ἀκούσας δὲ ὁ Ἱερεμίας, ἐδόξασε τὸν Θεόν·
καὶ ἀπελθὼν συνῆξε τὸν λαὸν σὺν γυναιξὶ καὶ τέκνοις, καὶ
17 ἦλθεν ὅπου ὁ ἀετός. Καὶ κατῆλθεν ὁ ἀετὸς ἐπὶ τὸν τεθνηκότα,
18 καὶ ἀνέζησε· γέγονε δὲ τοῦτο, ἵνα πιστεύσωσιν. Ἐθαύμασε δὲ
πᾶς ὁ λαὸς ἐπὶ τῷ γεγονότι, λέγοντες ὅτι, Μὴ οὗτος ἔστι ὁ Θεὸς
ὁ ὀφθεὶς τοῖς πατράσιν ἡμῶν ἐν τῇ ἐρήμῳ διὰ Μωϋσέως, καὶ
ἐποίησεν ἑαυτὸν ἐν σχήματι ἀετοῦ καὶ ἐφάνη ἡμῖν διὰ τοῦ
19 μεγάλου ἀετοῦ τούτου; Καὶ εἶπεν ὁ ἀετὸς τῷ Ἱερεμίᾳ, Δεῦρο
λῦσον τὴν ἐπιστολὴν ταύτην, καὶ ἀνάγνωθι αὐτὴν τῷ λαῷ.
20 Λύσας οὖν τὴν ἐπιστολήν, ἀνέγνω τῷ λαῷ. Ἀκούσας οὖν ὁ λαός,
ἔκλαυσαν, καὶ ἐπέθηκαν χοῦν ἐπὶ τὴν κεφαλὴν αὐτῶν· καὶ ἔλε-
21 γον τῷ Ἱερεμίᾳ· Σῶσον ἡμᾶς καὶ ἀπάγγειλον ἡμῖν, τί ποιήσω-
22 μεν, ἵνα εἰσέλθωμεν πάλιν εἰς τὴν πόλιν ἡμῶν; Ἀποκριθεὶς δὲ
Ἱερεμίας εἶπεν αὐτοῖς· Πάντα ὅσα ἐκ τῆς ἐπιστολῆς ἠκούσατε,

v. 13 επιστολην; c adds εν τω τραχηλω αυτου | ανεπαυσατο c aeth; ελθων ανε-
παυσατο ab | τι ξυλον ab; c στυλου; aeth auf einer Säule and explains the τόπος
ἔρημος as eine Stelle des unbebauten Landes | ου διηλθεν; c αν παρελθη | αυτος κτε;
ab αυτος γαρ και ο λαος εξηρχοντο; c αυτος γαρ και αλλοι τινες του λαου· απηρχοντο
γαρ | v. 14 νεκρον; ab add εξω της πολεως | και γαρ ητ.; c ητ. γαρ | του Ναβουχ.; ab
του βασιλεως Ναβ. (not c aeth) | που c aeth; ab οπως | αυτω; ab add ο βασιλευς |.
v. 15 κατεναντι; c εναντιον | σοι λεγω ab aeth; c om | απαντα c aeth; ab om |
ελθωσιν ωδε; ab ελθε εντανθα; aeth (?) es soll hieher kommen | του κ. κηρ. ο ην.
aeth; c τ. κ. κη. του θῦ ο ην.; ab επιστολης ης ηνεγκα | του Βαρ. και του Αβ.; c Βαρ.
και Αβ. | v. 17 και κατηλθεν ο αετος; c om (ὁμοιοτ.) | ανεζησε; ab add και ανεστη | γεγονε
δε τουτο ab | τουτο δε εγενετο c; aeth und dieses that er | v. 18 μη...θς c; ab εστιν θς;
aeth vielleicht ist dies der Gott | και εποιησεν...τουτου c (aeth); ab και νυν εφανη
ημιν δια του αετου τουτου | v. 19 τω Ιερ.; ab σοι λεγω Ιερ. | αυτην τω λαω c aeth; ab εις
τα ωτα του λαου | ανεγνω; c adds αυτην (not aeth) | v. 20 ακουσας ουν c (? aeth);
ab ακουσαντες δε πας | εκλαυσαν ab aeth; εκλαυσεν c | επεθηκαν ab aeth; επεθηκεν
c | την κεφαλ. αυτων aeth; ab τας κεφαλας αυτων; c την κεφαλην αυτου | v. 21 σωσον
ημας και c aeth (rette uns!); ab om | ινα; c πως | παλιν; c om | v. 22 αποκρ. δε Ιερ.
ειπεν αυτοις c; ab και ειπεν προς αυτους; aeth und Jeremias erhob sich und sagte zu
ihnen | εκ της επιστολης; ab om (not c aeth) | ηκουσατε; c om.

φυλάξατε· καὶ εἰσάξει ἡμᾶς εἰς τὴν πόλιν ἡμῶν. Ἔγραψε δὲ καὶ 23
ἐπιστολὴν ὁ Ἰερεμίας πρὸς Βαρούχ, οὕτως λέγων· Υἱέ μου ἀγα-
πητέ, μὴ ἀμελήσῃς ἐν ταῖς προσευχαῖς σου δεόμενος ὑπὲρ ἡμῶν
ὅπως κατευοδεύσῃ τὴν ὁδὸν ἡμῶν, ἄχρις ἂν ἐξέλθωμεν ἐκ τῶν
προσταγμάτων τοῦ ἀνόμου βασιλέως τούτου· δίκαιος γὰρ εὑρέ-
θης ἐνάντιον αὐτοῦ καὶ οὐκ ἔασέν σε εἰσελθεῖν ἐνταῦθα μεθ'
ἡμῶν, ὅπως μὴ ἴδῃς τὴν κάκωσιν τὴν γενομένην τῷ λαῷ ὑπὸ τῶν
Βαβυλωνίων· ὥσπερ γὰρ πατήρ, υἱὸν μονογενῆ ἔχων, τούτου δὲ 24
παραδοθέντος εἰς τιμωρίαν· οἱ οὖν ἰδόντες τὸν πατέρα αὐτοῦ,
καὶ παραμυθούμενοι αὐτόν, σκέπουσιν τὸ πρόσωπον αὐτοῦ, ἵνα
μὴ ἴδῃ πῶς τιμωρεῖται αὐτὸς ὁ υἱὸς καὶ πλείονα φθαρῇ ἀπὸ τῆς
λύπης· οὕτως γάρ σε ἐλέησεν ὁ Θεὸς καὶ οὐκ ἔασέν σε ἐλθεῖν εἰς
Βαβυλῶνα· ἵνα μὴ ἴδῃς τὴν κάκωσιν τοῦ λαοῦ· ἀφ' ἧς γὰρ
εἰσήλθομεν εἰς τὴν πόλιν ταύτην, οὐκ ἐπαύσατο ἡ λύπη ἀφ'
ἡμῶν, ἐξήκοντα καὶ ἐξ ἔτη σήμερον. Πολλάκις γὰρ ἐξερχόμε- 25
νος ηὕρισκον ἐκ τοῦ λαοῦ κρεμαμένους ὑπὸ Ναβουχοδονόσορ
βασιλέως, κλαίοντας καὶ λέγοντας, Ἐλέησον ἡμᾶς, ὁ θεὸς Ζάρ.
Ἀκούων ταῦτα, ἐλυπούμην καὶ ἔκλαιον δισσὸν κλαυθμόν· οὐ 26
μόνον ὅτι ἐκρέμαντο, ἀλλ' ὅτι ἐπεκαλοῦντο θεὸν ἀλλότριον· λέγοντες, Ἐλέησον ἡμᾶς. Ἐμνημόνευον δὲ ἡμέρας ἑορτῆς ἃς ἐποιοῦ-
μεν ἐν Ἰερουσαλήμ· πρὸ τοῦ ἡμᾶς αἰχμαλωτευθῆναι. Καὶ μνησ- 27
κόμενος ἐστέναζον, καὶ ἐπέστρεφον εἰς τὸν οἶκόν μου ὀδυνώμενος
καὶ κλαίων. Νῦν οὖν δεήθητι, εἰς τὸν τόπον ὅπου εἶ, σὺ καὶ Ἀβιμέ- 28
λεχ, ὑπὲρ τοῦ λαοῦ τούτου, ὅπως εἰσακούσωσιν τῆς φωνῆς μου
καὶ τῶν κριμάτων τοῦ στόματός μου καὶ ἐξέλθωμεν ἐντεῦθεν.
Λέγω γάρ σοι, ὅτι ὅλον τὸν χρόνον ὃν ἐποιήσαμεν ἐνταῦθα, 29

---

v. 22 ημας; ab add Κυριος; not c aeth | for vv. 23...26; the text of ab is very
confused and varies a good deal from that which we have adopted from c aeth;
it runs as follows: ἔγραψε δὲ Ἰερεμιας ἐπιστολην εἰς Ἰερουσαλημ προς Βαρουχ και
Ἀβιμελεχ ἐνωπιον παντος του λαου, τας θλιψεις τας (b om) γινομενας εἰς αὐτους το
πως παρεληφθησαν· ὑπο του βασιλεως των χαλδαιων· και το πως ἑκαστος τον πατερα
αὐτου ἐθεωρει δεσμενομενον και πατηρ τεκνον παραδοθεν (b παραδοθεντα) εἰς τιμω-
ριαν· οἱ δε θελοντες παραμυθησασθαι τον πατερα αὐτου ἐσκεπον το προσωπον αὐτου
ἱνα μη ἰδη τον υἱον αὐτου τιμωρουμενον· και ὁ θεος ἐσκεπασεν σε και Ἀβιμελεχ· ἱνα
μη ἰδηται ἡμας τιμωρουμενους | v. 23 κατευοδευση; c κατευοδοση | δικαιος γαρ ευρεθης; c
δικαιοι γαρ ευρεθησαν; aeth du aber hast Gerechtigkeit vor Gott gefunden | μεθ' ημων
aeth; c om | v. 24 φθαρη; c φθαρει | ουτως; c ουτος | εἰς την πολιν ταυτην aeth;
ενταυθα c | v. 25 κρεμαμενους; c κρεμμαμενους | Ζάρ (= Heb צר, αλλοτριος); c Σαβαωθ |
mss aeth Zar, Sorot, Sarot | v. 27 οδυνωμενος (c) aeth; οδυρομενος ab | v. 28 νυν ουν
δεη. c aeth; ab δεηθητι ουν | εἰς τον τοπον οπου ει c aeth (wo ihr seid); ab om | εἰσα-
κουσωσιν...στοματος μου c aeth; ab εἰσακουσθη η δεησις υμων | κριματων; aeth ρηματων
(das Wort) | και εξ. εν. ab: c εξελθωσιν ενταυθα | v. 29 ολον; ab om (not c aeth).

κατέχουσιν ἡμᾶς λέγοντες ὅτι, Εἴπατε ἡμῖν ᾠδὴν ἐκ τῶν
ᾠδῶν Σιὼν, καὶ τὴν ᾠδὴν τοῦ Θεοῦ ὑμῶν. Καὶ ἀντελέγο-
30 μεν αὐτοῖς, Πῶς ᾄσωμεν ὑμῖν ἐπὶ γῆς ἀλλοτρίας ὄντες; Καὶ
μετὰ ταῦτα ἔδησε τὴν ἐπιστολὴν εἰς τὸν τράχηλον τοῦ ἀετοῦ,
λέγων, Ἄπελθε ἐν εἰρήνῃ, ἐπισκέψηται Κύριος ἀμφοτέρους.
31 Καὶ ἐπετάσθη ὁ ἀετὸς, καὶ ἤνεγκεν τὴν ἐπιστολὴν καὶ ἔδωκε
τῷ Βαρούχ. Καὶ λύσας ἀνέγνω, καὶ κατεφίλησεν αὐτὴν,
καὶ ἔκλαυσε ἀκούσας διὰ τὰς λύπας καὶ τὰς κακώσεις τοῦ
32 λαοῦ. Ἱερεμίας δὲ ἄρας τὰ σῦκα, διέδωκε τοῖς νοσοῦσι τοῦ
λαοῦ. Καὶ ἔμεινε διδάσκων αὐτοὺς τοῦ ἀπέχεσθαι ἐκ τῶν
ἀλισγημάτων τῶν ἐθνῶν τῆς Βαβυλῶνος.
1 VIII. Ἐγένετο δὲ ἡ ἡμέρα, ἐν ᾗ ἐξέφερε ὁ Θεὸς τὸν λαὸν
2 ἐκ Βαβυλῶνος· καὶ εἶπεν ὁ Κύριος πρὸς Ἱερεμίαν Ἀνάστηθι,
σὺ καὶ ὁ λαὸς, καὶ δεῦτε ἐπὶ τὸν Ἰορδάνην, καὶ ἐρεῖς τῷ λαῷ,
Ὁ θέλων τὸν Κύριον καταλειψάτω τὰ ἔργα τῆς Βαβυλῶνος,
καὶ τοὺς ἄρρενας τοὺς λαβόντας ἐξ αὐτῶν γυναῖκας, καὶ τὰς
3 γυναῖκας τὰς λαβούσας ἐξ αὐτῶν ἄνδρας. Καὶ διαπεράσωσιν
οἱ ἀκούοντές σου, καὶ ἆρον αὐτοὺς εἰς Ἱερουσαλήμ· τοὺς δὲ μὴ
4 ἀκούοντάς σου, μὴ εἰσαγάγῃς αὐτοὺς εἰς αὐτήν. Ἱερεμίας δὲ ἐλάλησεν αὐτοῖς τὰ ῥήματα ταῦτα· καὶ ἀναστάντες ἦλθον ἐπὶ τὸν
Ἰορδάνην τοῦ περᾶσαι, λέγων αὐτοῖς τὰ ῥήματα, ἃ εἶπε Κύριος
πρὸς αὐτόν. Καὶ τὸ ἥμισυ τῶν γαμησάντων ἐξ αὐτῶν οὐκ ἠθέ-

v. 29 κατ. ημ. c aeth; ab ελεγον | και την; aeth καινην (sagt uns einen neuen
Gesang) | υμων; b ημων | αντελεγομεν ab; λεγωμεν c (? aeth) | ὑμιν c aeth; ab την ᾠδην
κυριου | v. 30 αετου; ab add Ιερεμιας | κυριος αμφοτερους ab; c υμας αμφοτ. ο κ̅ς̅ | v. 31
επετασθη ab aeth; c om | αετος; ab add και ηλθεν εις (b om) Ιερουσαλημ | και ην...
Βαρουχ c, adding ο αετος after ηνεγκεν; ab και εδωκε την επιστολην Βαρουχ; aeth και
ηνεγκε την επιστολην τω Βαρουχ | εκλαυσε ab aeth; c εμεινε κλαιων | του λαου ab aeth;
c αυτων | v. 32 διεδωκε ab; εδωκε c (?aeth) | διδασκων; c ενδιδασκων (sic) | αλισγηματων
ab (a αλγηματων); c πραγματων; aeth das Thun und Treiben.
VIII. 1 ο θεος c aeth; ab κυριος | λαον; ab add αυτου (not c aeth) | προς Ιερεμιαν
ab; τω Ιερεμια c | end of verse ab add λεγων | v. 2 επι τον; a προς τον | τα εργα;
c aeth add των εθνων (from vii. 32) | λαβοντας ab; c (aeth) γαμησαντας | λαβουσας ab;
c (? aeth) γαμησαντας (sic) | v. 3 διαπερασωσιν ab; περασωσιν c | σου; b σοι | τους δε
μη ακουοντας ab; οι δε μη ακουοντες c | εισαγαγης ab; ενεγκης c | εις αυτην c aeth; εκει
ab | v. 4 αυτοις c aeth; ab προς τον λαον | ανασταντες ηλθον ab; ηνεγκεν αυτους c;
aeth (?) | κυριος προς αυτον; c αυτω ο Κυριος | και το ημισυ; at this point the text of c
abruptly drops from its level of excellence, and the manuscript ends with trivial
matter chiefly taken from the Septuagint; perhaps his copy was imperfect after the
word γαμησαντων; at all events his text proceeds as follows: και το ημισυ των γαμησαντων εξ αυτων αρω και στησω αυτοις διαθηκην αιωνιον του ειναι με αυτοις εις θεον· και
αυτοι εσονται μοι εις λαον· και ου κινησω τον λαον μου Ισραηλ απο της γης ης εδωκα
αυτοις· Κυριε, παντοκρατωρ, ο θεος Ισραηλ· ψυχη εν στενοις και πνευμα ακηδιον εκε-

λησαν ἀκοῦσαι τοῦ Ἱερεμίου, ἀλλ᾽ εἶπον πρὸς αὐτόν· Οὐ μὴ
καταλείψωμεν τὰς γυναῖκας ἡμῶν εἰς τὸν αἰῶνα· ἀλλ᾽ ὑποστρέ-
φωμεν αὐτὰς μεθ᾽ ἡμῶν εἰς τὴν πόλιν ἡμῶν. Ἐπέρασαν οὖν 5
τὸν Ἰορδάνην, καὶ ἦλθον εἰς Ἱερουσαλήμ. Καὶ ἔστη Ἱερεμίας,
καὶ Βαροὺχ καὶ Ἀβιμέλεχ, λέγοντες ὅτι, Πᾶς ἄνθρωπος κοι-
νῶν Βαβυλωνίταις οὐ μὴ εἰσέλθῃ εἰς τὴν πόλιν ταύτην. Καὶ 6
εἶπον πρὸς αὐτούς· Ἀναστάντες ὑποστρέψωμεν εἰς Βαβυλῶνα
εἰς τὸν τόπον ἡμῶν. Καὶ ἐπορεύθησαν. Ἐλθόντων δὲ αὐτῶν 7
εἰς Βαβυλῶνα, ἐξῆλθον οἱ Βαβυλωνῖται εἰς συνάντησιν αὐτῶν,
λέγοντες· Οὐ μὴ εἰσέλθητε εἰς τὴν πόλιν ἡμῶν, ὅτι ἐμισήσατε
ἡμᾶς, καὶ κρυφῇ ἐξήλθετε ἀφ᾽ ἡμῶν· διὰ τοῦτο οὐκ εἰσελεύ-

κραγεν προς σε· ακουσον, κυριε, και ελεησον· οτι θεος ελεων· και ελεησον οτι αμαρτανωμεν
εναντιον σου· οτι σοι καθημενος τον αιωνα ημεις απολλυμενοι τον αιωνα· κυριε, παντοκρατωρ,
ὁ θεος Ἰσραηλ, ακουσον δη της προσευχης των τεθνηκοτων Ἰσραηλ και υιων των αμαρτα-
νοντων εναντιον σου· οι ουκ ηκουσαν της φωνης θεου αυτων και εκολληθησαν ημιν τα
κακα· μη μνησθης (cod μνησθεις) αδικιων πατερων ημων· αλλα μνησθητι χειρος σου και
ονοματος σου εν τω καιρω τουτω· εγενετο δε μετα την συμπληρωσιν των εβδομηκοντα
ετων μεχρι του βασιλευσαι Περσας εν τω πρωτω ετει (cod ετη) Κυρου βασιλεως Περσων·
του τελεσθηναι λογον Κυριου απο στοματος Ἱερεμιου εξηγειρεν κυριος το πνευμα Κυρου
βασιλεως Περσων· και παρηγγειλεν φωνην εν παση τη βασιλεια αυτου και αμα δια-
γραπτων λεγει· Ταδε λεγει Κυρος (cod Κ.) ὁ βασιλευς Περσων· πασας τας βασιλειας
της γης (cod om) εδωκεν μοι κυριος ὁ θεος του ουρανου· και αυτος επεσκεψατο επ᾽ εμε·
του οικοδομησαι αυτω (cod αυτον) οικον· εν Ἱερουσαλημ τη εν τη Ιουδαια· ητις ουν
εστιν εκ του εθνους αυτου εστω ὁ Κυριος αυτου μετα αυτου· και αναβας εις την Ἱερου-
σαλην την (cod τηνι) εν τη Ιουδαια οικοδομειτω (cod οκοδομιτω) τον οικον του θεου
Ἰσραηλ· ουτος (cod ουτως) ὁ Κυριος ὁ κατασκηνωσας εν Ἱερουσαλημ· και ὁ βασιλευς
Κυρος εξηνεγκεν τα αγια σκευη (cod σκευει) του Κυριου· ἁ μετηγαγεν Ναβουχοδονοσορ
εξ Ἱερουσαλημ. και...(cod απερησατω) αυτα εν τω ειδωλιω αυτου· εξηνεγκεν τα παντα
Κυρος ὁ βασιλευς Περσων και παρεδωκεν αυτα Μιθριδατη (cod Μηθρηδατη) τω εαυτου
γαζοφυλακι (cod γαζοφυλακη)· δια τουτου δε παρεδοθησαν Σαραβαρω προστατη της
Ιουδαιας· αμα Ζορωβαβελ ὃς (cod ως) και ητησατο επι Δαριου βασιλεως Περσων την
οικοδομην του ναου. ην γαρ κωλυσας επι τον Αρταξερξου χρονον ως ιστορησε Ἐσδρας·
τω δευτερω ετει (cod ετη) παραγενομενος εις το ιερον του θεου εις Ἱερουσαλημ μηνος
δευτερου ηρξατο Ζοροβαβελ ὁ του Ραθαληλ και Ἰησους ὁ του Ἰωσεδεκα και οι αδελφοι
αυτων και οι ιερεις και οι Λευιται και παντες οι παραγενομενοι εκ της αιχμαλωσιας
εις Ἱερουσαλημ· και εθεμελιωσαν τον οικον του θεου τη νουμηνια του δευτερου μηνος·
εν τω ελθειν εις την Ιουδαιαν και Ἱερουσαλημ· προφητευοντων Ἁγγεου και Ζαχαριου
υιου Ἀδδων· τελευταιων (cod τελευτεων) προφητων· ανεβη δε ὁ Ἐσδρας εκ Βαβυλωνος
ως γραμματευς ευφυης ὢν εν τω Μωυσεως νομω· ὃς (cod ως) και επιστημην πολλην
ειχεν τω διδασκειν αυτον (cod αυτω) απαντα τον λαον τα δικαιωματα και τα κριματα
επι τον Αρταξερξου χρονον· και εποιησαν εγκαινια του οικου του θεου, υμνουντες και
ευλογουντες τω κυριω επι τη εγερσει του οικου του θεου.

v. 4 εις την πολιν ημων aeth; ab εις Βαβυλωνα | v. 5 κοινων; b κοινωνων | ταυτην;
aeth ημων | v. 6 και ειπον; aeth adds οι γαμησαντες γυναικας (welche eine Weib
geheiratet hätten) | εις τον τοπον ημων; aeth om | επορευθησαν; aeth adds και υπε-
στρεψαν | v. 7 ου μη...ημων; aeth om | εμισησατε; aeth adds vorher.

σεσθε πρὸς ἡμᾶς. Ὅρκῳ γὰρ ὠρκίσαμεν ἀλλήλους κατὰ τοῦ
ὀνόματος τοῦ θεοῦ ἡμῶν, μήτε ὑμᾶς μήτε τέκνα ὑμῶν δέξασθαι,
8 ἐπειδὴ κρυφῇ ἐξήλθετε ἀφ' ἡμῶν. Καὶ ἐπιγνόντες ὑπέστρεψαν·
καὶ ἦλθον εἰς τόπον ἔρημον μακρόθεν τῆς Ἱερουσαλήμ, καὶ
ᾠκοδόμησαν ἑαυτοῖς πόλιν, καὶ ἐπωνόμασαν τὸ ὄνομα αὐτῆς
9 Σαμάρειαν. Ἀπέστειλε δὲ πρὸς αὐτοὺς Ἱερεμίας, λέγων·
Μετανοήσατε· ἔρχεται γὰρ ἄγγελος τῆς δικαιοσύνης, καὶ εἰσάξει ὑμᾶς εἰς τὸν τόπον ὑμῶν τὸν ὑψηλόν.
1 IX. Ἔμειναν δὲ οἱ τοῦ Ἱερεμίου, χαίροντες καὶ ἀναφέροντες
2 θυσίαν ὑπὲρ τοῦ λαοῦ ἐννέα ἡμέρας. Τῇ δὲ δεκάτῃ ἀνήνεγκεν
3 Ἱερεμίας μόνος θυσίαν, καὶ ηὔξατο εὐχὴν λέγων· Ἅγιος, ἅγιος,
ἅγιος· τὸ θυμίαμα τῶν δένδρων τῶν ζώντων, τὸ φῶς τὸ ἀληθινὸν Joh. i
τὸ φωτίζον με, ἕως οὗ ἀναληφθῶ πρὸς σέ, περὶ τῆς φωνῆς τῆς
4 γλυκείας τῶν δύο Σεραφίμ. Παρακαλῶ ὑπὲρ ἄλλης εὐωδίας
5 θυμιάματος· καὶ ἡ μελέτη μου Μιχαὴλ ὁ ἀρχάγγελος τῆς
6 δικαιοσύνης, ἕως ἂν εἰσενέγκῃ τοὺς δικαίους. Παρακαλῶ σε,
Κύριε παντοκράτωρ πάσης κτίσεως, ὁ ἀγέννητος καὶ ἀπερι-
νόητος, ᾧ πᾶσα κρίσις κέκρυπται ἐν αὐτῷ πρὸ τοῦ ταῦτα
7 γενέσθαι. Ταῦτα λέγοντος τοῦ Ἱερεμίου, καὶ ἱσταμένου ἐν
τῷ θυσιαστηρίῳ μετὰ Βαροὺχ καὶ Ἀβιμέλεχ, ἐγένετο ὡς εἰς
8 τῶν παραδιδόντων τὴν ψυχὴν αὐτοῦ. Καὶ ἔμειναν Βαροὺχ
καὶ Ἀβιμέλεχ κλαίοντες, καὶ κράζοντες μεγάλῃ τῇ φωνῇ ὅτι,
Ὁ πατὴρ ἡμῶν Ἱερεμίας κατέλιπεν ἡμᾶς, ὁ ἱερεὺς τοῦ Θεοῦ,
9 καὶ ἀπῆλθεν. Ἤκουσε δὲ πᾶς ὁ λαὸς τοῦ κλαυθμοῦ αὐτῶν,
καὶ ἔδραμον ἐπ' αὐτοὺς πάντες, καὶ εἶδον Ἱερεμίαν ἀνακείμενον
χαμαὶ τεθνηκότα· καὶ διέρρηξαν τὰ ἱμάτια αὐτῶν, καὶ ἐπέθηκαν
χοῦν ἐπὶ τὰς κεφαλὰς αὐτῶν, καὶ ἔκλαυσαν κλαυθμὸν πικρόν.
10 Καὶ μετὰ ταῦτα ἡτοίμασαν ἑαυτοὺς, ἵνα κηδεύσωσιν αὐτόν.

v. 7 προς ημας; aeth εις την πολιν ημων.
IX. 1 οι του Ιερεμιου; aeth om | εννεα; aeth επτα | v. 3 το θυμιαμα...ζωντων; aeth
angenehmer Wohlgeruch den Menschen | προς σε; aeth ich flehe dich an wegen deines
Volkes und ich bitte dich | v. 4 παρακαλω υπερ (b περι)...θυμιαματος; aeth und um
des Weihrauchduftes der Cherubim (και περι ευωδιας θυμιαματος των χερουβιμ) |
v. 5 aeth ich bitte dich dass doch ja der gesangskundige Michael, der Engel der
Gerechtigkeit ist er, die Pforten der Gerechtigkeit offen halte, bis sie in dieselben
einziehen | v. 6 Κυριε; b om | κυριε...γενεσθαι; aeth Herr über alles und Herr welcher
alles umfasst und alles erschaffen hat, welcher erscheint und welcher nicht geboren
ist, welcher alles vollendet hat und bei dem die ganze Schöpfung verborgen war, ehe
die Dinge im Verborgenen gemacht wurden | v. 7 ταυτα...Ιερεμιου; aeth und dies
betete er und als er sein Gebet geendet hatte | v. 8 και εμειναν; aeth und alsbald
fielen B. und A. nieder.

Καὶ ἰδοὺ φωνὴ ἦλθε, λέγουσα· Μὴ κηδεύετε τὸν ἔτι ζῶντα· 11
ὅτι ἡ ψυχὴ αὐτοῦ εἰσέρχεται εἰς τὸ σῶμα αὐτοῦ πάλιν. Καὶ 12
ἀκούσαντες τῆς φωνῆς, οὐκ ἐκήδευσαν αὐτὸν, ἀλλ᾽ ἔμειναν
περικύκλῳ τοῦ σκηνώματος αὐτοῦ ἡμέρας τρεῖς, λέγοντες καὶ
ἀποροῦντες, ποίᾳ ὥρᾳ μέλλει ἀναστῆναι. Μετὰ δὲ τρεῖς ἡμέρας 13
εἰσῆλθεν ἡ ψυχὴ αὐτοῦ εἰς τὸ σῶμα αὐτοῦ· καὶ ἐπῆρε τὴν
φωνὴν αὐτοῦ ἐν μέσῳ πάντων, καὶ εἶπε· Δοξάσατε τὸν Θεὸν,
πάντες δοξάσατε τὸν Θεὸν, καὶ τὸν Υἱὸν τοῦ Θεοῦ τὸν ἐξυπνί-
ζοντα ἡμᾶς Ἰησοῦν Χριστὸν, τὸ φῶς τῶν αἰώνων πάντων, ὁ
ἄσβεστος λύχνος, ἡ ζωὴ τῆς πίστεως. Γίνεται δὲ μετὰ τοὺς 14
καιροὺς τούτους ἄλλα ἔτη τετρακόσια ἑβδομηκονταεπτὰ, καὶ
ἔρχεται εἰς τὴν γῆν· καὶ τὸ δένδρον τῆς ζωῆς τὸ ἐν μέσῳ τοῦ
παραδείσου φυτευθὲν ποιήσει πάντα τὰ δένδρα τὰ ἄκαρπα
ποιῆσαι καρπὸν, καὶ αὐξηθήσονται, καὶ βλαστήσουσι, *καὶ
ὁ καρπὸς αὐτῶν μετὰ τῶν ἀγγέλων μενεῖ.*   Καὶ τὰ βεβλα- 15
στηκότα, καὶ μεγαλαυχοῦντα, καὶ λέγοντα, Ἐδώκαμεν τὸ
τέλος ἡμῶν τῷ ἀέρι· ποιήσει αὐτὰ ξηρανθῆναι μετὰ τοῦ ὕψους
τῶν κλάδων αὐτῶν· καὶ ποιήσει αὐτὰ κλιθῆναι* τὸ δένδρον
τὸ στηριχθέν· καὶ ποιήσει τὸ κόκκινον ὡς ἔριον λευκὸν γενέσθαι.
Ἡ χιὼν μελανθήσεται, τὰ γλυκέα ὕδατα ἁλμυρὰ γενήσονται 16
ἐν τῷ μεγάλῳ φωτὶ τῆς εὐφροσύνης τοῦ Θεοῦ. Καὶ εὐλογήσει 17
τὰς νήσους τοῦ ποιῆσαι καρπὸν ἐν τῷ λόγῳ τοῦ στόματος τοῦ
Χριστοῦ αὐτοῦ. Αὐτὸς γὰρ ἐλεύσεται, καὶ ἐξελεύσεται, καὶ 18
ἐπιλέξεται ἑαυτῷ δώδεκα ἀποστόλους, ἵνα εὐαγγελίζωνται ἐν
τοῖς ἔθνεσιν· ὃν ἐγὼ ἑώρακα κεκοσμημένον ὑπὸ τοῦ Πατρὸς
αὐτοῦ, καὶ ἐρχόμενον εἰς τὸν κόσμον ἐπὶ τὸ ὄρος τῶν ἐλαιῶν·
καὶ ἐμπλήσει τὰς πεινώσας ψυχάς. Ταῦτα λέγοντος τοῦ 19

gn.
rall.

v. 11 κηδευετε; b κηδευσατε; aeth wickelt ihn nicht in Leinen; so in v. 12 |
v. 12 εμειναν...αναστηναι; aeth sassen indem sie um ihn drei Tage wachten bis
seine Seele in seinen Körper zurückkehrte | v. 13 μετα...φωνην αυτου; aeth und eine
Stimme erscholl | τον θεον (2°); aeth τον χριστον (den Gesalbten) | εξυπνιζοντα;
aeth auferwecken und richten | v. 14 ετη τετρ. εβδ. ab; aeth 303 (codd. 330, 333)
Wochen von Tagen | και το δενδρον aeth; των δενδρων ab | φυτευθεν; aeth war
und nicht gepflanzt war | και...μενει; ab om; aeth und ihre Frucht wird bei
den Engeln wohnen | v. 15 βεβλαστηκοτα; a βεβληκοτα | μετα...κλιθηναι (b κρι-
θηναι); a om | the whole verse thus in aeth; und um der Pflanzschule der Bäume
willen, damit sie grün werden und hoch wachsen, wollen wie der Luft Verherrlichung
spenden damit ihre Wurzeln nicht ausdürren wie eine Pflanze deren Wurzel nicht
Boden gefasst hat | και ποιησει aeth; και ab | ως aeth; και ab | v. 16 τα γλυκεα...γενη-
σονται; aeth adds και τα αλμυρα γλυκεα γενησονται | εν...θεου; aeth mit grossem
Frohlocken und die Freuden Gottes | v. 17 χριστου; aeth υιου | v. 18 ινα ευαγ....
εωρακα; aeth damit ihnen gezeigt werde was ich gesehen habe | κεκοσμημενον ab;
aeth geschickt | πεινωσας a aeth; ταπεινωσας b.

64 ΤΑ ΠΑΡΑΛΕΙΠΟΜΕΝΑ ΙΕΡΕΜΙΟΥ ΤΟΥ ΠΡΟΦΗΤΟΥ. [ΙΧ.

Ἰερεμίου περὶ τοῦ Υἱοῦ τοῦ Θεοῦ, ὅτι ἔρχεται εἰς τὸν κόσμον,
20 ὠργίσθη ὁ λαός, καὶ εἶπε· Ταῦτα πάλιν ἐστὶ τὰ ῥήματα τὰ
ὑπὸ Ἡσαΐου τοῦ υἱοῦ Ἀμὼς εἰρημένα, λέγοντος ὅτι, Εἶδον
21 τὸν Θεὸν, καὶ τὸν Υἱὸν τοῦ Θεοῦ. Δεῦτε οὖν, καὶ μὴ ἀποκτεί-
νωμεν αὐτὸν τῷ ἐκείνου θανάτῳ, ἀλλὰ λίθοις λιθοβολήσωμεν
22 αὐτόν. Ἐλυπήθησαν σφόδρα ἐπὶ τῇ ἀπονοίᾳ ταύτῃ Βαρούχ
καὶ Ἀβιμέλεχ, καὶ ὅτι ἤθελον ἀκοῦσαι πλήρης τὰ μυστήρια,
23 ἃ εἶδε. Λέγει δὲ αὐτοῖς Ἰερεμίας· Σιωπήσατε, καὶ μὴ κλαίετε·
24 οὐ μὴ γάρ με ἀποκτείνωσιν, ἕως οὗ πάντα ὅσα εἶδον διηγή-
25 σωμαι ὑμῖν. Εἶπε δὲ αὐτοῖς· Ἐνέγκατέ μοι λίθον. Ὁ δὲ ἔστησεν
αὐτὸν, καὶ εἶπε· Τὸ φῶς τῶν αἰώνων, ποίησον τὸν λίθον τοῦτον
26 καθ' ὁμοιότητά μου γενέσθαι. Ὁ δὲ λίθος ἀνέλαβεν ὁμοιότητα
27 τοῦ Ἰερεμίου. Καὶ ἐλιθοβόλουν τὸν λίθον, νομίζοντες ὅτι
28 Ἰερεμίας ἐστίν. Ὁ δὲ Ἰερεμίας πάντα παρέδωκε τὰ μυστήρια,
29 ἃ εἶδε, τῷ Βαρούχ καὶ τῷ Ἀβιμέλεχ. Καὶ εἶθ' οὕτως ἔστη
ἐν μέσῳ τοῦ λαοῦ, ἐκτελέσαι βουλόμενος τὴν οἰκονομίαν αὐτοῦ.
30 Ἐβόησε δὲ ὁ λίθος, λέγων· Ὦ μωροὶ υἱοὶ Ἰσραὴλ, διὰ τί
λιθοβολεῖτέ με, νομίζοντες ὅτι ἐγὼ Ἰερεμίας; Ἰδοὺ Ἰερεμίας
31 ἐν μέσῳ ὑμῶν ἵσταται. Ὡς δὲ εἶδον αὐτὸν, εὐθέως ἔδραμον
πρὸς αὐτὸν μετὰ πολλῶν λίθων. Καὶ ἐπληρώθη αὐτοῦ οἰκο-
32 νομία. Καὶ ἐλθόντες Βαρούχ καὶ Ἀβιμέλεχ, ἔθαψαν αὐτὸν,
καὶ λαβόντες τὸν λίθον ἔθηκαν ἐπὶ τὸ μνῆμα αὐτοῦ, ἐπιγρά-
ψαντες οὕτως· Οὗτός ἐστιν ὁ λίθος ὁ βοηθὸς τοῦ Ἰερεμίου.

v. 20 και; aeth om | v. 21 μη αποκτεινωμεν κτὲ; aeth wir wollen an ihm
handeln wie wir an Jesaias gehandelt haben; und ein Theil von ihnen sagte, Nein,
fürwahr, mit Steinen werden wir ihn werfen. Und Baruch und Abemelek schrieen
ihnen zu, Durch diese Todesart tödtet ihn nicht | v. 22 πληρης b; πληρη a |
v. 24 end; aeth adds και ηνεγκαν αυτω λιθον | v. 25 εστησεν; b ανεστησεν | μου;
aeth αὑοῦ | γενεσθαι; ab adds εως ου παντα οσα ιδον διηγησωμαι τω Βαρουχ και τω
Αβιμελεχ | v. 26 λιθος; ab add δια προσταγματος θεου | v. 29 ειθ' ουτως; b ειθ' αυτως
(sic) | v. 30 εν μεσω; b εις μεσον | v. 32 ο λιθος; aeth om | end of verse ab add και τα
λοιπα των λογων Ιερεμιου και πασα η δυναμις· ουκ ιδου (a om) ενταυθα εγγεγραπται εν
τη επιστολη Βαρουχ.

www.ingramcontent.com/pod-product-compliance
Ingram Content Group UK Ltd.
Pitfield, Milton Keynes, MK11 3LW, UK
UKHW042152280225
455719UK00001B/293